Also By Jacquelin Smith

Talking With Animals

Animal Communication—Our Sacred Connection

Star Origins and Wisdom of Animals

Talks With Animal Souls

Jacquelin Smith

Foreword by Brad and Sherry Steiger

authorHOUSE

AuthorHouse™
1663 Liberty Drive
Bloomington, IN 47403
www.authorhouse.com
Phone: 1-800-839-8640

© 2010 Jacquelin Smith. All rights reserved.

No part of this book may be reproduced, stored in a retrieval system, or transmitted by any means without the written permission of the author.

First published by AuthorHouse 9/1/2010

ISBN: 978-1-4520-5244-1 (sc)
ISBN: 978-1-4520-5246-5 (hc)
ISBN: 978-1-4520-5245-8 (e)

Library of Congress Control Number: 2010910082

Printed in the United States of America

This book is printed on acid-free paper.

Because of the dynamic nature of the Internet, any Web addresses or links contained in this book may have changed since publication and may no longer be valid. The views expressed in this work are solely those of the author and do not necessarily reflect the views of the publisher, and the publisher hereby disclaims any responsibility for them.

Cover artwork, "Tour Guides," by Eva M. Sakmar-Sullivan (www.stardolphin.com)

Dedication

This book is dedicated to all of the animal souls who shared information about their star origins and about the animal bodies they inhabit on Earth. They've shared great wisdom about multiple realities, universes, the soul, and changes that Mother Earth is continuing to move through. Everything these beings shared came from a place of deep love, joy, and at times with sadness.

My mind and spirit have expanded as a result of these incredible conversations. They took me on adventures within myself as well as into other dimensions I shall never forget.

This book is also dedicated to Q, Chloe, ET, and Bella who are my teachers.

Acknowledgments

I thank my dear friend, Connie Parkinson, for the wonderful work you did editing this book. Thank you for your love, support, and for the excitement you had about the communications between the animals and me from the beginning. You have midwifed this book!

Thank you, Lynette Carpenter, for your talents and generous support in editing this book. Your skills as an editor have helped to make this a better book.

With love, I thank all of the animal souls for sharing their wisdom and insights so that humankind can better understand who they truly are as souls.

Contents

Acknowledgments vii
Foreword By Brad and Sherry Steiger xvii
Introduction: Star Origins xix

1. **My Journey** 1
   Animal Communication. Communication with interdimensional/star beings. My work as an animal communicator. Conversing with animal souls. Animals are here to teach. We belong to a cosmic family.

2. **Galapagos Giant Tortoise** 9
   We are a part of creating the original grids on Earth. The star system from which we come is not far from Sirius. We work with Earth's meridian systems. Emotions are a common bond between other species and humans.

3. **Manta Ray** 15
   We are angels. We are a group consciousness. We care about humans but they are not our focus. We anchor our frequencies into Earth's grid. We keep interdimensional lines open for communication for other beings. We come from a fluid world.

4. **Octopus** 23
   We are ancient elders from another star system. We have existed longer than Earth. Our etheric bodies are round with tentacles of light. Our ability to shapeshift is intrinsic to our species. You are a cosmic being.

5. **Dolphin** 29
   Dolphins are linked to the moon. We are open-hearted beings. We enjoy communicating with humans. We are from Sirius. We are one of the first species to come to Earth. We work from many realms/dimensions.

6. **Deer** 37
   We grace Earth with beauty and gentleness. We were created by an assistant creator. Mother Earth is balancing the energies' of the human species. We love Earth.

7. **Cat: Melinda** 41
   My home star's name is Ee-ah. We sing the language of vibration, color and sound. I came to Earth to assist with her evolutionary process. We are androgynous. Not all cat species are from one galaxy, planet or universe.

8. **Cats: Mittens and Milo** 47
   I am from Earth's moon. I am an energy form. Milo is from one of Jupiter's moons. I am visiting Earth for a short time. The moon separated from Earth. Wake up and remember that the All is energy.

9. **Cat Elder** 53
   Cats have missions in the same way that humans have missions and purpose. Cats are healers, teachers, meditators, mediators, interdimensional shifters and workers. Cats are telepathic by nature and are showing humans that they are also telepathic. Cats can shapeshift. Humans are ready to live from the heart rather than from the ego. Cats are here to share, love, and communicate. A cat can help clear and align a person's energies.

10. **Lion** 61
    The "beginning" was not as violent as humans think. The lion body disguises my true essence. I am a being from a higher equation. I am in a number of dimensions at once. I balance energies in deep space. I know love from the I AM.

11. **Lion Elder** 65
    I have lived on Earth for fifteen years. I come from a planet north of Andromeda. My planet is a very warm climate. Lions are reminders of the primitive aspect every being possesses.

12. Yellow Butterfly **71**
Butterflies are songs. Our realm of an energetic matrix is one of beauty, love and joy. There are angels and other beings in this realm. Beauty wakes up every living being. Earth is precious and beautiful. I am an aspect of your soul.

13. Cockatiel: Etheria **79**
I am from a world where we have wings, even though it is an etheric realm. The spirit world is much more than humans think. There are many galaxies, worlds and dimensions. Fly like a bird into other dimensions.

14. Double Yellow-Headed Amazon Parrot: India **83**
I discover new things by looking through others' eyes. I come from a group consciousness. We can be as one or individuals. I have twenty-eight key chakra centers. Earth is not a random creation.

15. Barred Owl **89**
Owls bridge the Earth and sky. We agreed to be a part of this gathering on Earth. We keep the interdimensional highways clear and open. Trees play a big part in the awakening on Earth. Look at the bigger picture of your lives as well as details.

16. Jellyfish **95**
There are multidimensional worlds/realms within the oceans. We expand in vast ways beyond our bodies. It is time for humans to understand the deeper workings of spirit. Your chakra systems are not linear. New energies usher in the new evolved human.

17. Overseer of Oceans and Waters **101**
The oceans are spiritual beings. Beings within the waters help maintain the health and balance of the oceans and Earth as well as the moon. Humans can be shortsighted. I ask humans to respect the oceans and all waters on Earth.

18. Council of Diverse Beings **107**
Every living being is a mirror reflecting the Key Creator's life force. Animals express and reflect unconditional love. Look into a spider's essence and see the divine. Animals are more than symbols. Engage in conversations with other life forms.

19. Dog: Marilyn 115
My person Todd and I are aspects of the same soul. I am from a distant star system. Humans have forgotten what they truly know. Just because I am in a dog body, does not make me an expert on dogs. Universes are connected like a vast Internet system.

20. Dog Elder 119
Dogs are probably humans' closest friends worldwide. Dogs can teach people how to listen telepathically. Dogs have agreed to be guides for humans. Unconditional love is present within humans. Dogs are not humans.. Those souls living in dog form have chosen to care about humans. Dogs are here to remind humans how to love and accept themselves, others, and life.

21. German shepherd/wolf: Rainbow 127
I am dog and wolf. This allows me to do my healing work with people. My galaxy is small in comparison to this galaxy. We take on physical form when we choose to visit denser galaxies such as the Milky Way. Loving allows humans to evolve spiritually. Each family group on our home star is of a particular tone and frequency.

22. Marine Iguana Overseer 135
Being coldblooded does not mean that we are heartless. We are interested in the future of Earth. There is a key Earth vortex in the Galapagos Islands. We communicate with each other telepathically. We were seeded on Earth. Humans did not evolve from apes.

23. Waved Albatross 143
Galapagos is the heart of Earth in many ways. We are from the Pleiades. Many humans are waking up and recalling their spiritual origins. You are our future and we are your future. We weave love and balance through the sky. Every island of the Galapagos is alive and has its own spirit. We have dances that express love and affection.

24. Groundhog 149
You were my first direct alien encounter here on Earth. Our light bodies have different shapes and colors with long flowing ribbons of light. We were invited to Earth. Groundhog is inconspicuous. I am currently living in three bodies on Earth.

25. Large Sea Turtle **155**
Our presence helps to bring balance to the oceans. We are like an orchestra creating music deep in the oceans. Dive into the oceans and you will find vast universes. We sea turtles are about light, love and truth. We work with Earth's grids. Water is simply a different frequency than Earth's air and deep space.

26. Horse: Jonah **161**
I had trouble adjusting to living in my horse skin. I come from a planet beyond Pluto. I chose to be a horse because of their grace, power, and healing abilities. The material world is simply a stage or dream for souls to learn, grow, and evolve.

27. Horse Elder Council **165**
We were invited to assist with helping set up frequencies for Earth. We chose to be in partnership with humans. If you drop all bodies, every being is one light. Emotions connect all living forms. Tap into your spiritual heart. Horses assist humans in learning about grace, beauty, and balance.

28. Bat Elder **173**
Our core vibration feels like a soft gentle breeze across your cheek. Humans create some strange ideas about bats. We work energetically to uplift human consciousness. Echolocation is a spin-off from our natural talents. Our DNA was implanted on Earth. Bats are a part of the balance of Earth's entire ecosystem. Follow your hearts.

29. Sea Horse **179**
We come from a planet where can can reproduce another of our species from within one body. We are older than Earth. Our energy fields can expand for hundreds of miles. We have met many beings from various galaxies on Earth.

30. Roach **183**
Thoughts and emotions you send us you send to yourselves. We come from a nebula within a star system. The Creator's spark dwells within us. We offer humans the opportunity to accept and love their own shadow aspects. We transcend and transmute lower vibrations into love. Humans can learn how to survive by listening to us.

31. Llama: Jocelyn 191
Having conversations with Earth would benefit humans. I was queen of the mound. We are interdimensional travelers and time travelers. Part of our mission is to assist humans in raising their consciousness. We are assisting with the energies changing on Earth. We bring love and light from higher dimensions.

32. Polar Bear and Bear Species Council 197
Bear energy protects Earth and gateways. We are gatekeepers. We are from a dimension deep within Earth. The energies are of purer vibrations at the North and South Poles where there are less humans. Bears carry the full spectrum of frequencies.

33. Grasshopper Council.. 203
Love is the underlying code of the All. We come from a world that is shimmering silver. The human species was put to sleep. We weave our loving energies through grasses, gardens, fields, and everywhere else on Earth. Imagine what it would be like to leap.

34. Firefly 207
We bring wonderment to Earth. Our mission is to spread light and love. We come from a fire world. We are mainly here to interact with trees, bushes, grasses, and Earth. Our light helps to balance Earth's meridians. Teach children to observe us.

35. Raccoon 213
Love is the greatest gift we can give to one another regardless of species. Humans refer to us as pests. I am from Sirius B. My species is individuals who live in community. Love and joy is what my species is about. We travel through intention.

36. Serpent Creator.. 219
Snakes bless the world by offering their gifts of healing. Serpent energy is creative, wise, and powerful. My origin is that of many dimensions. I am one of many assistant creators. There are positive and negative portrayals of serpent. Earth has chakras.

37. Electric Eel **235**
We are benders of light and beings of bending light. We are from Amereta. We are frequencies. Earth's codes are being activated. We came to Earth to introduce our frequencies. It is always the "core essence" of a being that matters.

38. Gorilla Elder **243**
The spiritual awakening is Earth centered. We are a gentle species. We live in the now. We are completing our mission. More humans than Earth can handle. We send humans love and light. Love, and harmony can exist in a wonderful and orderly way within a family. Your roots are in nature. We are becoming extinct.

39. Bee **251**
We are a group consciousness living in multiple bodies. We possess many emotions. The physical body is only one level of experience. Pollution and chemicals affect us greatly. The act of creation involves setting our intention. Meditation to bless Earth and humans.

40. Dragon Council **259**
We come from an interdimensional fold. You have much in common with the planet Mars. We were programmed for breathing fire. Humans are evolving. Learning never ends. Consider loving all species, all beings.

41. Dragonfly **267**
We are messengers of love, joy, beauty, balance and peace. We are connected to higher beings. We are menders and healers. The plant and tree beings on our star are not physically stationary like those on Earth.

42. Viceroy Butterfly **273**
Butterflies are of etheric realms, and also shapeshifters. We are connected to angel-like beings. Butterflies bring beauty to Earth. We work with the bees and dragonflies. We were born from energy blooms. See the truth of beauty within.

43. Red-Tailed Hawk **281**
Hawks spread beauty, joy, love, peace and balance. I wanted you and me to meet eye to eye. My wings are used for more than flying. We teach humans how to look at life from a larger perspective. My essence is light. The hawk body suits the needs of my soul.

44. Squirrel **287**
Squirrels and trees communicate telepathically. We help maintain balance and harmony in neighborhoods. We chose to be in relationship with humans. We came here from a planet beyond this universe. Take walks in the woods.

45. What Is Your Animal Companion's Star Origin? **295**
Star Being Traits. Difficulties Star Beings Can Encounter As Animals. Telepathic communication is natural. Guidelines for Communication. Practice and have fun with communications. Remembering who you are.

Epilogue 305
Glossary 307
About The Author..309

Foreword by Brad and Sherry Steiger

Never let anyone tell you that animals cannot speak to you. Anyone who is sensitive and really knows how to listen and to watch will be able to hear every animal communicate his wants, wishes, and displeasures.

As we have written in so many of our animal books, animals are highly intelligent, compassionate, and capable of teaching each of us the wisdom of the universe. Animals have guided, comforted, and lead many humans who have gone astray to return to the spiritual path. With their astonishing unconditional love, animals have become master therapists for the elderly, for children, for the depressed, for wounded soldiers returned from war. Even children judged autistic have been brought to a shared awareness between animal, humans, and the greater world around them.

Although there are many fine men and women who serve as effective animal communicators, Jacquelin Smith steps over boundaries that others have not yet traversed. Animals actually asked her to write this book, to alert other humans of their true origins. The spirits within many animals come from other planets, other galaxies, and take on the form which would best enable them to teach humans about the interconnectedness of all life.

Many of the animal souls who blended with Jacquelin's consciousness are the elders of their species. On occasion, an entire council of spirit beings would communicate with her, but thoughtfully utilize a single voice to speak to her.

These unselfish souls discuss their origins, emotions, and missions, as well as provide detailed descriptions of their home planets, stars, and the multiverse. There are multiple dimensions within our oceans and within the Earth, and through the abilities of Jacquelin, each reader may have the pleasure of experiencing the All, the oneness of these multidimensions first hand.

Some of these loving spirits have been here since the time our Earth was first being formed, and they have returned to guide us through the massive energetic changes that are about to occur on the planet. Others have come to help our own human evolution as spiritual, rather than physical beings.

Because she is in possession of such abilities, Jacquelin by no means considers herself superior to other humans. As so often throughout history, she says, "the least" have been chosen. By a blessed awareness, her body, mind, and spirit have been selected to express the thoughts, advice, wisdom, and warnings of the animal souls.

—Brad and Sherry Steiger,
Authors: *Animal Miracles, Pet Miracles, The Mysteries of Animal Intelligence, and Starborn*

INTRODUCTION: STAR ORIGINS

It's natural for me to communicate telepathically with animals as well as with other living forms. Every person is gifted in particular areas. My talents happen to be conversing telepathically with animals and star beings, and working psychically with people. I have spent over thirty years offering my skills as a psychic, animal communicator, and lightworker to people globally.

As an animal communicator and psychic, I'm able to see, feel, hear, and know what an animal is communicating to me. Also, being clairvoyant, I can see an animal's aura and essence. I teach people in my workshops how to look beyond an animal's physical form and how to connect heart to heart with the essence of an animal. An animal friend may be a handsome cat, cuddly dog, awesome horse, beautiful bird, or any other species. The key to hearing our animal companions' essence is to look beyond the body and to connect with the amazing soul of the being. The body happens to be a physical form that the soul has created in order to learn and to fulfill a purpose.

The animals asked me to write this book. This book emerged from the many spontaneous telepathic conversations that occurred between animal souls and me. The chapters are arranged in the order in which each animal soul communicated with me. There was a natural flow and order with every conversation.

As I began writing this book, I asked for souls of the highest vibration to share whatever they wanted to share with me and other humans. Every time I sat down and prepared to communicate with a soul, someone would show up. Also, councils, elders, and those of shared-group consciousness conversed with me. What I enjoyed was that the souls would often, a day before our conversation, give me a hint of who was preparing to communicate with me. The animal souls shared their essences and information flowed from them with love and joy. They have literally bared their souls.

The conversations the animal souls and I had were inspiring. I had a great deal of fun writing this book. They were open-hearted and answered many questions I asked them.

There are many beings whom humans can't see but who exist in various realms. The beings in this book state that their origins are based in other star systems and dimensions. These beings are clearly from other neighborhoods. All this could sound sci-fi, but I had so many outrageous synchronicities while writing this book, all I could do was laugh and keep writing.

These beings are much more than they appear to be. They have come to Earth from various stars, planets, and dimensions.

All living forms are connected. The common denominator that all living forms share is that we all have the divine light and life force within us. This is what allows the telepathic communications to be possible. I have had countless experiences through the years of feeling and knowing the oneness of all life, which includes life throughout the cosmos.

This book was a natural progression for me, going from communicating with animals to communicating with the deeper aspect of animals' souls. The process of writing this book came with ease and was exhilarating for my soul.

In this book, the animals talk about their origins, emotions, and missions. They discuss their original home planets, stars, and dimensions. These wonderful souls showed me the multiple dimensions that exist around Earth as well as throughout the cosmos, and the work they do interdimensionally. There are multiple dimensions within our oceans and within the Earth. I had the pleasure of experiencing many of these dimensions firsthand. My consciousness swam with dolphins, manta rays, and others through the network of the oceans' many dimensions. Other animal souls guided me on journeys deep into the Earth where I experienced countless dimensions of fantastic complexity and beauty.

In some conversations, the animals have a sense of humor in regard to humans who are concerned that those from other worlds might land on Earth. Many beings, whom we refer to as "animals," arrived here long before humans existed on Earth The irony is that animals' origins are rooted in various dimensions, galaxies, and universes. But this is true for every being that exists. All souls originate from the Creator. Yet, every soul is influenced by the bodies it creates as well as the various star systems, dimensions, and other places it experiences.

There came a point in my work as an animal communicator that I chose to step out and voice to clients what their animal companions were communicating to me about their origins from other galaxies and universes, what they were doing on Earth, and their star connections to the humans they were living with on Earth. This was scary at first, but what I discovered is that when I shared the animals' messages, their people resonated with what I was saying. In fact, some people would sob because they *knew* it was the truth. More and more people are embracing what their animals' souls have to say about their star origins and missions.

Perhaps you remember the films, *Men in Black I* and *II*. They are not so far-fetched as you might think. In both films there's a pug named Frank. We could say his soul was wearing a disguise so that he could accomplish his mission on Earth without attracting a lot of attention. If he were to appear as his star essence, humans would scream and run or even pull out a gun. In both films, many star beings disguised themselves in animal or even human form so that they could move about Earth without being identified or without risking terrifying humans.

In this book, one dog tells about being an interdimensional traveler. A cat discusses how difficult it was adjusting to his cat body because he's only lived on Earth twice. You will read about a groundhog who walked up to me and put his paw on my shoe and a hawk who flew to me after I had communicated with her telepathically. There is a mind-altering experience with squirrels that I witnessed in my own backyard. Some souls brought up the issue of pollution. And the gorillas and bees and lions discuss extinction while dogs and cats discuss their roles in helping to raise their peoples' vibrations just by living with them. Many of the animals discuss their feelings about humans.

The conversations between the animals and me are filled with love, joy, humor, and seriousness as well as play. These souls felt it was time for them to share with humans the truth about their origins. People are ready to understand the deeper spiritual truth about those whom we call animals.

Some of my clients' animal friends whom I've communicated with in regard to behavioral, physical, and/or emotional issues, including those who are now in spirit form, were some of the souls who showed up and wanted their messages to be in this book. A number of them appeared after I had sent out an energetic call asking for volunteers to speak to me about their spiritual origins. Our conversations were joyful and brought tears to my eyes.

A number of souls discuss their roles involving the creation of Earth. Others talk about being here when the Earth was first formed. Many discuss the changes going on with Earth and why they are here. Even though most of the animals discuss Earth changes in a similar way, which may seem repetitive, each one talks about different aspects of these changes from their own perspective and mentions different points. Also, the animals refer to the "All" throughout this book. The "All" refers to the Key Creator's creations as well as Itself.

Today, there are huge energetic shifts occurring in, on, and around the Earth as well as within our universe. Some people refer to this as "transition." Higher frequencies are pouring over the Earth and are creating dramatic shifts in the Earth's electromagnetic fields as well as within the Earth. The Earth is transforming. These energies are also creating shifts within us as well as all living forms on Earth, which the animals discuss in detail. The new paradigm being created is one of unconditional love, peace, and joy. Humans' consciousness and frequencies are being raised. The animal souls give important information about changes with the Earth, our solar system, the universe, and humankind. The changes are positive. Animals are assisting the Earth and all inhabitants on Earth with becoming more conscious spiritually.

As we all progress, we are shifting away from three-dimensional reality and fear and are moving into deeper dimensions of light and love. We have the opportunity to see through the illusion that we are separate from one another and to remember that we are all One. This is one of the most important points the animal souls discuss in the book. It is a fundamental truth which I have been teaching in my workshops as an animal communicator for over thirty years. Since we are all energy literally, we are all One.

As we evolve, we are releasing the ego and old behavioral patterns and learning how to live from our hearts. Humans are returning to the path of the heart. Love and joy is who we truly are.

The animals' souls give suggestions on how we can assist ourselves in evolving spiritually and how we can be a part of assisting Mother Earth in a truly conscious way. From my perspective, since so many souls discuss the ongoing energetic changes, it gives validity to how important it is for us to be aware of these shifts. These transitions affect us and all beings on Earth in dramatic ways.

We can learn a great deal from what the animal souls share about themselves, the Earth, humans, and other beings as well. We learn that what we think of as reality is not reality. We come to understand the basics of reality through their communications. The animals shared and showed me their basic essences as well as multidimensional selves. One soul used the analogy of an artichoke, saying, "The heart of an artichoke is like the core of a soul. The leaves are multiple lives being lived simultaneously."

This book will help you view animals, including your own animal companions, in a new light. What the animals reveal will allow you to see deep into their souls and discover who they are as spiritual beings and yourself as well.

Some animals share that they are here for an adventure, while others are here to assist the Earth and humankind. Many of them discuss their emotions. And numerous beings are helping with the interdimensional shifts that are taking place at a very fast pace. These essences talk about growing spiritually from their experiences, which is no different than the process that a soul in a human body goes through.

The bee offers a meditation you can do to bless the Earth as well as yourself. And the last chapter gives step-by-step guidelines on how you can converse with your animal companions' souls to discover their star origins, to receive messages they want to share with you. Also, you can find out what their original home is like, why they are with you or what purpose they are fulfilling on Earth, and more.

It's time for humans to understand the true nature of souls who are living and expressing themselves through animal bodies. Some of what the animal souls say may challenge your current beliefs, but will expand your way of thinking about everything. Explore and have fun while reading what these loving beings have shared through conversations.

The Overseer of Oceans and Waters showed up one evening to speak with me. It asked me to include the conversation that took place between us because it felt the information was important for humans to read.

This book will open your mind, heart, and soul to your animal companions in new ways. They are our teachers and healers. They are ambassadors and emissaries from afar.

You will come to know your animal companion's soul for the magnificent evolved soul that it truly is. These conversations will open you to animals, nature, and the Earth, as well as other worlds, and to yourself.

Read what these loving animal souls share from their hearts. Get ready for a wild cosmic ride!

Chapter 1

My Journey

I've had many interesting rides throughout my life. I've always been psychic and would dream about events or circumstances in regard to particular people, and they'd come true. At eighteen, I began delving into metaphysics in a bigger way.

In 1972, I started studying animal life and behavior. Also, I studied psychology to better understand animals. After receiving my animal technician's license, I worked in that field for a number of years. In 1977, I was involved in a serious car accident which resulted in having a near-death experience. Then I was forced to leave my position because I could not recover fast enough to resume my duties.

After the car accident, I began studying metaphysics more in depth. Within a few months of practicing meditation, my psychic abilities blossomed very quickly. As my knowledge and experience in using my natural abilities grew, I offered my consulting services to people concerning personal issues. At the same time, I was part of an apprenticeship program with a woman who taught me about training dogs and working with behavioral issues.

I began to wonder if there was a way for me to combine my psychic work with my love for animals. I thought to myself: if telepathic communication exists between people, why not between humans and animals? So in 1979 I decided to see if I could communicate with an animal telepathically. One of my first experiences was with a zebra. I was at a zoo and asked a particular zebra to come stand in front of me. Within a minute, the zebra walked from the far side of the exhibit and stood in front of me. Then I heard the zebra ask, "What do you want?" I was off and running into communicating with animals.

Telepathic communication with animals is a natural way of communicating. It is like a telephone conversation between two people. The telephone wires are the available lines of consciousness open between us that make the call possible. The electrical current, or the energy that the two beings send to each other, flows through the telephone wires and enables the beings to connect and have a conversation.

Since we are human, we receive words, pictures, thoughts, and feelings. Animals perceive whatever feelings and images we send to them. The vibration, the intention behind the word or thought, is translated in ways that both the animal and we will comprehend.

My work continues to expand and grow with the animals. I offer a wide range of services to people globally in regard to their animal friends' behavioral and physical issues, and those who have transitioned back into spirit form. Also, I do long distance healing, which involves working with animals' energy bodies and chakra systems to help align them with their high self and soul so they can better fulfill their purpose.

While continuing to grow as a communicator, I became a board-certified clinical hypnotherapist. Also, I got involved in studying shamanic work with an anthropologist. Then I read a book on soul recovery which inspired me. The next thing I knew, my spiritual guidance taught me how to do soul recovery work with people. Then I decided to try soul recovery work with an animal. Soul recovery is basically shamanic healing. The powerful work of soul recovery involves gathering the pieces of an animal's soul and/or pieces of their energy bodies that have fragmented due to emotional and/or physical trauma and integrating them back into their proper places so that the animal's mind, body, emotions, and soul are once again intact and aligned.

My first experience was when Mary called me, "Help! If you can't help I'm going to have to get rid of my dog Mike." So, I did a soul recovery for Mike, who was being aggressive with his dog sister. I wanted to see what would happen with SR work. To my amazement Mary called the next day. "Oh gosh, there were miraculous results overnight. Mike is now sitting next to my other dog." And to this day, Mike sits next to his sister with a heart full of love. (You can read my chapter on "Soul

Recovery Work" in my first book, *Animal Communication—Our Sacred Connection.*)

During these years, I also began experiencing a number of kundalini risings, which opened me to visions and telepathic communication with star beings and interdimensional beings. My first conscious telepathic communication with a star being occurred in 1982.

Some people may perceive these beings as highly evolved beings of light, star beings, and/or angels. It doesn't matter what name we call them, because it is just a name or label. Every person categorizes and labels everything in life from their basic foundation of personal beliefs and experiences. From my perspective all these beings are interdimensional, regardless whether they are labeled as angels, beings of light, and/or star beings because they all travel and work interdimensionally. So I may use these terms interchangeably.

As I was experiencing the kundalini openings, a group of star beings showed up at my house one evening. I knew immediately they were the same group who had communicated with me beginning in 1982 and for a number of years thereafter.

The one whom I refer to as Q shared with me that I was expanding spiritually and would be experiencing more communications with interdimensional/star beings. This started a series of conversations between Q and me, as well as with many other interdimensional beings. I could see and feel the star beings as well as angels with an increased clarity that was wonderful. They poured out information about dramatic shifts going on with the Earth. I responded by telling them I had no interest in the "shifts" and that I was simply an animal communicator. With that, Q and others let out a hearty etheric laugh, which I could hear quite clearly. "We have news for you, beloved one. You are expanding multidimensionally and remembering who you truly are. Your soul agreed to come to Earth during this major transition period to share your talents and skills as an animal communicator and psychic and to communicate with star beings."

I remained in denial of this reality for months. I was busy managing the hot energies moving through my chakras (energy centers.) Light bulbs were bursting all around me from the kicked-up kundalini energies. My clocks were showing different times due to the high energies; my computer would turn off and on whenever I walked past it. The star beings actually left a transmission on my answering machine. But when I went to record it onto a tape, the power was knocked out, which deleted these incredible frequency/sound transmissions. And they wanted me to listen to what was happening with the Earth? Eventually, I surrendered because I could feel in my heart the truth of what they were saying. I began to understand the many weavings of events and circumstances throughout my life from early childhood. Synchronicity abounded at every turn. All I could do was howl because it was so deliciously outrageous. My eyes and heart were more fully opened.

My work as an animal communicator continued to expand. The animals began asking me to assist them with aligning their chakra energies and to assist them with integrating their multidimensional selves with their physical bodies on Earth. Today, I do a great deal of this work with these beings who inhabit animal bodies. They need support with all the ongoing energies shifting, since they live in physical bodies. If you would like to know more about this, read the last chapter in my book, *Animal Communication—Our Sacred Connection*, which is about the transitional energies and the work that I do in this area with animal beings.

All of these experiences have brought me to where I am in my life now. I never thought I would write a book such as the one you are holding in your hand. Some could say I've flipped. Perhaps I have, but I've flipped into experiencing multiple dimensions and multidimensional selves which we all possess.

I haven't read books about Earth transition, let alone about animals being from other galaxies and universes before writing this material. And just as the animals taught me how to communicate with them, they've taught me how to see and hear their deeper soul essences.

As I was completing this book, I asked the star being, Q, if I should print out pages to share with a particular friend. Before my question was fully formed, my printer automatically began printing out the pages. I laughed out loud because it was clear that I was supposed to share the conversations with animal souls with my friend.

One of my clocks would stop at times while I was having a conversation with an animal soul. I had many similar experiences while writing this book.

I love my work as an animal communicator and continue to learn more and more. My work continues to evolve even though I've been communicating with animals for over thirty years. I'm filled with awe and gratitude as I continue to delve into the deeper aspects of communicating with animals and star beings and travel with my consciousness into multiple dimensions and multiverses.

Communicating with animals can seem strange enough to some, but sharing communications with people and telling them that their dog or cat companion is from Sirius or another universe can certainly seem totally off the wall. But, all this is beyond any walls and that's the point.

Near the end of the kundalini experiences, I began seeing the deeper layers of soul essences of animals with crystal clarity. They were revealing themselves to me as star beings. They showed me their otherworldly auras and what they look like on their home worlds or in their home dimensions.

When I started sharing this information with animals' people, they validated what the animals were telling me about their star origins and who they were as souls. Also, I began learning that the star beings in animal bodies sometimes had particular physical traits, emotional reactions, communications, and energy fields.

The process of communicating with soul essence telepathically is the same process I've developed and employed through the years when communicating with animals. It's a heart-to-heart connection.

I've learned a great deal through the telepathic conversations with all the beings who volunteered to converse with me. I typed down what they were sharing as they shared it and set aside any judgments about what they conveyed. Meeting these highly evolved souls has been a fantastic journey.

What they shared with me rang true within my core even though, at the time, it was beyond some of the beliefs I held. In writing this book, I have expanded beyond boxes of beliefs that I had no idea I was existing in despite the psychic work I continue to do with people and animals on a daily basis.

These inspiring souls not only showed me what they look like on their original planet, star, or the dimension they come from, but they whisked my consciousness through wormholes to other galaxies and universes filled with beauty and wonder that left me breathless. They have given me countless gifts that I can't begin to thank them for.

It's time for humans to open and explore other worlds and beings who live with us so that we can learn about them and ourselves. They can teach us about our souls, our cosmic roots and love. Also, they can help each one of us to evolve and explore our multidimensional selves and our own soul.

I have been involved with and concerned with not only endangered species, but all species for a long time. As I moved through my own process and was given information about the transitions going on globally, being concerned about other species and the environment took on a different light for me. Many species have communicated that they are helping to activate not only the Earth's chakras (energy centers) but those of humans as well. These souls also informed me that the communications were literally raising the frequencies in my chakra system. Your animal friends are activating your chakra system as well.

Because of the global shifts going on, many species are leaving the Earth. They have shared with me that the work they came to do on Earth is almost completed and that they are ready to go home. Every soul plays a part with these shifts. A number of animal souls communicated, "What we were once needed for on Earth we are no longer needed for. We have completed our missions with love." Some have left, some are leaving, while others will remain here until their souls decide to leave. Many of these animal beings were here long before the human race, as we know it, existed.

Some of the animal souls who conversed with me are the elders of their species. Also, if a council communicated with me, one voice spoke for the group. Some species who are a group consciousness also spoke to me with one voice. There can be individuals who are a group-shared consciousness who can speak individually or as the group with one voice. Sometimes they will say, "we, she, he, they," and at other times "I." I looked beyond their usage of pronouns.

Also, what the souls are communicating about is nonverbal: energies, sounds, tones, light, and concepts which are not linear. So it gets very interesting. Some would access my language base in order to speak to me, since they don't have a spoken language or similar framework. This is why the souls would invite me, my consciousness, to go with them so they could show me what they wanted to share with me through firsthand experiences. It was, to say the least, out of this world. These experiences reminded me over and over again that I am a soul who created a body (bodies) in order to grow spiritually and a soul which has a purpose to fulfill. And by growing spiritually, I am evolving. My body is a wonderful vehicle for my soul to express itself.

The animal souls, who are innately aware of and connected to who they are, are helping humans to remember who they are. They are assisting us in raising our consciousness. A key message that they shared with me and that I have taught for over thirty years is that we are all One. And regardless of where a soul originates, whether it be from Andromeda, Sirius, or another universe, we're all brothers and sisters filled with the divine spark.

Let's get to know and embrace our cosmic kin. At times they may look strange, but it doesn't mean they're a threat. And humans could perceive them as a threat if we don't look into the hearts of those who look different from us. We're accustomed to seeing horses, dogs, cats, praying mantises and many other beings, but if we had never seen them before we might feel startled or scared by their appearance. It makes sense when the animal souls talk about putting on a cute puppy or kitten costume so that they can fit in and so we don't go running off in another direction.

Communicating with animals opens the door to communicating with all other beings and life forms, whether they be rocks, trees, dragonflies, or interdimensional beings from the seventh universe beyond the Milky Way. It's a heart to heart and soul to soul language that can't be experienced through logic or ego.

This is why it has been, in some ways, a somewhat smooth transition for me to expand from communicating with animals into communicating with their deeper soul essences as well as other beings from other dimensions and worlds whom we would not refer to as animals. Yet, I had begun communicating with star beings in 1982 and then expanded into animal communication work. The star beings have greatly expanded how I think and who I am. We've communicated on a regular basis. The truth is, the communications with animals (who are star beings) and other beings throughout the cosmos is the same. Whether I'm communicating with an animal soul or a star being who doesn't live in an animal form involves the same process. I have come full circle with these communications.

Many beings are composed of various energy forms. Some look like globes of light, others appear as lightning. Some exist in physical form on their planet while others are etheric or what they refer to as in-between.

The key is being open and receptive to what we receive from these beings through images, feelings, words, and in other ways.

The following chapters tell what the animal souls communicated to me about some of the reasons why they are here. "We are here to experience life on Earth. Some of us want to know what it is like to feel through physical senses. We are here to experience the physical realm. Some of us desire to experience duality, emotions, touch, smell, love, and joy through a physical body.

"We have missions. We are here to teach, guide, and re-awaken humans. We are here to assist with the evolutionary process of the All. Not just Earth, but this entire universe and beyond."

In the end, some part of our soul is living in the stars, on Earth, and elsewhere simultaneously. Your dog or cat could be an aspect of your very own soul whose essence is from Saturn, Pluto, or beyond.

Deep within us we know we belong to the cosmic family and many humans are awakening to this truth and reality. This helps each of us as individual souls to remember who we are, which allows us to grow spiritually and to embrace the All. Our souls are growing spiritually and evolving in ways we can't begin to imagine. What powerful beings and co-creators all of us are.

What you read on the following pages may jog your own cosmic memory. You will feel or simply know the truth in what these souls have communicated. Let go and enjoy what the animal souls have so freely shared with me from hearts filled with love and joy.

Chapter 2

Galapagos Giant Tortoise

We are keepers of the garden

I traveled to South America and decided to spend some time on the Galapagos Islands. It was here that I had the opportunity to visit the tortoises of the Galapagos Islands for which the islands are named. The tortoises are hundreds of years old. When in their presence, I knew that I was standing among elders. They began communicating with me through a lower frequency sound that I could hear clairaudiently. Perhaps in the same way, elephants' lower frequencies can now be heard with special equipment.

Why are you here on Earth?
We are but one species, along with many others, who were here long before humans were seeded on this Earth. We are ancient ones, along with whales, eagles, llamas in the Andes, and many others who were here preparing the way for other species to enter through the interdimensional gateways to become inhabitants on Earth.

We are a part of creating the original vibrational grids on Earth. We were invited to be a part of helping to set Earth up, so to speak, and to prepare her for seeding from many cosmic species who were going to be coming to Earth.

Now, we are assisting with creating a new order or holographic blueprint with the interdimensional frequency shifts. We are anchoring in these frequencies to assist with setting up the new paradigm, not only on Earth but within your entire solar system. These shifts are happening in many universes.

At this time, we are but one of many species who are creating spirals (vortexes) for the higher frequencies to implant themselves deep into Earth. This is to help raise the frequencies in and around Earth. There are those beings living in other dimensions within Earth who are helping as well. Do not think a worm is a worm or a beetle is a beetle. We are all collectively doing our work as every being is shifting or spiraling into higher and higher frequencies.

What do you mean when you say, do not think a worm is a worm or a beetle is a beetle?
What we mean is that when you look at a worm, there is a much greater being with the worm body that most humans do not see or sense. The same with the beetle. If you see the true essence of a worm, their essence is much bigger than their body and the essence doesn't resemble a worm at all. Yet the body of a worm is perfect for what that race of beings' purpose is on Earth and how they nourish and care for Earth not only physically but spiritually and energetically as well. A worm and beetle are multidimensional beings just as humans are. All energy is energy. Therefore, no being is higher than another. We are all different frequencies.

Thank you. Are you the tortoise elder or the group consciousness?
Actually both. My group consciousness is just that, but also we are a part of the tortoise elder simply because we are in tortoise bodies and connected to this species energetically.

Where are you from?
We are not of Earth. We are an ancient race doing our work not only from where our bodies are but from the stars and from our other bodies that travail at times in working with Earth's energies. We help to maintain balance and help heal Earth's meridians.

Remember that looks can be deceiving. Our bodies move slowly, but our spirits are mighty and soar on starlight; moonlight. We travel on the sea's rhythm and energies. We are keepers of the garden along with other ancient races.

The star system from which we come is not far from Sirius. Yet, it is a star system that has not been seen by any humans on Earth. Or at least not seen through any kinds of radio waves or telescopes. The world from which I come exists in an etheric realm. There are many dimensions within dimensions and star systems within star systems. Humans would have a difficult time believing how vast the cosmos is and how many races of beings exist. There are more than you could count.

What do you look like on your home star?
We are a group consciousness, yet can be individuals, too. We can be anywhere we desire in an instant. We do not have physical bodies on our home star, yet can manifest whatever body we desire to and to place a part of our consciousness in that body or in a number of bodies. To you we would look like a group of sparkles of light.

Why a tortoise body?
Being in tortoise bodies serves our purpose well. We can simply be and do our work energetically. We work with Earth's meridian systems in and around her by never moving. We are able to set our intention and the work is done. We have no need to be moving fast or over great distances. This is one of the reasons why we were invited to be a part of the initial council who helped prepare Earth to receive many other species.

Galapagos Giant Tortoise: Photo by Jacquelin Smith

Are all those in tortoise form from your home star?

No, but many are from my home star, because all aspects of our group consciousness felt comfortable inhabiting the tortoises on the Galapagos Islands. It was a place where we could be removed from many species and simply do our work on Earth creating the original Earth grids. But later on, we were discovered and treated horribly by humans.

What happened?

Humans ate our flesh without regard for who we were and why we were on Earth. We communicated with them telepathically, but they were not ready or open to hear us for who we truly were. They had forgotten that we are all One. It was very difficult to experience the body's feelings and great pain as we were butchered. Yet those who remained continued the work on Earth. And those who had left their bodies continued to work from other dimensions because it was and is a more comfortable way to work with Earth's meridians.

But the tortoises are now protected, so it is much easier to be in the body now. Yet those of us who work from our bodies are working mainly with certain aspects of Earth's meridian system while those in spirit form are alternately working with other aspects of Earth's meridian system. It is an intricate system that is difficult to explain in words. We do not typically use words but communicate telepathically as well as through tones and sounds, which is how we communicate with others in the universes.

Do you experience feelings on your home star or is this new?

We experience feelings but in a different way. We can experience pain even though we are in etheric bodies, because we still have a body. We feel love and joy and can also feel sadness and anger.

Are emotions a common bond between other species and humans?

Humans feel all these feelings too, so all of the species on Earth have this in common. It is a very important bottom line in terms of bonding and connecting. It is important for empathy and for species to understand one another.

Many humans do not remember that other species have these feelings and hurt them without intending to do so. Some humans intend harm, yet there are those who intend to love other species. This is important for humans to remember. What one does to another they are doing to themselves, whether it be harmful or loving. This is what the human species is hoping to remember and evolve in ways that allow them to grow spiritually. We desire for them to recall that we are all interconnected without exception.

Thank you.
> You are welcome.
> Tortoise

Chapter 3

Manta Ray

We are angels

Hello. Are you of this world?
We are not of this world. We come from a world of energy similar to water. So we will refer to our world as a water world. In coming to Earth, our essence vibrates most with the oceans. Your oceans are truly beautiful with the many life forms that have lived here for billions of years.

Some think of us as ugly, but you see our angelic essence. You see how graceful are our water wings.

We thank you for acknowledging us. We were here long before humans. We watch over the oceans with the whales, dolphins, starfish, octopi and others who care about Earth and the oceans.

Are you individuals or other?
We are of a group consciousness. We are in numerous bodies to experience various places and spaces in the oceans to help raise the vibrations of the oceans. It was foreseen long ago that humans would pollute the oceans, so we agreed to come and anchor in higher frequencies as many species are doing not only in the oceans but on land as well as in the sky and Earth's center.

We are seen as primal. Our gills are many to sustain our large bodies. We look similar to where we are originally from. Not of this solar system, but of another solar system that exists within another dimension just beyond the Milky Way that cannot be seen visually by your scientists' instruments. We travel home to our worlds when our oversouls say we can, but we are needed here physically to continue to assist with shifting the vibrations of Earth. Yet an aspect of our soul always remains on our home water world.

Tell me more.

We see prey move easily with our eyes because of the way our eyes are positioned on our bodies. Our tails allow for streamlining through waters. We are aware how alien we look to you. Especially since you walk on land with two legs, which is foreign to us and to the world from which we come. There are many other beings here from other galaxies who resonate with the vibration of water on your planet. Thank you for caring about us.

Do you care about humans?

We care about humans but they are not our focus. We're here to assist as well as to learn about other worlds for the sake of our souls. We are many, we are one.

Our vibration designed the form of our bodies just as your vibration determined your physical body. We are angels to some and devils to others. It is all a matter of perception. This is why it is good that you teach humans about seeing the essence of all beings.

Second Visit From Manta Rays

Hello. It's nice to see you again.

We are glad to visit with you again. You seem fascinated by our tails.

Can you tell me more about your tails?

In the physical world, they help us to maintain balance somewhat; but they are long and thin because as we mentioned, it streamlines our movement in waters. If we had a big tail fin it would not work with our water wings. Our tails are like antennae and we can sense what is behind us, including the electromagnetic fields.

Can you say more about anchoring energies into Earth?

Many of the sea beings anchor their frequencies into Earth's grids. For billions of years, we have helped to anchor in the energies that are appropriate for every age that comes and goes.

We are now in another shifting zone. And we are helping to transmit the higher frequencies from deep space and anchor them into Earth's center and grid systems. Look and see the brilliant crystalline.

Water is a magnificent transmitter for energies, so it is easier for us to anchor in the electromagnetic energies coming from deep space as well as those from inner Earth. We are anchoring in the higher frequencies to help shift Earth's paradigm to one of peace and love once again.

We are assisting because we can and because we care. Humans are often fearful of our appearance, calling us devil rays, yet we are kind. We have reached out to humans to communicate physically and telepathically. We have given dreams to those who care about us.

Tell me more about your experience with the waters.

There are many secrets about Earth that science cannot even begin to explore because they have not thought of the questions. There are many invisible worlds and wondrous dimensions for those of us who live in the sea experience. The whales and dolphins and the others can all tell you about this.

There are dimensions of such glorious shimmer and color you cannot fathom. You experience many dimensions within the air, but beneath the ocean, it is a very different vibration of sound and sight and feel and hearing. A different universe, as you know.

We were not a part of Lemuria but Atlantis. We understand how important the oceans are for all living forms who inhabit Earth. We know the currents and when a current shifts in an unusual way, we recognize this.

We were able to recreate our bodies on Earth that are similar to what we experience in our own water-like planet. This enables us to function in a much better way on Earth.

What is your home like?

Our home is beautiful, beautiful water. There is no land where we come from, so we have had to learn the boundaries of where water ends and land begins. But it is a beautiful universe in the oceans here on your planet. We travel through various dimensions daily. There are interdimensional doors and portals we can travel through and be anywhere we desire. We can travel between Earth and our water world at will. More doors are opening, and other doors are closing because of the shifts.

Tell me more about your work with Earth.

We are angels living beneath and in the sea. We can and do affect energies throughout the waters and Earth. There is a worldwide network of manta rays, dolphins, and all other ocean beings who are helping to maintain Earth's grids and to anchor in new vibrations. We hear the tones and sounds beneath the waves. We, as a network of sea beings, communicate telepathically. We are all like points of light that create an intricate web, just as the creatures on land create a web of intercommunications via different soul frequencies. And we are all frequencies in this cosmic web of life.

Earth was here before it was here. It was manifested through the guidance of councils and other beings who helped to give her physical form after a black hole spewed out a new universe. Your galaxy, the Milky Way, was created, and Earth of course became a part of your immediate galaxy. Earth is a soul who desired and agreed to become physical for the sake of experience as well as for the evolutionary process of the All.

There are many Earths. Earth has her various etheric bodies, as you do, and many of these are being affected by humans' lack of understanding that she is a living, breathing being. More recently, humans are opening and looking beyond themselves in order to understand that Earth is alive. And that the flow of life isn't one only they possess. We feel, too.

Manta rays are said to be solitary beings who exist in very small groups. We are busy doing the work we are here to do as star beings.

Thanks for sharing.

Thank you for seeing our beauty.
Manta Rays

Third Visit From Manta Rays

Hello. It is good to hear from you again.
Hello, we had more information we wanted to share with you.

Great!
The moon is more than Earth's satellite. The moon helps Earth to maintain balance and rotation in space. The sea and the moon are necessary for all of the water beings to be on Earth. The moon allows Earth to maintain rhythm as well as the seas. This includes the interdimensional Earth as well as many other realms.

We are in contact with the moon and her electromagnetic energies. Remember we are all connected whether it be human to human, human to starfish, starfish to moon. The moon is connected to the Earth, the sun, and the rest of creation.

Manta rays assist with keeping the interdimensional lines open for communication and travel so all beings and energies can communicate and interact with each other.

We have spacecraft, so to speak, in our galaxy. You think we and the whales look like spaceships. We can create spacecraft from energies with our thoughts and intentions or we can dissipate it with our thoughts and intentions, whether we are here on Earth or in another universe. It matters not, since there is no distance or space when you are communicating telepathically; and as we mentioned, we can travel back to our home any time through portals beneath the sea that exist in many dimensions. You might think of them as wormholes.

Do you have families?
We do not have families in the way you think of family. We are one large community that's linked as one through telepathy; yet we can be individuals if we want to. We are individual manta rays on Earth. We see we now have a sacred space within your heart and are happy about this. We are happy you will be sharing this with many humans.

Tell me more about your world.
Our water world is difficult to put into words. It is different from your oceans. It is of a different texture, but we call it water. Our entire

world is water, no land. It is a sphere of a very high frequency that is light which conducts electrical fields with ease. Our world is fluid. There is no struggle to move, no struggle of any kind from where we come. It is of a different kind of density.

Since the group and individuals are linked electrically as energy, we know each other's thoughts and intentions in an immediate way. There is no need for policing as there is on Earth.

Is there love in your world and what are your feelings about love?
Oh, yes. We do not know discord or disharmony in our world. It is difficult here on Earth experiencing duality, chaos, disharmony. Even though we live beneath the sea, we feel the wars, the bombs, the intentions and thoughts that humans create on Earth. These are lower vibrations that humans are slowly transforming into higher vibrations within themselves and within the world. We do not mention this to bring up feelings of shame and guilt, but to speak the truth. We are befriending humans.

Whales and dolphins are meant to be reaching out more than we are to humans. They are teaching about the sea, love, joy, and healing. They are helping humans to raise their vibrations by being openhearted and simply by connecting to them. Also, they are helping humans shift into their hearts as well as teaching them about how to shift interdimensionally. There are many species doing this work now.

We also, are part of the whole creation and are doing a great amount of energy work with grids, too. Every life form has its place and mission. The fact that people are understanding that manta rays are gentle, loving beings who like their bellies rubbed is a part of fulfilling the divine plan. With people acknowledging us, even though we are very strange foreign-looking beings in the sea, this spreads love and does wonderful feats with lifting energy.

We know you wish this was coming from a more familiar and acceptable group like dolphins and whales, but we can say, basically, or with the fundamental base of zero that everything else has come from, we are. The whales and dolphins will validate this. All of us beneath the sea talk telepathically, and throughout the universe as well.

What colors are in your water world?
When we go beneath your sea what colors do you observe? What

is before you? To keep it simple you could say we come from a globe of fluid rainbow light. It is something you can understand, because we do not have words to convey the colors or texture. Our world is of a high frequency beyond what you perceive as white light. The rainbow light is of different colors than those of Earth. As I mentioned, this is difficult to put into words.

We can be on our planet while being on Earth, too. We can travel back and forth. An aspect of our energy is both places and living in other places and spaces as well. We are really living in multiple locations just as your soul is doing this moment.

We do not walk, we swim, or we could say we fly through this fluid world of light. It is not dense like Earth's water, yet water was the element on Earth that we could adjust to the best.

Why are you here?

We are here to help Earth, humans, and some other species evolve, in the same way you might help a child learn how to walk. We do not have to have direct physical contact with you. We set our intention with thought and send it into the world to be received through the electromagnetic fields, or you could say, the global energy network. This could be compared to sending our energies through telephone wires or the Internet. We are not influencing humans in any negative way, but only putting out high frequencies to assist Earth, people, and others if they choose to integrate these frequencies in order to evolve and live from their hearts. There is no force involved with this.

Thank you for blessing us this evening. You bless us with your open heart.

Thank you for blessing me and for opening your thoughts and your world to me.

You are welcome.
Manta Ray

Chapter 4

Octopus

We are ancient elders from another star system

Hello. What would you like to share?
The inner dimensions of the oceans are composed of stable frequencies which create the form of water. I swim through frequencies, the sounds, the geometric forms that compose water. Water has many sounds and tones within it. Just as you hear many sounds as you walk through the woods, we hear and feel many sounds, vibrations and frequencies as we live our lives in the waters.

This has become more challenging because of the pollution in the waters. It is interfering with the purity of vibration and frequencies that once were. So it is becoming more difficult for many sea creatures to function and remain in their physical bodies.

Many sea beings are leaving their bodies and moving into higher dimensions, while others are simply slipping into higher frequency dimensions.

Are you from another world?
We octopi are of another world, one similar to that of the manta ray and other beings living in the sea. Our souls made a decision to manifest into physical form on Earth and to live in the sea for many and varied reasons. We come from a star system where we are born as shapeshifters

and so we chose a form on Earth that would allow us to continue our natural way of being. The sea is perfect for shapeshifting (smile).

Why are you on Earth?

Some of us came to visit and explore Earth's oceans. Others have come because they have agreed to be a part of the interdimensional shifts. It is not that we are so different from you, even though we look very strange and different to you. We have all been created by the Key Creator.

You are not totally comfortable with how we look, but you are amazed by the innate talents an octopus possesses and you are curious about us. Our ability to shapeshift physically is intrinsic to our species. We can change color and shape whenever it is appropriate to do so. We can change the shape of our eye in a flash. Other beings shapeshift in that they place their consciousness into another being, but we literally shapeshift. This is to show humans and other species that shapeshifting is very real and possible.

How old is your species? Tell me more about your world.

We are high frequency and have existed much longer than Earth. We are from a distant galaxy. It is a galaxy that your scientists have not discovered and probably will not. We come from billions of years ago and from an incalculable distance. Your universe and others are older than you know.

We are ancient elders of another star system which we oversee. Our bodies adjust best to your oceans. The world from which I come is of fire and ice, water and stone. These are the best words I can offer to you to describe our world. There is no temperature on our world. No time. We are a species which interacts with others similar to us.

Do you assist humans?

We did not come initially to help humans. But as we became more familiar with you as a species, we understood that you might destroy this wonderful planet unless there was and is intervention from others.

Where I come from there is only peace and harmony. On Earth, we adapted to being in the physical and killing in order to eat and remain in the physical. We learned that this is the natural order of life on your planet. This is foreign to us, but we were interested in learning about other species and being in physical form.

Are you one of the elders?
Yes.

What other star system do you oversee?
It is a star system that is not a part of your universe. The star system we oversee is one we were asked to oversee by a council of assistant creators. It is many dimensions deep and of high frequency in comparison to where Earth is.

What type of form do you have on your world? Are you individuals, group consciousness, or other?
We are in etheric physical form. Our etheric bodies have a round shape with tentacles of light and we can materialize or dematerialize at will. In other words we shapeshift at will.

We are individuals but we can become a group consciousness if we so desire. We remain individuals but if there is a need for us to be group consciousness then we can become that. For example, let us say there are a hundred birds in a few trees. When some begin to fly, all the birds flock together and fly in sync. The only difference is that we truly merge and could fly as one being in one etheric body.

Do you have families and how do you reproduce?
We have families, but they are not structured in the same way as Earth families. A family on my star is those born of one frequency and another family is of yet another frequency and so on. We reproduce through means of using energy. There is not a physical process since we are in etheric form. Those within our family units are able to all set their intention to create another being of the same frequency and the being comes into creation on the etheric realm.

Is this a fun process for the family who creates a new being?
Yes. The new being is always created with and from the intention of love and joy.

Sounds fun to me. Please share more about the ocean and changes going on.

There are spacecraft beneath the waters. There are also other universes and worlds and star systems beneath as well as within the oceans. The water is a wonderful conductor of electrical energy and we use it in a variety of ways. Hard to imagine (smile)? We can link with any other being. We can link and be with our others at our home planet for a visit or to report home what is happening on Earth.

What do you mean link?

Those of us in the waters communicate telepathically with each other. There is another way to communicate that is different, which I call "linking." We have the ability to link with other species if we desire by sending an aspect of our energy bodies to actually be there and link with another being. This is not a merging process, but simply being present, and communicating. This energy body is palpable, and other species see this aspect of ourselves and receive it with open hearts.

Thank you for explaining this. Can you say more about what's going on with energy shifts?

The galactic federation is a part of this entire plan that is taking place cosmically. They oversee the energy shifts and events going on around Earth. There are councils consisting of many star beings who consult with one another and make decisions to determine how many energy shifts humans can tolerate and still remain sane and in their physical bodies. Other sea beings and animals on land can adapt fairly well since they are aware of what is going on and continue to play their part with shifting energies.

Remember, nothing is solid, so we can travel through Earth's land as if it were water. Remember your dream about the dolphin. (*I had a dream about a dolphin springing up through soil and leaping high into the air. I realized in the dream that land and water are simply different forms of energy and learned to see past the illusion of what seems to be solid.*)

Do your auras expand for quite a distance?

Yes. See our auras. They expand for miles as do those of the manta rays. We can expand or contract our auras as you do. You now think my eight tentacles are beautiful. The suction cups are amazing, you say. You think we look holy swimming through the waters with our tentacles moving in the waters behind us as we swim (smile).

Yes, you are correct. I have come to admire you.

We thank you for opening to a more expanded truth of the universes. You began as a psychic, then expanded into telepathic communication with animals and teaching others how do this for many years. Later, you learned or actually remembered that you are a cosmic being connected to the cosmic family. And within the last number of years, you began recognizing the basic star being essences within the familiar forms around you such as cat, dog, and others, oh, and octopus, too (laugh). What a journey you have chosen to embrace. We admire you, too. All this is stepping up your spiritual evolutionary process. You are now able to look beyond what you were fearful of in the past. Our big heads and tentacles. Boo! (Haha). We love you.

We are very gleeful to communicate with you this evening. Peace and gratefulness from the stars, and from our world to your world.

Thank you for this conversation.
You are welcome.
Octopus

Chapter 5

Dolphin

We leap for joy

Last night while I was lying in bed, in a twilight state, the dolphins appeared to me. They guided me into the ocean and let me experience what they see and hear using sonar. It's difficult to describe in words, but I will try. I saw a radar screen within and heard, saw, and felt various frequencies. I could scan any being whether it be a fish, shrimp, or rock, and hear, see, and know the density of the being or object instantly. I could experience all this on my brain's screen as well as in my body. I saw numerous energy fields beyond the density of bodies or all other objects. I knew the intention of beings around me by the frequencies they were giving off, which I picked up; I could smell whatever beings were around me, too, in some strange etheric way.

(Dolphins know whoever and whatever is around them by using echolocation. This is the dolphins' language. It is a language of sound, light, frequency, and holographic images, which they shared with me. They experience all this in an instant. I wonder if this can be compared to the way our human brains take in millions of details in an instant, even though we aren't conscious that they are doing so.)

Welcome. Are you a dolphin elder?

Yes. Dolphins are linked to the moon. We are very attuned to the moon's magnetic fields, which we see and listen to during all of its phases. We feel the moon's energies through the waters, the shifting of tides. We would not be here without the moon.

Thank you.

We love life! We are openhearted and embrace all that is living. We leap for joy through the waves, we sing, and we speak. Our families are close-knit. Dolphins care about the All. We are teaching humans to care about not only us but about the oceans and other beings in the sea as well. Joy is our song. Love is our essence.

We come from another realm that is of very high frequency. The frequency is so high humans cannot hear it, but many other beings on Earth can and do hear it. A dog twenty miles away, a cat a million miles away can hear us sing.

We are working with many beings of the sea and in other dimensions to continue introducing a new paradigm. A paradigm of love, joy and peace. Love is everywhere if you but breathe it in and feel it. *(Note: dolphin means "breath" in the yoga system.)*

Thank you. I can feel your joy (laugh).

We understand that we are not our bodies, although we enjoy having these bodies to celebrate the waters. The waters are living forms, as is the entire Earth. In having a body on Earth one must eat, so we eat.

What's the key message you bring to Earth?

We have shown humans that we can learn their language. We are highly intuitive beings. Our language is more complex, but our message is simple. Love, joy, peace, and harmony. There is harmony within our pods. Now and then there is what you would call a rebel, who has a difficult time due to an injury or being affected by pollution or invasive frequencies from human-made machines.

Also, the magnetic poles are shifting as well as the sun's energies, which are creating unnatural behaviors in many species worldwide. This is true not only in the oceans but on the land and in the air as well. The body and mind can be affected, but the spirit is not. The soul is ever present and desires to fulfill its purpose.

What else would you like to share?

We love Earth and enjoy the sun, the waters, the sky. We value beauty and kindness. Earth is a beautiful place to live.

We have the capabilities to heal others which are now recognized by science and therapists alike. We choose cooperation. There are times, because of being in bodies, that we will create boundaries for others not to cross.

We enjoy communicating and sharing with you. We are giving and enjoy giving. This is why humans respond to us. We reach out to you with joy.

Joy is humans' true nature. Peace on Earth. Please share this information with others.

Are you from the stars?

Yes, we are from Sirius and other planets as well as other star systems. A number of us agreed to be in dolphin bodies, yet our souls have many different origins. We are not all from Sirius or Andromeda or Pleiades. We are from various systems meeting and agreeing to experience dolphin bodies.

Is every species from various dimensions, universes, and other places in space?

Yes and no. When we speak of dolphins from a star system, we are, yet every soul decides what type of body to incarnate into for its purpose. Also, remember that your soul can incarnate into a human form, a manta ray, a bird and a tree simultaneously. In reality, the soul does not live one lifetime at a time in a linear fashion.

For example, not all manta rays are from one planet. They spoke of their planet and said that they look similar to how they look on their planet. So, that too, is true. So some beings do incarnate as a group from another planet or somewhere else, while other beings' souls decide to incarnate in many and varied bodies. It is not just one way or another. There are many combinations of how life, incarnation, and soul expression work.

It is all of the above. This is not multiple choice (laugh). All answers can be correct when you are delving into other dimensions. Remember, not one body per soul at a time.

Thank you for explaining this.

We realize this is not the book you had planned originally within your mind, but this book of conversations with many species goes into much deeper space (smile).

A Visit From The Dolphin Elder

Hello. Good to hear from you again.

We are happy to speak with you today. We knew you would be inviting us back for a chat. We like to communicate with simplicity, yet the many types of work we do are complex when presenting this to the human mind. Yet, many other beings in the waters understand all that we do naturally.

Do animals on land also understand you?

Some do and some do not. The polar bears understand, for we meet with them as we are doing our work in multiple dimensions. Beings who live by water tend to better understand the energies we are working with. But we meet many other species while working in other realms. We work with many different species. We are but one aspect of a team or a group fulfilling our soul's missions, which is a part of fulfilling a higher mission for the good of the All.

Are all beings here to help raise the frequencies in and around Earth?

There are high councils who oversee the networks of beings who are involved with raising the frequencies in and around Earth. Not every being on Earth is here to work with humans or to raise frequencies, yet by just being present on Earth they contribute to raising Earth's vibrations.

Many beings are here for the experience or for an adventure. Some are here for a kind of vacation. The soul always decides what the purpose will be in creating a body or bodies.

Have dolphins been here a long time?

We were one of the first species to come to Earth. The council of assistant creators asked if we would come to Earth as she was being created to help set up some of the basic geometric holographic structure grids that would allow Earth to be who she is. We have existed far longer than humans and humanoids in other galaxies. You could say we are guides, elders watching over what we have helped to create. Also, there are other species involved with the basic set-up of Earth, including the whale.

Do you understand humans?
We are happy and are capable of learning many beings' languages in one way or another. We communicate with humans telepathically, yet most humans still do not understand or accept that this is what is natural. Not only for us but for them. We communicate in the best ways possible with humans, but we are saying so much more than they are currently aware of. If only they would open their hearts and listen. Also, we are always emitting various frequencies to help humans open up, to heal them, to guide them. We do not say this from an arrogant point of view, but simply speaking from an evolutionary standpoint (smile). An analogy would be that we emit all the colors and frequencies of the rainbow and many more. We do not have words to describe this.

We see the best in humans and encourage love and joy to be expressed through them. This helps raise their frequencies and assists them with their evolutionary process as humans and souls, which also assists Earth with the evolutionary expansion she is moving through.

Do dolphins exist in other worlds besides Earth and Sirius?
Oh yes. We swim in multiple dimensions as beings and in the interdimensional creations that we assist with. We assist with helping to shift frequencies, basic grids, and holographic geometric structures when they are called for by the All. It is the Key Creator and the All who by divine design decide to create basic changes within universes. And this includes every living being and life form, whether they are aware of it or not.

So you are doing major work in creating the new paradigm for Earth as well as within this and other universes?
Simply put, yes. We are one of many species of beings who are a part of orchestrating creation and holographic shifts in many universes.

Are the whales also a part of this?

Yes. We are kin. The whales and dolphins along with many others helped to set up the basics on Earth. It wasn't a one-species job (laugh).

Will dolphins be staying on Earth in physical form much longer?

Some of us will remain here in physical form so that our frequency will continue to assist Earth, yet many of us are and will be leaving. Yet understand that this does not mean that we will not still be assisting Earth and doing our work. We simply will be working from other realms.

We work from many realms/dimensions now since we are multidimensional beings. The physical body is a way for us to anchor in the frequencies with Earth since Earth is physical, too. Yet Earth exists in many dimensions as well. Every living being is multidimensional and this is what we are trying to show humans as well as some other species who are unaware of this or who have forgotten who they are as a soul as well as group soul.

Group soul?

What I am referring to is that every soul belongs to a group of souls who have the same or similar purpose and mission to fulfill.

Do you know most of the other beings here on Earth?

We know many soul groups here on Earth, but not all of them in terms of direct communication. As we mentioned, we meet many of them through the teamwork we do interdimensionally.

What does your essence look like?

My particular essence looks like a brilliant rainbow of lights, which includes many unearthly colors that flow outward from my core like a sun. My energy radiates countless rays of light. But remember that other souls who have chosen to be dolphin have soul essences that look different from mine.

What other realms do you live in?

I am still living on Sirius, while also on Earth. I am living lives in two other universes currently helping to create new paradigms. Also, I am living about fifteen other etheric and semi-etheric existences within other dimensions.

Are all aspects of yourself aware of the other aspects of your soul self?
Some aspects are more aware than others of the multidimensionality of my soul.

Are dolphins mirroring and teaching humans about their own multidimensional selves?
Yes. One body on Earth does not constitute the whole of your soul. Humans are multidimensional beings living many lives at once. This can be difficult for humans to comprehend, especially since time does not really exist except within the dream of physical life on Earth. In many other realities, everything is happening simultaneously, which is very difficult for the human mind to process, yet this is the way of the soul.

Are all aspects of you working with creating paradigms or are some of them doing other things?
Some aspects are assisting the All with creating and setting up holographic geometric structures while some of my aspects are fishing (laugh).

Fishing?
I thought that would catch your attention (laugh). A phrase I felt humans would understand—taking a vacation. I love to have fun and to enjoy life. I love being joyful because that is who I am. It is my soul's essence. So, you could say, some aspects are enjoying the luxuries that exist within other dimensions. This is about balance with the soul. Yet, I love the creativity of creation that I have the wondrous opportunity to express.

This makes sense (laugh). Are you shapeshifters?
Yes. Even though my physical form on Earth is dolphin, I am often creating in other dimensions with various etheric bodies that are continually changing shape, form, and quality of energies. Remember, every being in truth is frequency.

Are you here to assist humans?

Yes. But we are here to assist in whatever we can with many beings, with the waters, the entire Earth. The moon's energies help us to accomplish what we are here to do. We are not here specifically to assist humans, although they seem to need more assistance in remembering who they are and what wonderful beings they are.

Can you say more about the moon?

The moon's energies help maintain Earth's balance and to keep her in sync with the rest of your solar system. This is very important for humans to understand. It would be nice to thank the moon as well as Earth for all that they give and for the work that they do so magnificently.

What would you like to say to humans?

We would love for you to listen to us with your hearts. You do not need all the instruments to understand us. You have seen we can learn your language. We have a much more complex language of light, sound, and frequency that we truly wish you would focus on rather than trying to measure how intelligent we are. As you see, we are intelligent, but there is so much more to us, dear ones. Connect with our hearts and you will know us better as well as yourselves.

Thank you.

Love and Joy to you.
Dolphin Elder

Chapter 6

Deer

We grace Earth with beauty and gentleness

Hello. Wonderful to see you. Please tell me about deer.
Deer are Earth-based beings. We are not an ancient race like many other species are. In fact, we are younger. Our souls are of a young nature. We were created to bring beauty on Earth. We were created to leap and mingle with the trees in the forest. Deer keep the energies around Earth grounded, as do trees, rocks and other beings. We were created by an assistant creator who oversees certain kingdoms on Earth. But we carry the divine spark of Key Creator within.

Are the souls who live as deer from other galaxies?
Yes. Souls who inhabit deer form are from various other galaxies, but deer as a species is not from a particular planet or star. Some souls who dress themselves in "deer clothing" are from other galaxies and some are from this galaxy. These souls want to know what it is like to live as a deer. And when we talk about *core deer energy*, it comes from another dimension. Not all souls who are in deer form are from this other dimension, but the basic energy of deer comes from another dimension. This may seem confusing or like a paradox, but it is not.

We are gentle and grace Earth with beauty and gentleness. We were created to come to Earth and to be a part of the diversity of many and varied beings from different galaxies as well as this galaxy. Do not forget that there are beings from this galaxy on Earth.

Some of the key or fundamental energies of species are stored in interdimensional templates. Vast amounts of information are stored and coded in holographic templates and can be accessed by those who possess the key.

Key?

Yes, those who have access to the templates must have a key. The key is a series of frequencies that allows those beings to access the templates. Be still and let us lead you to this particular deer template.

I see a ring of templates in a circle. The first template in this ring showed me what is known as deer leaping. I opened the second and there was a reindeer. I opened another and there were Thomson's gazelles. I opened the next one and it showed me a holographic blueprint of a construction of core deer energy. I opened the next and it showed me another blueprint of deer energy. The next template I opened had vast amounts of information about deer DNA. The next one I opened contained notes about someone's observations about deer on Earth. I opened the next template about deer and saw nothing but darkness. It was an energy void from which beings could be created. Then I opened the next one. It was a chakra system along with stored DNA material. I opened another template and there was a family of deer in a forest. The last template opened and the vibration and frequency of deer were stored here.

We have shown you a part of what creates a particular species on Earth. Not all species are created by assistant creators in the way that we were. But this is another aspect of what is true when you focus on the multiple energy levels of the All.

What about your soul and spirit? Are you living in other bodies elsewhere?

We are soul and spirit as you refer to it. One of the templates holds the collective soul energy of deer just as there is a holographic template for the human collective. There is also the individual level where deer are individuals. Every deer belongs to a group soul just as every human does. Remember to focus on essence, not physical bodies (smile). There is a group soul of beings in which one might manifest as a deer, another as a human, and another as a cat or tree. You can see traits or flavors of each soul's origin in every living being.

I can be a deer on Earth since we are basically Earth-based, but my soul might also desire to be a rat, a human, or some other kind of being on another planet.

Thank you, deer, for all the amazing things you have shown me. Humans say there are too many deer. I've always felt that there are too many humans on Earth. We humans don't think about how to procreate in a responsible way which would benefit all species. What do you think?

Yes, it is a big lesson. It is amusing when humans think that there are too many deer who are destroying the environment and decide to kill us, because they are blind to what their own species is doing to Earth. Humans would not consider killing other humans just because there are too many of them on Earth, correct?

We are reflecting to humans their own creation of overpopulating the world. The difference is that deer are attempting to survive by eating what is in the area in which they live.

Humans kill deer, they say, to save the forests. Yet all this began because of too many humans on Earth. And humans are destroying more and more sacred forests to make more room for more and more humans. In the process, they continue to destroy the forests and areas where deer live. So, what are we to do?

The lesson here is about balance. We reflect back to humans what they have created and are continuing to create on Earth. This is not intended to judge. These are simply the facts.

So what do we do with all the humans?

As you know, Mother Earth is and will be balancing the energies of the human species. The souls who leave Earth's plane agree to leave in their proper timing.

Thank you for communicating with me. These concepts are very important for humans to hear.

Peace, love, joy, and groundedness. We love Earth. Dear one, we thank you for opening to receive our messages (smile).

Deer

Chapter 7

Cat: Melinda

Earth is beautiful

Melinda woke me up this morning singing. She's a cat with a bright soul whom I've been doing energetic work for many years. Originally, at the request of her person, I had done a Soul Recovery with her to bring back and integrate her dissociated aspects from past trauma. After regaining her wholeness through this process, Melinda began to ask me to align her chakra systems, balance her aura, and assist her in balancing her multidimensional selves. (You can read more about Soul Recovery in my book, Animal Communication—Our Sacred Connection.)

Melinda is one of the first animals who showed me her star being energies in a direct fashion. Her aura was flashing rainbows that swirled around her in a way that was different from many auras I had seen.

Hello, Melinda. Good to see you.

You and I are the same. We are light. We come from different galaxies, actually different universes. What fun! Relax with this chat and listen with your heart.

The star I have traveled from is distant. There are many dimensions intertwined with dimensions of other worlds, galaxies, universes and beyond. I come from a star that is beyond the Milky Way. My universe is a few dimensions from the universe from which you come. You could say our universes are twin universes.

This beloved etheric star from which I come has the most beautiful frequency. Listen to my home star sing.

I can hear your home star singing. It's glorious and unearthly.
My home star is of a high, high frequency. You and I have known each another in past lives. Our souls are connected.

The star I come from literally sings in harmony with countless sounds and chords of many frequencies. Those who come from this star sing as well. I decided to awaken you this morning with my singing. Did you enjoy it? (smile).

Oh yes. What is your home star's name?
My home star's name is Ee-ah. This really is not the name, but this is the vibrational sound. We sing the language of vibration, color, and sound. There is no time or space, yet there is space; but not in the way there is space from a human's perception. I do not view space through physical eyes, but through my beingness of vibration.

Thank you. What do you enjoy doing on Ee-ah?
We dance, sing, and create whatever we desire to create. There is only light, unconditional love, and consciousness on our star.

Do you have different sexes on your star or families?
We are androgynous beings. We do not experience sex or families in the way humans do. We create whatever we desire from our essence. We combine our essences to create other worlds, other beings, other selves.

What do you mean other selves?
What I mean is that I can create another aspect of me from my essence if I desire. For example, if I am a song in the moment, I can sing a rainbow or anything else into existence. It is difficult to give examples since there is not much to compare between my home star and how things are on Earth. But I can create a rock, tree, motorcycle or spacecraft if I set my intention. And all this happens instantaneously.

The etheric worlds as you know are malleable. The energies are present to be shaped and molded into whatever we desire to create by setting our intention. And the truth is that all worlds are malleable even though they may appear solid.

Sounds like fun!
It is great fun! You have experienced this yourself in etheric realms during the night.

Why did you come to Earth, Melinda?
One reason I have come to Earth is to be with my person Mary, who is my star sister and soul sister. Thank you.

I was asked to come to Earth by a friend of a friend, you might say. A friend shared what they knew about Earth and had experienced when they were here at one point. I was up for an adventure. But also, I made the choice to come and assist Earth with her evolutionary process along with countless others from many worlds and universes. You know the beat.

So you're here to help with the energetic shifts happening with Earth?
Many of us are shifting energies interdimensionally with Earth for the sake of the All. This involves helping the Milky Way shift into a higher vibration and integrate with other galaxies and universes that are doing the same.

What are you doing personally to help with this process and why did you choose to be in a cat body?
I am fulfilling my purpose. I am meditating and shaping energies in various dimensions from my wonderful cat body. It is inconspicuous. I chose to be a cat because cats live with people yet do not in certain ways. This was a way to be with Mary. Our souls decided that it would be this way before we came into the bodies we are living in. Also, I am a teacher for Mary, you, and others; and both of you are teachers for me. We have all come full circle in meeting here on Earth.

Are all cats from one world, galaxy or universe?
Not all species of cats are from one galaxy, planet or universe. The souls in cat bodies are from various galaxies, universes, dimensions, and other. The essences in human bodies are from other galaxies and beyond. The soul decides what species of body will best suit its needs for its mission, growth, and experiences.

Jacquelin Smith

A cat body suits you well!
　Earth is beautiful. A cat body fits my vibration well in regard to my home star's singing frequencies. This way, I could be with Mary as well as be on my own in the world (as an outdoor cat) to do the work I have come to do in helping to raise and shift Earth's vibrations. Also, I do quite a bit of shapeshifting, as Mary has shared with you. It is a much easier way to be wherever I desire to be at any given nanosecond.

Melinda: Photo by Lynda Sowers

What would you like to say to humans?
　Sing sing sing. I love Earth's music. I an referring to the song that Earth sings and that other beings sing. Humans are still trying to regain harmony within and with one another. The human species was experimented with long ago, but is now getting back on track. LOVE is always the song of the All. Every being is connected as One.

Thank you, sweet Melinda.
　You are welcome. This was fun.
　Melinda from Ee-ah

This telepathic conversation between Melinda and me came through in

her singing frequencies, yet my high self and brain were able to translate it into words. This is the same way we can process communicating telepathically with animals. All of our basic essences are different musical notes or vibrations that make up a harmonious symphony which IS the Creator.

Chapter 8

Cats: Mittens and Milo
(A neighbor's cat companions)

I rode in on a beam of moonlight

One night while I was looking at the full moon, I heard a silent voice shout from my neighbor's yard, "I am from the moon." There sat my neighbor's white cat, Mittens. She shouted again, "I am from the moon." I thought I might be making this up, yet I had learned to trust myself with these kinds of happenings. I thanked Mittens and asked her to share what she wanted me to know about all this.

It is true. I am from Earth's moon. I rode in on a beam of moonlight and entered this cat body. Milo is from a different place. (Milo is Mitten's cat mate.) I am moon white (smile).

I have an extra toe to prove it (laugh). Some bodies that vary from the norm can be a star being. Look at my aura. Different, is it not? You never noticed it since I live next door and have not talked to me much. Yet, you have tried to befriend me when I am in your yard. Look at my energy. My aura is not the same as yours or many other cats'. Look at the shimmering silver and white light around me.

Yes, I do, Mittens. It is beautiful (smile).

Milo is from Jupiter, or I should say one of Jupiter's moons. He and I are shapeshifters and elusive, and love living with Nancy. She talks to us and watches over us. We watch over her. She is a delightful soul. We love communicating with the flowers and plants in her yard.

Do the flowers and plants communicate in the same way that you do with me?

Yes, but you already know that. The same living force that fills every living being connects all living beings.

Tell me more about your origin from the moon. Are you really from the moon?

Why not from the moon? (chuckle). The moon may appear cold, icy and dead to humans. Why would that exclude us from the list of worlds where there might be life? Maybe not life as you know it, but we exist in a different form. I am an energy form, a beam of moonlight, which has a different frequency and vibration than sunlight. You too are a beam of light or frequency.

I am visiting Earth for a short time and will return to my original home. Yet the moon and Earth are one, even though it appears that they are separate. Earth could not maintain its place in space without the moon and where would the moon be without Earth? The moon separated from Earth long ago in order to create balance and for new species to be seeded on Earth.

How did the moon and Earth separate into two spheres?

A major collision between Earth and an asteroid is what created Earth's moon.

Thank you. Are there other dimensions in and around the moon?

Yes, there are multiple dimensions within and around the moon that humans do not see and most are not aware of on a conscious level. But at a deeper level, humans know the truth, that the moon was once a part of Earth.

Humans see craters on the moon due to her violent birthing process. I see my family when I look at the moon. You see light when you look at her, and I am able to see intuitively the dark side of the moon.

Do life forms from the moon visit Earth?

The moon and sun help humans to remember the light even though their vibrations are different, yet not. There are simply different life forms on the moon. These other life forms on the moon visit Earth often. It is easy for us to be on Earth in the blink of an eye. Remember, in reality they were one before the moon was created from Earth's energies. It is easy to simply come to Earth on a moonbeam.

There are many beings on Earth that visit the moon regularly. Why not? Many amphibians and birds visit the moon. Bats and other nocturnal animals love the moonlight's energy. They listen to the moon sing and communicate through her light and vibration. And the light reflecting from the moon is our sun's light, but when synthesizing with the moon, this creates yet another vibration.

Everything is connected.

Every living form is a being which is connected to all other beings. A planet is connected to its moon or moons. And the moons are connected to its planet and stars. There are complex interconnections within every galaxy and all other energies and beings. Every galaxy is interconnected, interdimensionally speaking, with all other galaxies and universes. They all commune through the language of light, frequency, sound, and color.

Thank you. Do you and Milo get along well?

Milo and I enjoy lounging in your yard. We were happy when you moved in. Milo is shy, so don't mind him. He gets freaked out by earthly things whereas I am accustomed to Earth.

Ask Milo about Jupiter. Jupiter is another realm. Earth is not solid, nothing is solid, gas is just another form of energy. It does not make it less inhabitable unless you are human I suppose.

Milo

Milo is an orange cream color with brilliant blue eyes.

Jupiter and its moons are more beautiful than you can image. I come from a metallic kind of energy. It is hard to find words to share this with you. My original essence is from one of Jupiter's smallest moons, which is the farthest away from Jupiter. Jupiter's moons were formed after Jupiter was created. I was created on Jupiter and transmuted to one of the moons. I was asked by the council of creators to assist with balancing the energies of that area of space and time. Is it not sublime?

You have such intense blue eyes and lovely cream/orange fur, Milo. Does this have anything to do with coming from one of Jupiter's smallest moons?

Thank you. A cream/orange cat with blue eyes is not usual. This reflects the energies of my essence as a star being. This is no different than Mittens having white fur and gold eyes while her aura rays outward with white and silver.

I see.

Now, look at my aura. This will be a bit different and new for you to see (sly smile).

Yes. I see different colors of energy curls—like a young girl's curls. I see swirls of varied rainbow colors and other unearthly colors, which I realize are frequencies that don't exist on Earth. (Mittens's aura emits rays outward like a sparkler.)

Why are you two together on Earth?

Milo and Mittens

We are together because we agreed to meet here on Earth and spread our vibration and light, even though we act like ordinary cats. Our souls decided to be a part of the interdimensional shifts, to lift Earth's vibration during this time period. Also, this gives us the opportunity to be together in physical form, even though it is not easy being in physical form nor in this framework of time and duality.

Milo

In a way this is like a vacation of sorts from my home planet/moon. It is a very short time on Earth considering how long a cat lives. Many souls who know one another go on missions together.

Are there various councils you know about?

Different beings from various planets, stars, galaxies, and universes who make up many councils gather together and discuss alliances and what missions will help to create an atmosphere of peace, love and cooperation. They also discuss such matters as how to deal with renegade beings or those who have committed crimes against beings on another planet or star or in other dimensions. Various councils and very evolved beings decide how the renegades or criminals will be dealt with in regard to what they have done. These councils serve the All. They are busy doing very high work in many universes.

I am giving you the opportunity to look through the windows of the more basic truths of universes and beyond. Remember, what you think of as life on Earth is an illusion created by other beings. Wake up and remember that the All is energy. The All is spirit and the basis of All is love.

Do all beings have this knowledge within?
Every being knows these basic truths within their core essence. since their core essence is the Key Creator. Yet there are those who exist who want to be powerful. Humans might call them gods, and some of these gods do not always understand or know how their energies are affecting other living forms, including humans. This, in turn affects all others on Earth and everywhere else.

Thank you, Milo.
You are welcome.
Milo, from one of Jupiter's moons

Chapter 9

Cat Elder

Cats keep the lines of telepathy open

Hello. Are you a cat elder?
Yes. I already sense a few of your questions so let me begin with some basics. Those who inhabit cat form are from various galaxies and universes, not just one world. There are many souls who decide they want to live in a cat body while on Earth. You have heard Melinda, Milo and Mittens talk about their homes and why they are here.

When a soul chooses a cat body, they understand that they will be living with humans or in close proximity to humans. Those who choose to be cat understand that they can get a great deal of work done, energetically speaking, because many of their needs will be cared for by their people. This frees them up to pursue their missions on Earth.

What about feral cats who roam the streets in some countries where people cannot care for them?
Cats who roam the streets in other countries, such as India, China, Japan, Africa, and many other countries are cats who are pursuing their particular missions despite the fact that it is a more challenging lifetime physically as well as emotionally.

What difficulties do cats encounter when living with humans?
Many cats who live with humans must deal with their human's

attitudes and feelings on a daily basis. This can be very challenging if a cat is living with an unhappy human. But it is much easier if the cat is living with a happy person. Sometimes cats do not desire to take on their person's negative feelings and attitudes (which are energies) willingly. This is more so for cats who live indoors than for those who are outdoors on a daily basis.

Animals who live indoors with humans have a more difficult time setting psychic boundaries, so they end up taking in their person's energies in the same way that a child does from his or her parents. If a cat lives with an unhappy person, it can help them to go outside. This allows them to release any energies they have taken on. Some cats are willing to take on a portion of their human's feelings, but do not wish to take on the entire energy of who their person is.

In what ways do cats benefit from humans?

Cats benefit a great deal from humans who understand cats. Cats feel the love a person sends them. Also, they can perceive what a human is thinking and feeling. Therefore, if a cat lives with a happy, upbeat person this uplifts the cat. They benefit from people who know how to respect "cat boundaries."

What kind of work are cats doing on Earth?

Cats have missions in the same way that humans have missions and purpose. Cats are healers, teachers, meditators, mediators, interdimensional shifters and workers along with many other roles. This is not so different from the dog in some ways, yet very different in the way they approach and fulfill their missions.

Those who incarnate into cat bodies choose to assist humans with raising their vibrations. Most humans are not aware of this, but cats are working diligently to wake humans up to their own natural intuitive gifts and multidimensional selves. A large part of working with humans is to assist humans with opening their hearts and recalling what intuitive and powerful beings they truly are.

Cats are very telepathic by nature and are showing humans that they, too, are very telepathic. Actually, all beings are telepathic and have telepathic connections since we are all One. Cats help to keep the lines of telepathy open interdimensionally. Cats are excellent communicators telepathically and have their paws on the pulse of what is going on not only with humans but with Mother Earth.

Cats as well as all other beings are continually communicating telepathically with humans. It is just that humans often are not open to receiving messages from other animals because they have been taught the lie that other beings cannot "talk." It is very important to continue to teach humans that telepathic communication with other animals is not only possible, but is natural. Cats are great at teaching this lesson.

I realize animals are constantly communicating with each other telepathically. What about cats?

Cats are highly intuitive and telepathic. They are often communicating with one another throughout neighborhoods and great distances. Their communications depend on every soul's purpose and physical position while in a cat body. As I mentioned, cats are shapeshifters working interdimensionally and multidimensionally with one another as well as with many other species. Some of these species live on Earth while others exist only in other realms.

Say more about shapeshifting and interdimensional shifts.

Cats are shapeshifters by nature. Many species are shapeshifters, but the cat has chosen to be in partnership with humans to wake them up to their gifts and abilities as shapeshifters, too. This is becoming more evident as the veils thin and other realities are now more readily accessible. For example, you have a friend who saw her cat companion leap over her backyard fence and disappear in mid-air. An instant later, her cat friend appeared in the middle of her neighbor's backyard. Your friend's cat companion wanted her person to see this interdimensional shifting to remind her of what she, too, is capable of doing.

Thank you. I know that animals are often mirrors for their people. What do cats mirror to humans?

Cats mirror the more evolved intuitive, heart-centered aspects of themselves with clarity to humans to remind them that they too have these talents and open-hearted qualities. Cats are typically clear in who they are and what they desire. Is this not true? (smile).

Yes. Do they act like tuning forks for humans vibrationally to help bring them to a place of inner harmony and alignment?

Yes. The human has the opportunity to learn how to resonate with their own basic inner tone or song. Every soul has a song which it sings. Whether or not the human ever hears it is another question. It depends on if the human is willing to open and listen to not only their own heart but to other living beings who communicate from their hearts. By cats being present in your lives you have teachers and mirrors and healers who can remind you how to align and balance within.

Those in cat bodies have agreed to do quite a bit of work with the human species. They have chosen close interaction in order to help to raise humans' vibrations.

How else do cats assist humans?

Cats are wonderful protectors. They have the ability to physically and psychically protect those whom they are around. Cats also protect their people's homes by keeping them clear from lower vibrations and entities who need to be in a different dimension.

Cats are savvy interdimensional travelers. They can assist humans with remembering how to travel in such a way that their consciousness can be anywhere they want it to be in an instant, whether it be on Venus or in the seventh universe from Earth.

When a cat's person is ready to cross over, their cat will help them to cross over into the light. You remember when a human friend of yours was getting ready to cross over that her cat companion, Smokey, sat quietly beside her for a few hours. Your friend crossed over that night. You saw how he was helping her spirit detach from her body.

Yes. It was an experience I'll always cherish.

Cats help humans to remember who they are and to connect with their core essence. I am not insinuating that cat is better or of more value because all beings are of equal value, but cats are simply more evolved since they have been around a lot longer than the human species.

What would you like humans to remember about themselves?

All beings are co-creators. Cat is asking humans to remember that they, too, are co-creators, and to remember that all other living forms are also co-creators. Humans tend to think they are the most evolved and powerful species, but this is a myth they have created. This myth was created from the ego. Humans are ready to live from their hearts rather than from ego; and this is a huge shift in consciousness that is and has been taking place for awhile. These shifts are not only happening with Earth, but with your entire solar system and beyond.

Humans are from the stars as are all other species. Earth was seeded long ago by assistant creators with the DNA of countless species. Humanoids exist in many other galaxies and universes.

Do cats feel the same emotions as humans?

Yes. Cat feels the same range or spectrum of emotions that humans experience. Cats have hundreds of ways in which to express their feelings. These expressions come through body gestures, vocalizations, and in many other ways. Anyone who knows a cat knows this to be true. Just think of how many ways cats share their feelings through their eyes. What about the tail, ears, whiskers—I could go on and on (smile).

Do you know if most species share the same spectrum of emotions?

Long ago, humans decided that animals did not have souls, yet this is not the truth. It was a false belief constructed by humans.

Souls who incarnate as cat, or any other living form on Earth for that matter, and many from other universes, experience feelings and have a wide range of emotions as does the human species. Of course, every species has their own specific ways of expressing feelings and emotions. As you know, plants have a full spectrum of emotions and feelings as well.

For centuries humans did not accept that animals had feelings, but were simply like machines without souls. It has become clear to most humans that cats and other living forms possess feelings and express emotions. Cats feel love and joy as well as sadness and pain.

Also, cats are learning lessons when they come together with a particular human or humans. Those who live in cat bodies have not "arrived" (smile).

Who oversees the cat species?

Look at the Creator's light within cat, or any living form, and see that they all have spirit and soul. Every cat has an individual soul. There is also the Cat Overseer Soul or Cat Guardian who guides the cat species. Cats are not a group consciousness, yet there is a cat species consciousness level just as there is a human species consciousness level. Every species has their own consciousness and collective level.

I'm curious about cats' attitudes. At times, cats seem to act as if they are superior or as if they think humans aren't very bright (smile).

Well, every species has certain inclinations and basic makeups, don't they? (laugh). Cats are one of the few species that humans accept in terms of their independent nature. As I mentioned, cats know who they are and why they are on Earth, so they may sometimes become impatient with humans who seem at times to run in circles, not listening to their own basic intuitive core or self.

Most cats do not seek approval from their people or anyone else. This is a very valuable lesson to be learned from cat. This does not mean that they do not desire to be loved and cared for, but they live from their essence. Cats ask for respect and space yet cats also ask for love and to be cared for so there is a balance in living that cat mirrors for humans. Cat offers these lessons. We wish for humans to allow themselves to become students. Does this make sense?

Oh yes. Also, many humans have the need to make cats and dogs their "children." I am hoping that humans will open to what you are sharing with me.

It is important for humans to respect animals for the beings they are rather than boxing them into the role of "children" or their alter egos. It is not appropriate for a human to project and attempt to get many of their needs met through their cat friend, or any other animal for that matter. A mutual exchange is wonderful, but when a human is extremely dependent on an animal to have needs met, this indicates that they are out of balance and need to go within themselves to find a way to meet their own needs.

How would you feel if someone tried to keep you a child? It would stunt your growth in many ways, which cat and other species do not desire.

Cats are here to share, love, and communicate. There can be a healthy mutual exchange between cat and human if the human can relate to and treat the cat as an equal life form.

Can you say more about this issue with humans and love?

Love does not mean that a cat sits on a human's lap or follows a human around. A mature love is about mutual respect, giving one another space, and coming together when it is appropriate. Being overly dependent on an animal only creates imbalance within the relationship.

Some humans have misperceptions about cats as well as other species. This is why communicating telepathically is so important. It is a heart-to-heart communication which takes place so both species see each other's essence. This goes far beyond the physical interactions. The telepathic communication experience allows a human and other animal to *know* one another at the deepest core level.

Cats are God's love in expression. Many humans misunderstand cats. They may view cats as aloof and not as loving as dogs, but this is not the truth. Those in cat bodies love the human species, but simply express it in a different way. Cats would not have chosen to live with humans if they did not love them.

The Key Creator's love within cat is loving you even when you may not think so. Look at a cat's essence. It radiates with great love. Take time to sit down and listen to what your cat friend has to communicate with you. It will open your heart and mind.

Cats assist humans in many ways. Can you mention some practical ways?

They do a great deal of healing work with humans whether it be in close proximity or from a distance. As many humans know, a cat will sit on your lap or lie beside you when you are ill. A cat can help to clear and align a person's energies.

Cats help the elderly in nursing homes as well as those who are labeled as psychotic and schizophrenic. Cats are great companions for those who are lonely or feeling unloved in general.

Cats reflect the Creator's love in a healthy way. A cat is happy to see you when you come home and will "let" you pet them if they are in the mood. In subtle ways, cats will let you know that you are appreciated and loved.

Cats have a wonderful ability to teach humans how to respect boundaries if the human is needing to learn that lesson. They are trying to teach humans how to be in *partnership* rather than dominating over them. Cats offer nurturing to not only your physical presence but to your soul. Thank your cat for these wonderful gifts that they give so freely.

Thank you. Is part of the problem that humans come from need because they don't know what love is or how to express love? I have talked with people who cry and say their cat doesn't love them or may even dislike them because he or she won't sit on their lap.

Yes. This is about mature love as I have mentioned. When one truly loves another, regardless of species, there is a deep desire to let the other "be" who they truly are without trying to change them. I am talking about this at the deepest level of true love. And it is this *true* or *honest* love that humans are being asked to remember by opening their hearts. And to remember that this love *is* the Key Creator's love.

Can you address what humans label as misbehaviors with cats?

Issues can occur if a cat takes on too much of a person's negative energies. This can also happen when a cat is mistreated, neglected or ill. If a human knows how, they can assist their cat friend with coming back into alignment and harmony once again. But, at the core essence, the cat knows who he or she is regardless of the "misbehaviors."

Sometimes misbehaviors are humans' misperceptions about how they think their cat friend should act or be. This can be in conflict with the cat's inner self. At times humans ask cats to "be" and "act" how humans want them to be and act. And if the cat does not respond to what they want, the person gets frustrated and then labels it as a problem, which only creates more misunderstanding or tangled energies.

These comments are not intended to be criticisms, but to offer humans' insight into themselves and cats.

Humans who love cats offer cats the gift of heart-felt love.

I hope we humans take this message to heart. What incredible gifts cats have to offer us if we open and listen with our hearts.

I, Cat Elder, am delighted to share these messages with you this evening. I am happy that you will be sharing these messages on a larger scale so humans can open their hearts and expand their minds in regard to cats.

Thank you from my heart and soul. Blessings of love and gratitude to those beings who are dressed in cat elegance.

You are welcome (smile).
Cat Elder

Chapter 10

Lion

I am a part of matrix energies

Hello, lion. What would you like to share?
Earth scientists talk about the Big Bang as if they were there. We were all there in one way or another. They can see through the windows of time and space to a certain point from the human perspective, but much of it is conjecture and limited theories. The beginning was not as violent as science states. I am referring to the "beginning" from what humans think of as the beginning.

Stars blow up and spew outward creating new galaxies, don't they?
Yes, but the very first light was silent. There was a point of light, of geometric form, that created a frequency that created the very first light of your universe.

Was the beginning of this universe an accident?
No. It came into being by divine design. The light is/was/will be the first dawning or birthing of this universe and other universes. This is difficult for the mind to grasp since it is beyond mind and logic. All is, was, and will be in perfect order. This is the higher order of design which the Creator created. And from there, it was a chain reaction of life begetting life in numerous forms that humans cannot imagine.

Why do you come to me as a lion?

This lion body disguises my true essence. I am a being from a higher equation. I am an energy that creates the inner form that you are seeing now that initially unnerved you. You are familiar with a lion so I appear as a lion. If you had initially seen me as I am, you might have sent me away. I am.

I see you as a static kind of energy that's constantly vibrating with many legs arms or antennae - kind of tall and thin with three segments?

This is because I am. I am in a number of dimensions at once. So are you, but you do not look at your other selves the way you are perceiving me. So I can look a bit scary to you.

What do you mean you're an equation? What's your spiritual origin?

I am not from a planet or star. I am a being of multiple universes whose purpose it is to be a higher equation. I am a part of energy matrixes. An energy. I am. A small portion of my energies are in a lion on Earth. Other aspects of my energies are on other planets and stars and dwell in deep space. They are distributed in a way that serves the All. A certain percentage is in the lion form. Other percentages are in many other forms and geometric constructs. One aspect of my equation is in the constellation you refer to as Leo.

You could say being in the lion body and existing in other realms in other forms and energies allows me to fulfill my mission. I balance energies in deep space, which includes the material and interdimensional realms. I see this is hard for you to grasp, but I wanted to offer you this communication.

Thank you. I appreciate your communication, but it might be beyond me. Why are you in lion form?

Being a lion, I can do my work on Earth without much interruption from humans. I am living in Africa.

Are you being hunted by humans?

Not where I am. I can do my work from a fairly clear space and place on Earth. I have never experienced what I am experiencing being in lion form before. It is refreshing. Having a lion's senses is quite new and interesting for me. The mating habits of a lion are different from what I have known. It is all interesting.

Why are you on Earth?

I am in many places and spaces at once. Earth is but one place I have agreed to be in order to help shift the frequencies of your solar system, your universe, and other universes.

Do you understand and experience love?

Yes. Not in the way that you understand love. I know love from the I AM and I am.

Are you created from the Key Creator?

All energies are from Key Creator. There are other creators creating many and varied worlds. Just as humans create to an extent what happens in their lives, other creators are manifesting worlds, galaxies, and universes. This can be difficult for humans to grasp or accept. I serve and am an aspect of the Key Creator. Look at me.

When I look at you now, I see a pure white light.

Your mind wants you to stay within a certain framework in order to try to understand all this. Do not worry about trying to understand it all. You know the truth but the mind cannot comprehend it all. That is fine. Love and consciousness is the foundation of the All. Key Creator is love. I am from love.

Why do you sound like a robot?

I am not accustomed to bringing my vibration to this level in order to communicate with a human using their primitive language. Words cannot show or tell the truth. You must feel and know truth within you. I am not as smooth-flowing as many of the others who have communicated with you. Understand?

Yes. Thank you for giving me further insights.
You are welcome.
Lion

Chapter 11

Lion Elder

We are a primal reminder

Hello. Are you a lion elder?

Yes. I am happy to be here. The equation who is in lion form speaks the truth about who it is. But you asked to speak to a lion elder who could give you a broader view of lions and that would be me.

Thank you. Tell me about lions.

Lions are powerful beings. Many souls desire to experience being a lion for at least one lifetime, sometimes more. It is difficult in many ways to be in a lion body because of the conditions on Earth. Yet many souls who come from planets that are more desertlike or of a drier climate choose to be in bodies that live in drier climates on Earth, although there are some beings from drier climates who choose to experience the wetter areas on Earth for an adventure and for a different kind of experience. In general, beings from arid climates choose to take forms that live in dry areas.

Are all lions from a particular planet or realm or can any soul in the cosmos experience being a lion?

Lions are not from the same planet by any means. There are many very dry-climate planets that your world does not know about. Earth is a mix of dry and wet climates and in-between, which is not always the case on other planets.

What is it like to be in a lion body? Are you in a lion body now?

Yes. I am a very old lion and will not be on Earth much longer. This is part of the reason why I wanted to communicate with you before I cross over. Being in a lion's body can be simply wonderful or it can be very difficult depending on the life circumstances. My body is living in the Serengeti region right now. I have greatly enjoyed living my life as a lion. I have experienced wounds because I have had to defend my territory, but I have been fortunate in that I have lived many years.

Lion in Africa: Photo by Jacquelin Smith

How many years have you been on Earth?

In Earth time, it would be calculated to be about fifteen years. Earth is a luxurious planet from my point of view. Even though lions reside only in Africa now, we are aware of Earth's beauty. Lions used to exist in other places on Earth, but now we live only in Africa. To be able to roam through the grasses, to hunt, to sleep, to run is glorious! These are physical pleasures I do not experience on my planet since I am composed of a different physical form.

Where do you come from?

I come from a planet that is north, you would say, of Andromeda in another universe that humans cannot perceive.

What is your planet like?

My planet is smaller than Earth. It is of a very warm climate and there are many species on my planet, but they are vastly different from the species on Earth.

How so, and what do you look like on your planet?

My species' physical form is very, very tiny, and might be compared to the size of a bacterium that you can see under a microscope. There are other species that could be compared in size to microbes, viruses, and gnat-size beings who are all very powerful. They understand the energetic basics of light, sound, color and of life. We are all intelligent, although humans would not recognize this from their point of view.

Are there larger beings on your planet?

The largest being is about the size of a pencil eraser. We do not focus on size on our planet but on energy interactions. I am giving size comparisons so that you can get a sense of the beings on my planet. Humans tend to do comparisons, but we do not view other beings from the framework that you do. Every being simply is. We respect one another and live in perfect harmony and peace. We love one another. It does not take a large brain or even a brain to love or to be intelligent.

Thank you. Why are you here on Earth?

We were invited here to offer our particular frequencies to Earth. We thought about it for a long while and decided that we wanted to experience Earth as well as all of the other beings who were agreeing to take physical form on Earth.

You mentioned that not all lions are from your planet, but that particular souls decide to have an experience as a lion. What do you mean you were invited to be on Earth?

I am in lion form. Some other species on my planet are living in camel and llama form. Others decided to take big leaps and are living as clams, fiddler crabs and fish. But I did not want to take such a big leap. It was important for me to focus on lion energy since I am an elder.

Thank you. Why are lions on Earth?
Lions offer a primitive energy and wildness that Earth needs in order to maintain balance. Lions are reminders that every living being has a raw, primitive aspect. Since we do not have hunting on our planet, we view it as an adventure to experience being a carnivore. This may sound strange to you, but remember that this level of physicality on Earth is illusion, with every being playing their part.

Lions can be fierce but they can also be regal and loving. There are many different aspects to every life form and soul.

Lions work multidimensionally to keep energies in balance on Earth. We offer beauty and are a primal reminder to those on Earth. While lions sleep they are doing a great deal of work with not only Earth's energies but with your entire solar system. Lions travel interdimensionally. We are focused and act as gatekeepers guarding numerous interdimensional portals. We act as guides for beings and energies who are traveling continuously through this universe.

It sounds like lions have quite a few tasks they are doing.
Yes.

I've always respected and admired lions. I saw many lions while in Africa and was told they sleep much of the day because of the heat.
This is true on the physical level, yet souls inhabiting lions are doing a great deal of energetic work as I have just discussed.

Do you enjoy the lions' mating rituals?
Yes. The rituals of combining, as we refer to it on our planet, are different than being in a lion's body and mating many times in very short periods of time. This is one of the perks of being a lion (laugh).

Thank you. Do lions care about humans?
Yes. Lions can teach humans how to respect one another's space as well as other beings living on Earth and throughout the universe. We are not here to serve humans, but to serve Earth and entire solar system.

The human species has a difficult time learning to listen to what all other species communicate.

We desire to communicate with humans and for humans to communicate with us, but their fear holds them back. It is important to respect the ways and boundaries of every species with wisdom. But communications can always take place whether one is in the physical presence of a lion or not.

Have many lions left Earth on purpose?

Many souls who were in lion bodies have departed from Earth and returned to their worlds since there has been much less understanding and valuing of lions. It will not be long before lions will no longer exist on Earth; and we never intended to be on Earth forever. Our intention was to be here for a period of time, but then for the souls in lion bodies to return to their original homes.

Thank you. And thank you for gracing Earth.

You are welcome. I will not exist in lion form for much longer so I am very happy to have communicated with you this day. I am glad many humans will read our conversation.

Blessings to you on your journeys.

Thank you.
Lion Elder

Chapter 12

Yellow Butterfly

*Butterflies are free and the lightest part
of the soul if you would but see*

Welcome! I love butterflies. What would you like to share?
    I bring joy into the world. Butterflies are free and the lightest part of the soul if you would but see.
    I am of an intense high frequency. The vibration I carry is beauty. Butterflies bless flowers, the air, trees, and many other beings around us. We are close to the angels, but not angels in the way that you think of angels since we manifest in physical form. We are light, love and beauty. We are light traveling on wings! Many kinds of angels watch over Earth and all beings on Earth.

Thank you. Tell me more.
    Humans feel we are beautiful. Butterflies are songs. And to choose to be in a butterfly body, one has evolved to the point of being able to flutter here and there while in physical form. You could say we have earned our wings (laugh).
    The soul manifests a wide variety of existences on various planes of frequency and dimensions simultaneously. Being a butterfly can be but one existence out of many.

Jacquelin Smith

Say more about many existences happening simultaneously.

Let us say your soul is like a flower petal. And each leaf is a different lifetime experience whether it be past, present or future. But there really is no past, present, or future because everything is simultaneous. Anyway, all of these lives overlay one another so they are all intertwined and connected. The soul projects a certain portion of its energy into each existence. Each existence, whether it is a physical or etheric existence, has a different amount of soul energy invested.

I have thought this to be the case. Thank you. Where are you from and do butterflies exist elsewhere?

We are not from Earth originally. We are from a high frequency energy matrix. Our energies are anchored in that realm. Our energies, or souls, extend a bit of soul energy to manifest in physical form on Earth. But most of our soul's energy remains in the matrix.

We shapeshift interdimensionally while on Earth and elsewhere. We are not only on Earth but exist on and in other worlds, realms, and universes.

Are you in physical form on Earth?

Yes. I have been in physical form on Earth ten times. I enjoy being in physical form. Earth is full of beauty and we are about spreading beauty, which is a high frequency. This blesses Earth which is what we are here to do. But I also enjoy being here just for the sake of being surrounded by the beauty of flowers, meadows, breezes, trees, and sunshine.

Are you individual or group consciousness?

We are a group consciousness that manifests in various individual forms: physical, etheric and in-between, throughout the cosmos. We help to uplift vibrations wherever we are invited to do so.

What does your group consciousness look like?

Our group consciousness consists of a number of different frequencies. These frequencies are what you would think of as a musical chord. We are unseen in your realm since we are frequencies, but in our energy matrix we look like flashes of various lengths of light waves and colors that humans would not recognize. In terms of our original form, we do not look like butterflies. But a butterfly body is perfect for

Star Origins and Wisdom of Animals

the work we do throughout the cosmos. As I mentioned, we take many different shapes and forms depending on what universe we are living in.

Are all souls in butterfly form on Earth from the energy matrix?
No. Many of us from the energy matrix manifest as butterflies in various realms and worlds, but there are souls from other planets and star systems who desire to experience being a butterfly and so they do so.

Can you say more about your energy matrix?
Our realm of an energetic matrix is one of beauty, love, and joy. There are swirling rainbows, beautiful songs singing, and light so bright that it would be difficult for you to imagine. Much brighter than your sun. It is an astounding realm of radiant light, love, and joy. There are angels, and other beings in this realm which you have no names for since humans are not aware on a conscious level of these beings. There are no limitations or boundaries in our realm. It just is—we just are.

Wonderful! Say more about beauty and how you're communicating with me.
Beauty wakes up every living being. Humans love beauty. Really all living forms value beauty. Earth is precious and beautiful. Let humans not forget to revel in nature's beauty. They forget to appreciate and enjoy the Creator's gifts.

Do not get lost, because as I speak to you, I weave together all that I am communicating to you. I am not linear and do not communicate in a linear fashion. Then again, nothing is linear. But everything can seem linear because of the way the holographic programs are set-up on Earth. Those programs are shifting dramatically even as we speak.

What else would you like to share?
If you notice my aura, it is like swirls of mist with bright morning sunlight shining through it. So bright, you must turn your eye. This is my essence.

Now for the fun part of this communication! I am also an aspect of your soul. One of the flower petals that have grown from the core of your soul. One of your highest frequencies is that of me—we (smile). So we communicate, you and I, as different aspects or expressions of the same soul.

I am not separate from you, although it would appear so looking through the skewed illusion of time and space on Earth. This part of you, me, can be near or far depending on your perception and acceptance since all is energy.

Wow! You're an aspect of my soul, really?

I am one of your multidimensional selves spreading light and beauty wherever I go. I say "I" for the sake of helping the mind to grasp and accept this. You feel this in your heart. You feel this deep within your core.

Yes! I don't have words to express how I am feeling.

This is a surprise to your mind. Do not worry about not having words. The energy matrix from which I come does not communicate through words.

Yes, you are butterfly beautiful! Crying is your heart feeling this truth and the beauty and vastness of soul. Sing sing sing with your wings. When I flutter in the world I am spreading love songs of heart and soul and helping to lift the vibrations on Earth since this is what I, you, we, have agreed to do (smile).

Have you always been aware of me?

Yes, I have been aware that there was an aspect of my soul living as a human on Earth currently. But you, we, also live in many other dimensions, universes and star systems. Now, you are aware of me, the butterfly aspect of your soul who flits in and out of various dimensions working with Earth and other living forms.

I've been aware of at least two lives I am currently living on Earth! I am connecting with my multidimensional selves in a more conscious way these days. I view these other selves like a constellation in the night sky; each star connected to another forming the constellation of my soul.

Yes (smile). Every soul is multidimensional and is living as many expressions in various realms and universes simultaneously. With all the energetic shifts happening on Earth as well as in your solar system, humans are remembering that they are spiritual, multidimensional beings. Humans are evolving, as is every living form, and are connecting in more conscious ways with what I call the interdimensional highways. Humans are reconnecting to their basic soul essence and the Key Creator.

Thank you. I realize this has been going on for many years. It is joyful to see the leaps humans are taking to reconnect with their souls and Creator. I am thinking now that I can consciously connect with the energy matrix?

Of course. Just tap into the energy matrix anytime you wish through butterfly. It can be fun and you will be getting to know another aspect of your/our soul (smile).

Thanks for this gift and for this wonderful connection.

Oh, what joy to help you connect with one of the highest aspects of who you are in a conscious way and for me to connect with you. You have always honored and held butterflies as beautiful and sacred in your heart.

You can always communicate with me. Your mind needs a little time to digest this direct experience of two aspects of your soul communicating, which is different from an intellectual understanding.

Yes, it does. It sounds like you love being a butterfly.

Oh yes! I love being a butterfly. And I am just one of many aspects of the same soul, which includes you, which includes me. You are growing beyond old beliefs you once held (smile).

Do butterflies exist in other worlds and dimensions? I know that there are about 28,000 species of butterflies on Earth.

Yes. There are many butterflies in other worlds and dimensions. They look quite different in certain ways, though not really, than those fluttering around Earth. Remember many of the butterfly drawings you have done?

Yes.

Some butterflies in other worlds have six or more wings with heads at both ends! (smile). Many have six or more antennae. There are butterflies who are what you think of as physical. There are also those who are etheric and of other textures that I do not have words to describe.

Most humans identify a being as intelligent if it has a large brain. What about butterflies?
You know that the physical size of a being and its brain size, or if a being has no physical brain, has nothing to do with magnificence of a soul and its brilliant creations. There are many beings who do not possess brains in the way you think of brains, but who are highly intelligent and evolved beings who have very high frequencies.

The universal intelligence flows through every living being. Humans have a particular perception of what intelligence is, but it is a very limited one at that. What humans often label instinct is spirit/body intelligence. Will humans be able to survive on Earth the way roaches will survive?

Probably not. I understand this because of my work as an animal communicator. What do butterflies mirror to humans?
Butterflies are often used as a metaphor in regard to a human experiencing a rebirthing or transformation process. Caterpillars metamorphose into totally new beings with wings before emerging from their chrysalis. It is an actual physical metamorphosis. It is a miraculous happening!

We mirror to humans that they too can transform and evolve into new beings, which is taking place on a grand scale. Humans are evolving into beings who remember their wings. Some do have wings depending on what star systems they have come from (smile). Yet it is about giving consciousness wings and remembering you are connected to the All and can be anywhere in the cosmos you desire to be by letting your spirit and consciousness soar with your intention. And as the subconscious within humans shifts holographically, they will remember that they are divine souls living in human bodies.

As humans progress and get in touch with themselves, they will remember that they are capable of creating what humans would think of as miracles. But for us, and soon for humans, this is what the norm is in most universes.

This is why butterflies are so abundant over Earth. We not only do our interdimensional work of raising vibrations through beauty and love, but are reminding humans and other living forms what great things they are capable of manifesting when they are fully awake. Humans are energetically and physically going through metamorphosis.

Thank you, butterfly, beautiful and elegant aspect of my soul.

It has been delightful having this communication. Let us do this again.

Flowers and flowers to you.

Yellow Butterfly

Chapter 13

Cockatiel: Etheria

I taught you about forgiveness and love

Etheria and I lived together for thirteen years. I loved her and she taught me many lessons about patience, forgiveness, spontaneity, joy and love. Etheria crossed over a number of years ago, but her spirit is often present and she speaks to me in my dreams.

Hello, sweet Etheria. This is a nice surprise to see you.
Hello. I loved the name you bestowed on me since it was fitting for where I have come from, even though you weren't conscious of it at the time.

See the higher spectrum of flashing lights around me like the rainbows of Earth? It is a higher frequency. And the colors that you perceive being neon, are intensified colors you see on Earth and beyond.

Where are you from, Etheria?
I am from a world where we have wings, even though it is an etheric world. See my beautiful giant green and blue wings? See my long body that kind of looks like a bird, but not any bird on Earth. There you have it. I have three eyes and three legs. I will call them legs because that is how you can relate to what I am saying. In this realm we have spirit bodies that can be seen in the ethers.

Etheria: Photo by Jacquelin Smith

What else would you like to share?

Is not it very interesting that your nickname for me while I was in physical form was ET? (laugh). Knowing, but not knowing consciously, that I was from another world. I come from a spirit world that rings like chimes through the ethers. Beautiful. Hear the music.

Oh yes. It's beautiful and sounds like chimes—lovely haunting tones and chords. By the way, I always felt you were a key teacher for me.

Yes. I was your teacher and guardian angel in many ways. We were a team. I taught you about forgiveness and love and about cockatiels (smile).

How are you doing in the spirit world?

The spirit world is much more than what most humans think it is. In what you refer to as the spirit world, there are many galaxies, worlds and dimensions. It is hard to convey this through words.

Is the etheric world you come from different from what humans think of as the spirit world or other side?

Yes. And it is easier for me and those who are from etheric worlds to cross over into the other dimensions because we do not have the physical form which is dense and has not learned how to teleport with ease. Your consciousness teleports to other planets and dimensions, and you remember your experiences. Some humans can teleport their physical bodies, but not the majority of them. Eventually humans will learn how to teleport their physical bodies.

Even though a dimension may be perceived as being directly in front of you, there are layers of dimensions accessible in any given moment for anyone to pass through if they are ready and believe that they can.

Tell me about the world you come from originally.

The world I come from is glorious. We have six globes of silver light, which you could compare to moons. And we have three globes which you could perceive as suns, although they are not hot or cold. They are simply beautiful. The dimension in which my world exists is of high frequency and vibrates, which creates the chime-like harmonies which you are hearing this moment.

It is not organized like Earth. To you it may seem that my world is chaotic, but there is an order of frequencies, colors, and sounds. We do not have a ground or sky like Earth and this is why it looks chaotic to you. We do not have an up or down or side to side or front and back, as you have on Earth. Earth was a challenge for me to exist on.

Thank you. I feel like you and I've been together many times.
You and I have known each other long before Earth existed. Our souls have sung together through the stars. We have traveled to many near and distant realities. See me with your soul, see the world which I come from with your heart.

What else would you like to share?
Those from my dimension create worlds around us to create beauty. I was spun from a globe of incandescent purple light and my soul took flight.

How beautiful. Why did you choose to live in bird form?
Being a bird was the most acceptable form for my soul to inhabit while on Earth. And I would not have survived without you on Earth. Remember when I flew high into a tree across the street from your house? You communicated with me telepathically and showed me visually how to come down toward the ground stepping on tree branches. You saved my body and you learned how to concentrate telepathically in a way you had not experienced before.

Oh yes. I remember when you flew across the street. I went deep within myself to be calm and to communicate with you telepathically. And thank goodness, we worked together, and we had the opportunity to live together for many more years.
Be at peace, my dear friend and soul mate. Continue to learn and reach toward the stars. I love you.

Thank you. I love you, too, Etheria.
Fly like a bird into other dimensions. Humans are remembering that they can do this with ease.
Etheria

Chapter 14

Double Yellow-Headed Amazon Parrot: India

I came to Earth to complete a mission I began long ago

I communicate with and do soul recovery work with India, who is a beautiful double yellow-headed amazon parrot. She lives with a man named John.

India asks me to balance her aura and align her multidimensional selves. Also, I align her chakra systems with her high self, soul, and Creator, and ground her in her body and with the Earth. When this is done, India remains clear and happy, and better able to fulfill her mission as an interdimensional being who's helping to raise the vibrations in and around Earth.

India is high, high frequency. The first time we met, long distance that is, she was flashing swirls of brilliant rainbows from her aura. It was like watching a light show.

After communicating with India for seven years, it is always a delight to watch her light show and how she continues to expand multidimensionally. Being a clairvoyant, I have the privilege of seeing these energetic shifts. She continues to teach me about multidimensional selves and holographic constructs.

Hello, India. What would you like to say?
You and I are connected on the soul level. Even though we are

seldom in conscious contact, we are in contact telepathically in order to carry out some missions which we have agreed to fulfill together in other realms.

Thank you. Why did you choose a parrot body?
I came into the physical body of a parrot for many reasons. Beings on my home star have wings. Not quite etheric, but not quite physical. I can shapeshift any time I desire to do so. It is fun for me to shapeshift. Many nights I travel and merge with other beings in this world which is foreign to me. This is so I can become more acquainted with other living forms on Earth.

I was sent to Earth with a mission. I did not want to take on human form. I have not been on Earth many times, so it is still a strange place in many ways for me.

Those of us who are in forms other than human are doing our work in quiet ways and from quiet places. I can work from my perch or while I am swinging on my swing. Most humans would think of me as less than bright and more as entertainment, but John knows I am very bright (smile).

Can you say more about merging with other beings on Earth?
I do a great deal of spirit traveling and discover new things all the time by looking through others' eyes. I do not actually merge, but it is hard to find words to describe the process. I do not take over another being. I simply project my consciousness into another being's aura while I am close to their physical body. By doing this, I can peek at a bird in a tree through a cat; or if I am looking through a dog's eyes, I can see grass, trees, concrete, toys, and food (smile). I can view the sky through a crow's eyes. I have seen cows, pigs, horses, hamsters, cockatoos, leopards, sunflowers, and many other magnificent beings who live on Earth.

Beings who live on my home star can access all that I see so they too can learn. I am like a camera and radio wave transmitter.

What do you look like on your planet?
I am like a bleep of light that looks like a cross between a butterfly and flamingo, with a little swan (big laugh). I can see this is hard for you to imagine, so let me show you.

I see clairvoyantly what looks similar to a flamingo body, long legs and feathers. I see another group of feathery wings like those of a swan. You have antennae like a butterfly as well as another set of butterfly wings that extend from your three dangling legs. Also, another pair of butterfly wings alongside of your head. So India, it looks like you have eight wings?

Yes, that sounds about right.

Why do you need all those wings if your body is the substance between what is etheric and the physical world?

In a way you just answered your own question. They are like wings, but they are *energetic* wings and have multiple functions. We can move through many dimensions but there are some dimensions in which we become more material and use our wings. Our wings are more or less like chakras that we use to propel us through what you call wormholes and many kinds of other energy vortexes. Our wings are helpful in many different and varied star systems throughout the cosmos. They help us to adapt to worlds that we visit such as Earth.

Why do you travel through wormholes and vortexes if you can be at your destination just by setting your intention?

We set our intention and manifest that intention. We set our destination and are there. Yet, it is just the way we were created and how we travel sometimes, but not all the time. It depends on the frequencies of whatever star system we are entering or leaving.

After you sit with this a bit it will make more sense. We can materialize and dematerialize, but it is difficult to match the frequencies in certain dimensional zones. I know this sounds strange to you. It is difficult to try to translate frequencies and energy into words. Of course it cannot truly be done, but I am doing what I can in order to share.

Thank you. I understand. Are you individuals or a group consciousness on your home star?

We are one—we are many. I come from a group consciousness. We can be as one or individuals. Whatever a being's frequency is determines what kind of body/bodies that soul will manifest in the cosmos.

Can you say more about your wings, form, and intelligence?

My basic frequency dictates wings. Your basic frequency manifesting on Earth dictates two legs, two arms, and two eyes. My frequency manifests eight or so winglike chakra centers. But I have twenty-eight key chakra centers and many other chakras. I have two long thin spindles or legs as you would call them. I do not have much of a physical brain but have a very evolved brain. A portion of my brain is within my form and the rest of it is around my form as well as connected to other star systems. My well-based brain functions on intuition and telepathy—sensing what is around me. We are very intelligent, but it is more of an instinctual intuitive intelligence rather than what humans think of as intelligence. By the way, there is a great amount of purple vibration around me. It is the vibration of what you perceive as purple through human eyes.

Why did you choose to come to Earth, India?

I came to Earth to complete a mission that I began long ago—long before humans were a part of Earth's landscape. There is another aspect of me that is pure energy without form. That aspect of me was exploring Earth after Earth was newly formed by a council of creators.

Say more about the Earth's council of creators.

Earth is not a random creation. There are various creators throughout the multiverses. Earth was created by a council of creator beings who gathered together from various realms, galaxies and universes. They created and have seeded Earth with many beings from countless regions of the cosmos.

There have been disagreements over the original holographic constructs as well as over some beings who inhabit Earth. This conflict, which is one of literal energies between the beings, is still going on, yet resolution is happening even now.

My soul essence is, along with, a number of other soul groups, intervening to shift the holographic constructs and grids of Earth. This affects all life forms that inhabit Earth in positive ways, raising their vibrations. Harmony and peace is what the All desires. It is what Earth desires.

India: Photo by Lynda Sowers

What about love?

Love is always the foundation within my galaxy from which we live. By the way, my galaxy is within the Milky Way. You just cannot perceive the star I live on since it exists between etheric and physical dimensions.

Pretty hifalutin' stuff, (laugh). There is so much more to the cosmos, to everything, than humans think.

See my beautiful cosmic rainbows.

Oh yes! (smile). Thank you, India.

This was fun. Talk with you later.
India

Chapter 15

Barred Owl

Owls bridge the Earth and sky

Last spring I was walking down a path that I walk on almost every day. I looked up and there was a barred owl perched on a very low branch of a tree. He was perched on this same branch for days when I walked by. Sometimes he ignored me. Other times he'd glance down at me. But one day as I looked up, admiring his beautiful feathers, beak, and black eyes, he looked directly into my eyes. His energetic eyes zoomed through my body. It was a weird, disarming sensation, yet was wonderful. He had projected the energy of his black eyes, which I could see clairvoyantly, through me in less than a second. What an efficient way for him to scan who and what is in his environment.

Hello. I am happy to see that you are volunteering to speak with me.
　Hello. You saw beyond what humans call owl. You saw the star being aspect of me. You visited many days staring up at me. I had not been in this world very long and was adjusting to the forest, the humans, birds, chipmunks, and squirrels.

Did you look through me?
　When you looked into my eyes and I looked into yours, you felt my eyes penetrate through your bodies. I was scanning you. I was checking out your aura as well as your physical structure. This unnerved you

somewhat because you felt my energy move through you, whereas most humans would not have felt my scan. For you, this was a close encounter with someone from outside Earth's realm (smile). But remember you are not of this world either. I am from the third universe beyond the universe in which Earth exists.

I did feel somewhat uncomfortable when you scanned me.
You were uncomfortable when I projected my energy through you with my eyes. This is what owls do with their prey. It is one way of scanning. My intention was for you to experience this scanning in a positive way. It is part of my natural function as a star being.

Why have you come to Earth?
My soul agreed to be part of an experiment on Earth. The assistant creators wanted to see if beings from a wide variety of galaxies could live in harmony and peace. They created a unique hub (planet) where all kinds of different beings could meet and come to know one another.

Are you an individual or group consciousness?
I do not come from a group consciousness but rather from a culture where there are individuals. We agreed to be a part of this gathering on Earth. A number of us fled from our planet because there were beings from a neighboring planet who were interested in taking over our planet. They liked our planet's environment and wanted our plants, trees, and flowers. We love trees, plants, and flowers. Their planet was not as beautiful or rich in surroundings. They could not get plants and trees to grow on their planet so many of us were driven away. Those who stayed behind to stand up for our planet ended up being slaughtered.

Some of us traveled to other planets. We travel faster than the speed of light by using our consciousness. We travel through star gates. Our atoms disseminate and then reorganize themselves back into our original DNA blueprint codes and forms without any disruption.

Were you physical on your planet and what did you look like there?
The physical form of an owl suits our energies. On my planet I was semi-physical, or in-between you could say. I am a round globe of light with many wings and many eyes. I can see in all directions at all times. We can be in physical form easily or what you think of as etheric form.

I would compare this to the color spectrum that you are familiar with; so, too, are the many and varied dimensions of density and pure energy. This is why owls are such great shapeshifters. We also tend to be rather solitary beings. And this is why owl suited me quite well.

Thank you. What's your mission while living as an owl?
Owls bridge the Earth and sky. We are part of a much larger group of beings and overseers who keep the interdimensional highways clear and open in order to be accessed and traveled on by the All.

Thank you. What other roles do owls play on Earth?
Owls are guardians for trees and forests. We care for trees a great deal and you could say trees and owls, along with some other living forms on Earth, are connected in multiple realms. We are in a kind of group partnership.

We are helping to lift the veils of illusion on Earth so that all beings can awaken and remember the truth that all living forms are One. In fact, all forms, even those that you would not normally identify as living, such as stones, mountains, rivers, and even objects in your homes are part of the One. Everything is energy. Trees are very important to Earth.

Why are trees so important to Earth?
Trees play a big part in the awakening on Earth. As you know trees are not really standing still in their roots. You have seen them dance rings around the moon. There is little energy in an actual tree. Most tree beings are working outside of their physical bodies in multiple realms with balancing and cleansing Earth's meridians and electromagnetic fields. They transform lower vibrations and help clear pollution. Also, their bodies help ground a multitude of energies into Earth's grids.

Thank you. What else would you like to say about the work owls do?
One owl can cover a great distance when helping to lift veils and shift interdimensional energies. Owls assist with creating intersections with the countless interdimensional highways so that connections are clear and energies are integrated. This is the Creator's plan. It is Earth's desire to be shifting into a higher frequencies and this takes integration of the All's energies. This is and has been happening throughout your

universe and beyond for quite awhile. All current creations are shifting into new creations, but then again, this is always taking place.

Why are all current creations shifting?
For the sake of spiritual evolution of the All. Every energy is always shifting, but old structures are dropping away and new structures are being created. Creativity is the fundamental basis of what the Creator is.

Yes. We're all meant to be creative, aren't we?
Yes. The creative force is within all whether these energies are visible or invisible to the human species. Every cell in your body is continually creating something new. What it creates depends upon your intention and feelings and those around you. It depends on those who hug you, since their cells rub onto you, and how your cells respond to their cells.

Humans were created to be creative. They have the power to be creative in many ways they do not yet understand. We are lifting the veils so humans and some other species can see this truth, rather than continuing to be trapped in the illusion that Creator is separate from them. The Creator is within All. The truth is simple, but this can be difficult for humans to grasp.

Why is this?
Many religions teach that the kingdom of heaven is a place beyond Earth. Humans' mind/ego keeps them ensnared in the misperceptions and illusions that have been taught for centuries. Humans have been taught that the physical world is the true reality, when it is the unseen holographic energies that are the basic foundation of realities.

Why is Earth in physical form and why are those of us on Earth in physical forms? Why not etheric or other?
Actually, the elders of many star systems gathered together and decided what kind of world Earth would be. They wanted to shape and create Earth in a way where everyone could relate. The common denominator is the natural connection of telepathic communication between all living forms.

Many of us agreed, like you, to manifest in physical form to experience the physical plane and duality, and to see how we would all coexist and co-create. Another reason was so that we all would experience manifesting energies in new ways. Earth is a meeting place for many beings from various dimensions and universes. Numbers of beings were transported or teleported to Earth from various planets, star systems, and universes to gather with others.

Are there many beings in etheric form on Earth?
There are many beings not only in physical form on Earth, but in etheric form and other forms as well. Some humans perceive them but many do not. These beings live throughout your human cultures on Earth, which is no different from me, except some choose to experience the human form or other forms. We are all playing our parts in the cosmos.

How do you feel about Earth?
We embrace Earth. It is a beautiful planet to coexist on with other beings. Humans are learning about their place in the cosmic scheme of things. Most other beings know that they are part of a wondrous cosmic family with no end.

Aren't humans from other planets and stars?
Yes, but many have forgotten their spiritual roots and origins in the stars, quasars, and beyond. Humans are exploring the universe from the point of view that they have never been beyond Earth before. But what they are reaching for innately is to remember that they come from the stars. Humans are made of stardust, moonlight, and love.

All of the beings whom you are conversing with for this book are giving you various points of view to show you the multifaceted truths of realities depending on which facet or point or self you are viewing things from (smile).

We who live in the trees on Earth like to see the overview of things. Look at things from an owl's point of view (smile).

Are all owls from your planet?
No. There are other beings throughout the universes who want to know what it is like to live in an owl body, so an aspect of their soul experiences being an owl. Other aspects of my soul may be living in a dog, horse, starfish, dragonfly, or in a being in the tenth dimension while also living on Sirius. All of this is happening simultaneously.

Are you living other lives right now?

I am living in six other universes right now as well as in multiple realms. There is less of my soul's energies living in some of those other consciousnesses. Remember there is no time. This owl body is the only body I inhabit on Earth currently.

Interesting. What message do you have for humans? What do owls mirror to humans?

We bring messages of *seeing the bigger picture* while being able to also focus on details. We can shift our sight from looking at an overview of a forest to being able to zoom in on small prey and details on a forest floor. Humans are able to do this if they view things using their inner eyes and consciousness.

If you choose to look at us as a mirror, we reflect to you the part of yourself that needs to remember to look at the bigger picture of your lives as well as goals and details. It is easy for humans to get lost in their everyday lives and too many details at times. It would be beneficial for humans to remember that they are just one aspect of a vast cosmos.

Owls possess an innate wisdom in the way that we live our lives. You have heard the expression, wise as an owl (laugh). Humans can tap into this wisdom that resides within them.

Owls also have the ability to see infrared and ultraviolet light, which humans cannot see with their physical eyes. But they can see these other spectrums if they view them with inner eyes and spirit.

What thought would you like to leave with me tonight?

Fly above the Earth, fly beyond the Milky Way, and experience the vastness of the creative All. Be wise and open your inner eyes. See all around you the wonders of the Creator. They are you.

Thank you.
You are welcome.
Owl

Chapter 16

Jellyfish

As above, so below

Good to see you. Jellyfish are exquisite beauty in motion.
Thank you. I live in a fluid world, a world of grace. It is an angelic realm. *As above, so below.* There is truly no difference between the stars and galaxies in the sky and the stars and galaxies in the oceans.

This is profound, since most humans don't think of the oceans and deep space being connected. Please say more.
There are multidimensional worlds and realms within the oceans. Humans see things from a particular perspective because of the way your physical eyes function. If you look into the oceans using intuitive vision you will see what we see and feel.

Did the assistant creators create waters on Earth?
Yes. The waters on Earth were created so that many of us from water worlds, water moons, fluid realms, and dimensions could feel comfortable on Earth. It came to be that all physical life on Earth needed water to survive. And Earth itself desired to have land and waters. Think about how much water your own body contains.

I thought Earth was originally a water world?
Logic would assume this, but it is not the case.

How long have jellyfish existed on Earth and do you have a mission here?

Life did not originate on Earth as you know it. Many of us living in the waters were here long before other beings came into being. We helped create the grids and holographic matrix energies that gave birth to Earth. Other species as you know were involved in this process as well.

Our powers are evolved, but we use our powers in subtle, inconspicuous ways. Those of us who grace the bottom of the oceans are working with and in countless dimensions, galaxies, and universes which exist in the waters on Earth.

What does your star essence look like?

Look with your intuitive eyes and see me. Our energies are connected to the physical as well as the interdimensional and multidimensional bodies. We expand in vast ways beyond our bodies. This is true of jellyfish, starfish, manta rays, dolphins, whales, octopuses, and various other ocean-dwelling beings.

My energetic body is etheric, yet you can see it now. My light bodies are oblong with many very long tentacles of light. I am a fluid light. That is the best way for me to describe who I am.

It's interesting that jellyfish do not have any bones and that they are transparent. How does this serve jellyfish?

Oh yes. This serves us well. We are less dense in terms of our body as well as energy. We flow in truly fluid ways. Being transparent, you can see we are are light beings. This works for us in terms of remaining safe in the waters.

What lessons can humans learn from you?

Humans can learn how to flow in much better ways by feeling our energy. We know how to flow with the currents. Also humans could learn a great deal about themselves by being transparent (smile). We are spiritual guides in this sense and offer these energies to Earth and anyone else who desires to learn about flow and being transparent.

Thank you. Are you an elder?

I am one of many who make up the jellyfish council. And I am one of a number of overseers and elders.

Is there a difference between the two?

Yes. I serve on what you could think of as two different committees (smile). The overseers watch over the councils of elders.

I myself am speaking as jellyfish, but it is also the council who is speaking to you. I am an elder, an overseer, an angel, an interdimensional being. I am more evolved and awake than humans are in this moment, yet that is changing. Earth is changing deep within as well as your entire solar system and beyond. The All is changing.

Thank you. What would you like humans to know?

It is time for humans to understand the deeper workings of life and spirit—the nuts and bolts of things as you would call it. The basic structure which makes up your universe and the cosmos is of holographic matrix structures and energetic geometric frequencies, which are all "fluid" energies.

What else do jellyfish do for Earth?

I am an angel of the deep. We are guardian angels or gatekeepers. We maintain balance and harmony interdimensionally and geometrically within the oceans. This assists the land and air in maintaining balance. You cannot have land without the oceans on Earth. It is a balanced ecosystem for all beings on this planet.

Humans must learn that the waters are sacred. The waters are living and breathing beings who have souls. Earth has soul, the land has soul, the air has soul. All of these souls which make up matrix energies are intertwined in this divine creation called Earth.

How beautiful to think of the various aspects of Earth as souls intertwined. What else can you say about jellyfish?

We seem silent beneath the sea, but we are not silent. Jellyfish communicate telepathically as do all beings. Our long tentacles are used as antennas to feel vibrations around us. We feel the vibrations of the oceans, Earth's moanings and shiftings, or a brother rock or sister fish. Our tentacles, on a practical level, protect us from predators.

We are glad you are able to read the vibrations we are sending you so that you can share these important messages from other beings whom humans have a difficult time relating to and understanding. Our common denominator is the wondrous gift of life and the divine within. Is it not a wondrous gift?

Yes. Please say more.

Water is a conductor which makes it easier for all beings of the sea to communicate vibrationally and to be in tune with the frequencies not only of this world, but of many other worlds among the stars and energetic material, what you call deep space.

We are capable of seeing and feeling with our frequencies all that is above as well as all that is below. Every being has this capability if they would but remember. This is how we are able to communicate with you since your consciousness is continuing to expand and awaken. Also, we would like to talk about the chakra systems.

What would you like to say about chakra systems?

The chakra systems are relevant and key not only for humans but for all other beings and for this universe and beyond. Every living form has chakras, or in other words, energy centers. These centers and the holographic geometric configurations they form determine how each being will evolve.

Humans often view their chakra systems as linear from head to toe or toe to head and somewhat above and below and around their physical bodies. This is fine but I am here to let you know the chakra systems are not linear. Yet, this way of viewing it helps the human brain to perceive the energy centers.

Yes, I understand what you are communicating. I was told by a star being that the chakra energies connect us to other planets and stars in the universe. Is this true?

Yes. And when you view the multidimensional selves and include these chakra systems as well, you are a galaxy unto yourself. You are more than a constellation (smile). You think of yourself as a constellation, but it is beyond a basic constellation. This is true for all beings.

As the many multidimensional chakra centers are activated, know that this connects you to yourself in superconscious ways. The multiple chakra energies connect you, as well as all other beings, to Earth, your solar system and the cosmic consciousness.

Thank you. Why is this important for humans to know?

It is important for humans who are waking up and assisting with the interdimensional intergalactic changes to better understand their energetic makeup. As the energetic shifts continue to occur on Earth many people will experience the energy moving through their chakra systems in new and profound ways. Some would refer to this as the kundalini that clears out old energies and aligns the human with their spirit, soul, and Creator. This ushers in the new evolved human.

What planet are you from?

I am a jellyfish glowing in the deep, but another aspect of my soul is home in my water world which is within the Andromeda star system. You seem surprised, since many of the others communicating with you are from beyond this universe. I am from one of the stars hidden within the Andromeda galaxy. It was easier for me to adjust to being in an ocean on Earth than being on land.

Are you from a star in Andromeda?

Yes, a water world. I see this is hard for your mind to accept (big smile). You could call it a water star in Andromeda's galaxy, I guess. I do not know how else to describe my world. It has not been easy adjusting to Earth, but we have been on Earth since its beginnings.

You have such elegant energy.

Thank you. This is a reflection of my star's energy.

Are all souls in jellyfish bodies from Andromeda?

Are all those in human form from Venus or Pluto? (laugh).

No (laugh). Are there other souls from Andromeda galaxy on Earth?

There are a number of life forms from Andromeda in Earth's oceans. There are beings from other stars in the Andromeda system who vary in shape and form. Some are somewhat physical while others are not. And there are those who exist in an in-between state.

Were you invited to Earth?

Yes. We were invited by a council of beings who congregated from numerous galaxies. Many star seeds were planted on Earth from

Andromeda. I am jellyfish, which is just one starseed species living on Earth. Others on Earth live in mosquito and walking stick bodies. And some souls exist in plant forms from Andromeda. There are a few souls, not many, from my galaxy who exist in humanoid bodies so as to fit in with your species.

Also, there are trees who are living breathing souls on Earth that have come from a universe (you might think of this as another dimension) within the Andromeda belt.

Thank you. Are you here to assist humans?
We are here to assist with and to be a part of all life, which includes those of us from the Andromeda Galaxy, the entire universe and the All, with the evolutionary process of the cosmos.

I invite you to flow with me beneath the sea with your consciousness when you are ready (smile).

Thank you. This has been wonderful.
From one I to another I. From one eye to another eye let light shine. One day it will be time for us to return to our original homes.

Peace.
Jellyfish

Chapter 17

Overseer of Oceans and Waters

I was chosen to help create the waters on Earth

This overseer of waters showed up when I sat down to converse with whoever wanted to volunteer to speak to me. It felt appropriate to listen to what it had to say and to include this in the book.

Hello. This is a surprise. What would you like to share?
　　I am the overseer of the oceans and waters. I am one of the creators who helped create waters on Earth. There are many intergalactic councils who gathered and made decisions about what kind of beings and ecosystems could thrive and evolve on Earth.
　　I began with a blank template with which to create waters. There are many councils who are a part of the Earth project. I am using terms that you can relate to. Since the universes, galaxies, stardoms and dimensions are interdimensionally and telepathically connected, the councils come together easily and communicate telepathically. There is an order with all of the assistant creators or co-creators. Of course, the Key Creator oversees the All and is the divine designer.
　　I know this is difficult for you to visualize. Do not worry about trying to visualize all this. It is not a linear or time-encased happening. It is beyond what many humans can even fathom (smile).

Are the oceans spiritual beings?

The oceans are spiritual beings of sorts and within them are billions of other beings: fish, manta rays, coral, extreme microbes, tube worms, sea horses, dolphins, whales, and many others. These beings are in the waters for safekeeping, since they play a major role in grounding and anchoring energies in the oceans and Earth, the moon's energies, cosmic rays, and the electromagnetic energies from deep space. Water is a superconductor for electricity and energy. It is much more efficient compared to electricity traveling on land.

Can you expand on beings living within beings?

The truth is that all beings are living within other beings living within other beings and this goes on and on without end. This includes worlds living within other worlds and so on. Just think of all the fantastic organisms that live within the waters and the human body. You cannot live without mitochondria within you, which has its own DNA. Without them you could not think or speak. Mitochondria live within every living form.

The beings within the waters help maintain the health and balance of the oceans and Earth as well as the moon. And the moon helps Earth maintain balance and health for Earth. The Milky Way exists within a bigger galaxy. And your universe exists within other universes. Layers and layers of the All, much like an onion.

Think of the *Men In Black* films you have viewed. They deal with beings within beings and worlds within worlds and many of these beings and worlds vary in size (smile).

There are so many worlds and dimensions just within and beneath Earth's oceans that you cannot fathom this.

I'm looking at the dimensions beneath the ocean clairvoyantly and see many geometric shapes and configurations.

Yes. The foundation of all energy patterns. Geometric shapes are determined by frequency, and the frequency determines the form of the body, whether it be physical or etheric or one that is in-between.

The oceans and seas are composed of holographic geometric (crystalline) patterns that dolphins, whales, manta rays, coral, eels, and others see, feel, and know. They are tuned into these frequencies in ways that most humans would have a difficult time understanding. Dolphins scan the waterscape with echolocation, which is very different from how humans perceive their environment.

Do humans see the truth about the oceans, Earth, and sky?

The overseers are watching and wondering how far humans will go before they destroy themselves. Humans do not understand that as they destroy the oceans and many other living ecosystems on Earth that they are sealing their own fate. They tend to be very shortsighted. Things can be different and humans are beginning to shift in positive ways.

Yes.

Humans are not special or better than a dolphin or coral or octopus. They are just different and use a small portion of their brain. Humankind faces the challenge of how they direct their intentions and energies. It is good to see the raising of consciousness that is happening with many more humans now.

What's the bottom-line message for humans?

The bottom-line message for humans is to live from spirit and heart. To live from love, joy and creativity.

When power is used to create in positive ways it is wonderful. For example, creating health, joy, prosperity, or even new worlds is wonderful. Humans are evolving spiritually, and their brains are expanding, holographically speaking. They are waking up to important coded information within their DNA, chakra systems and the subconscious. Humans were encoded before they entered the body.

Humans were encoded before they entered the body? Each soul chooses what form to create and live in, right?

Correct. I am referring to those souls who have chosen to live a human incarnation. The encoding happens within the soul's portion of energy that will be inhabiting the human form. The encoding also exists within the chakra systems.

Thank you. That's interesting.

I, the overseer energy that I am, and many others have helped to create and oversee the waters on Earth as well as on other planets and moons. There are stars that I call water stars that are not hot like your sun, yet they glow. These are in other dimensions that those on Earth cannot perceive or measure because they have not considered such wondrous beings.

Did you play a role in creating ocean beings as well as other beings?

Yes and no. Remember, many beings gathered from other worlds, galaxies and universes to create a new world—Earth—to experiment or play with, so to speak; and to see what we could create in positive ways from Light. Earth is a being who agreed to be the grounds for this ongoing experiment or creation.

Did you help to create the physical forms?

Many souls, such as yourself, volunteered to enter into physical form on Earth. We have created some forms, yet many beings from other galaxies helped design the bodies they exist in on Earth—in waters, on land and sky. Some of those bodies do resemble what they look like on their home stars and planets.

Remember, beings in other universes are not exactly like those of Earth. Some are more highly evolved and different from anything you can imagine. Some beings can span their energies across spaces as large as Earth, a universe and beyond.

The membrane of space which you can feel is an actual living being of sorts. And the All is connected like a vast Internet network of communications. This is the Key Creator communicating with itself and all that it has created in order to learn, grow, and expand.

Thank you. What a great description of the interconnections of the cosmos and all living forms. Can you say more about the waters on Earth and elsewhere and about the creation of Earth? What is the moon's role with Earth?

The oceans cannot exist in the way that they do without the land, and the land cannot exist in the way it does without the waters on Earth. The moon creates Earth's tides which assist in creating life in the waters. Of course, the tides affect the waters, so there is an intimate relationship between the oceans and the moon. And since the All is connected, the All works in harmony and order. Without the moon and the work that it does, life would not be what it is on Earth. If the moon were much closer to Earth, humans would not be able to exist since days would be shorter. As mentioned earlier, the moon helps maintain Earth's balance. So remember to thank the moon for the wondrous work that it does.

Yes. I often play music to the moon on my psaltry (an ancient form of harp).

This is a wonderful way to thank the moon. There are many water planets and different watery fluids that exist throughout the cosmos. It is too much to go into. But the water on Earth differs from forms of water on other planets and in other realms.

Were you asked to create the waters?

Yes. I was chosen to be the overseer of the waters. Because of my frequency I was chosen to help create the waters on Earth. Also, I was asked to invite souls who were interested to be a part of this grand creation.

Can you say more about assistant creators?

There are many assistant creators or co-creators who were a part of Earth's creation.

The Key Creator IS the All, and created All. It created others as well as me to assist in creating other worlds and galaxies. The Key Creator's divinity and consciousness exist in everything, since we are all born from the Key Creator.

Thank you. Does love enter into all this?

I hoped I had made myself clear but let me try again. Yes, love. Earth was created so that a wide range of beings with various frequencies could come together to meet and bless Earth as well. The intention of creating all this was and is created from love and light.

Were there other beings who had other intentions?

Yes. There were some who had other intentions. They were focused on power in regard to their creations. Some had more interest in controlling what was happening with their creations without thought to the beings they had created. Yet, there are those creators who serve the Key Creator and choose to step back and watch their creations learn, thrive, and evolve. I serve the Light and oversee the waters in the best ways that I can and will continue to do so.

What do you think or feel about how humans affect the waters?
Humans have a choice whether or not to wake up and see that they are destroying this incredible creation and the beings who live in the waters. More humans are waking up to the fact that Earth's waters are living, breathing beings.

There are many beings in the oceans who have never been seen by humans. They swim and live in the deepest depths doing their work. Also, there are many beings in the oceans' other dimensions and galaxies who are doing a mighty work for Earth.

Why are they doing this work?
Because they choose love and have chosen to be a part of this ongoing creation of Earth. They desire evolution for the All. It is that simple.

How do you oversee the waters?
I am in the waters and I am in deep space. I am in the moon, Mars, and in various places throughout multiverses. I am energy that continues to feel the pulse of what is happening with waters. I am a loving being of high frequency and am much larger than the oceans.

I oversee the waters from all aspects of who I am for eternity. I exist in many realms and worlds simultaneously. I oversee the many water beings who are working interdimensionally with Earth.

Thank you. Why have you come to talk with me?
This gives you a wake-up call. It helps you remember what you knew before you agreed to come to Earth. It is important to share this with others so they too will remember the truth. Think beyond the box (smile).

Just as Earth is seventy percent water, human bodies are composed of seventy percent water too. How could you not be connected to the waters and those who live in the waters? I ask humans to remember the importance of and to respect the oceans and all densities of waters on Earth. They are living breathing waters which give you life literally.

Thank you.
You are welcome.
Overseer of the Oceans and Waters

Chapter 18

Council of Diverse Beings
(Consists of animals, plants, bacteria, and many other beings that exist)

The lesson is to accept and love the All

I see and feel this council creating a circle around me as they begin to speak. The circle becomes a spiral flowing upward or perhaps downward.

Hello, welcome. Are other life forms like mirrors for humans and for one another? Humans tend to feel that their animal companions, (typically cats, dogs, horses, and birds) reflect qualities to them about themselves. Do dolphins, whales, butterflies, raccoons, and others mirror qualities to humans?

Yes. Every living being is a mirror reflecting the Key Creator's life force. We are all mirrors for one another. Every life is a miracle and reminds you what a miracle you are. The bottom line is that the core of all living beings possesses the divine spark. This mirrors the Key Creator in all its expressions, forms, and energies.

You already know that cats, dogs, horses, birds, and other companions can mirror what is happening on a number of levels with their people. Animals who live in humans' homes will often act out or reflect back whatever issues a person is dealing with consciously or not dealing with on the subconscious level. And beyond this, other beings mirror the beautiful divine spark to humans.

Thank you. Animals show and teach us about unconditional love, correct?

Yes. Animals express and reflect unconditional love which is Key Creator's love. Many animals and other forms of life on Earth spread love and help to raise the consciousness and frequency of humans. Also, they are to support Earth in her rebirthing process. It can be easy for humans to forget about love.

Other animals forgive and continue to love regardless of what has usually happened to them in the physical realm. But humans are remembering how to love and forgive as their frequencies are being raised.

What does the Earth reflect to us and what do we need to learn about other living forms?

Earth and every living being expresses and reflects the Key Creator's beauty. This beauty is all around you as well as within you. All of creation is beautiful. One example is butterflies, who are on Earth to spread beauty. Beauty is truth and offers magnificent transformative powers to All. Within beauty is love that lifts the heart and soul.

It does not matter what planet or star we come from—beauty, truth, and life mirroring life is how it is, and is the bottom line. Perhaps a human would think that a spider is ugly. Yet if you look into the spider's essence the spider is beautiful and sacred and has a soul that is no different than yours.

Also, consider that maybe a spider thinks humans are ugly. But if the spider looks within you, he or she will see the divine spark and know that they are a part of you since we are all One.

Yes. Also, humans need to learn to respect animals' natural instincts while loving them, right?

Yes. It is true that every living form has basic instincts depending on what physical form they inhabit. And humans can move beyond what may seem like barriers by connecting heart to heart with a being. For example, you can connect heart to heart with a lion and communicate with them, yet you use wisdom and natural instinct in doing this from a safe distance. This respects everyone's natural instincts and boundaries.

Send love to other beings. They will feel the love whether they are a cat, mouse, snake, horse, plant, or being from another planet or star system. This is the bare bones of life engaging with life.

The lesson is to accept and love the All. This includes all beings, regardless if a being has five legs, two heads, ten eyes, or no eyes. The beauty of a being is its divine core. This is what humans need to recall. All living beings are interconnected, and you are they and they are you since the All *is* the Key Creator.

You teach people as an animal communicator about how to look into the core of living forms on Earth. It is important to expand this teaching to include beings that live throughout the universe and beyond. The primary reflection or mirroring is to remember that we are all One.

Thank you. I've noticed humans tend to assign symbolic meanings to animals. For example, a bird means "spirit," or a cat may represent the feminine? What do you think about this way of thinking?

Well, humans associate what they have been taught with various life forms. So, there is no blanket statement. For some, dolphins mirror love, joy, friendliness, and intelligence. For others, the dolphin might be an annoyance to try to drive away. Some humans feel dogs are smart and love unconditionally. Other humans feel dogs are dirty, or dumb. So, what is the truth here? Moving beyond all human created perceptions, the All is love and love is the All.

Humans assign symbolic meaning to animals depending on the animal's energetic expression of who they are. But this is a human thing because no other being is a "symbol," but are living forms and energies of the Key Creator.

Do a human's mind/ego perceptions interfere with knowing other living forms?

Yes. The human mind and ego wants to categorize in order to create answers about animals and other living forms. Too often, humans seek to understand through intellect rather than from spirit and heart. When one comes from the mind there is no direct experience with, let us say, a dog, cat, or snake. In fact, the spirit is not usually considered or included when it comes to understanding other living forms. And yet spirit and soul are what is basic to understanding all living beings, including humans.

We are taking you beyond the layers of humankind's cultural

perceptions, or actually beyond the misperceptions about various forms and beings in general.

What do bacteria or microbes or snails mirror to us?
The wondrous diversity of life. They are the Creator's beloved children as are all living forms. Once again, they mirror the divine life force. When all is said and done, and after the soup is stirred, you are they and they are you. This is the truth of the All.

Humans tend to think in metaphor and symbols. That is what we are taught.
But to try to distill life forms, or diminish them into specific symbols, can lock humans into relating to other life forms as mostly symbols, rather than enjoying the wonderful divine beings that they are.

Humans search for their own qualities in other species. This is not negative but humans can take it too far. This way of thinking was created by human culture which then creates and perpetuates false beliefs and myths about other living forms.

Yes. I understand what you're saying. I know animals bring us messages, but to identify animals as mostly symbols for ourselves has always seemed inappropriate. Yet I find myself thinking this way at times.
Let us use a bird for an example. You yourself sometimes interpret seeing birds as having to do with your spirit. Yes, a bird can reflect a message to you about your spirit. Yet, the bird may be communicating with you telepathically about what a lovely day it is or that they cannot find a good place to lay their eggs. So to have a rigid system does not work well because it is not that simple. By doing this, humans limit their experiences with other living forms, rather than communicating with the being as a being in and of themselves. It would help humans to expand and embrace the incredible diversity of beings on Earth as well as Earth herself. Understand?

Yes. It's easy for us to fall into our cultural beliefs. How can we humans free ourselves of the habit of categorizing other living forms, which sets up false perceptions and barriers, to see others for who they truly are?
Look at and honor the Creator's light that exists within every living being. See beyond limiting thoughts you have about other species and

communicate with their essence. Relating heart to heart with other living forms is what's natural and what humans are remembering. This is what you teach in your workshops. And every person who remembers that this is the truth helps others to wake up and also remember.

You have seen light radiating from cockroaches, is not it grand? It is about moving beyond fears and old beliefs to expand and recall that all beings are of the Creator.

Yes, I understand. I suggest to people that they get out in nature and communicate with all kinds of living forms, such as squirrels, birds, rocks and rivers, which can help them expand beyond old beliefs.

Yes. Humans can let go of old, false beliefs about animals and other living forms. Let the walls disintegrate. It is that simple! A human can walk in the woods and engage in conversations with other life beings. And this would strengthen their innate intuitive skills. Humans can have conversations with deer and squirrels and learn from one another.

Sometimes animals get scared and their natural instinct is to protect themselves. This may happen because of lower energy that they may be picking up from a human who is nearby.

Yes. Other animals sometimes become afraid of humans out of natural instinct. Also, an animal can pick up on a particular human's limiting thoughts and intentions toward them as well as the human collective unconscious which holds the myths and misperceptions about them. And these are very real energies that the animal picks up on and reacts to.

If a person sends love and good intentions toward an animal, the animal feels the love energy. The animal may still be afraid, but they also feel the love energy in a positive way.

Are other animals, rocks and plants teachers?

Yes. We are all teachers for one another in the scheme of life. Is not it wondrous? (smile).

Jacquelin Smith

Thank you.
(As this conversation ended, I could see all the beings spiral around me and flow upward.)

Why do I perceive this council as spiraling?
It is our energetic signature.

Thank you.
We enjoyed this conversation.
Council of Diverse Beings

Second Visit From The Council of Diverse Beings

Hello. I am surprised to see you today since we just talked yesterday.
Since you continued pondering our discussion yesterday we decided to visit with you again and discuss the matter of "mirroring" in more depth.

Wonderful. What would you like to talk about?
There are mirror reflections that humans see when they look into the eyes or heart of another being. There can be the reflections of various emotions such as fear, anger, joy, and love. Our focus yesterday was intended to ask humans to move beyond what they often project onto animals as symbols. Often what they project onto an animal is not accurate.

I understand that humans often project their own emotions onto their animal friends.
As we mentioned, humans may think spiders are ugly. If a human responds with fear they will probably kill the spider. But if a human sees a deer or hawk, they might think, "What beautiful animals." Everything is a matter of perspective. We are asking humans to open their hearts and to see the beautiful divine within all beings.

Animals often act out their person's emotions. What would you like to say about this?
Yes, humans can watch their emotions and attitudes acted out by their companion animals. In this sense they are mirroring their person's emotions. But someone can look at a raccoon and think she is beautiful

while another may think that she is a scavenger with rabies, so once again *perception* is everything. This is the heart of the matter.

Humans often interpret animals in dreams as symbols. What do you think about this?

We understand there are many books on dream symbols. But what is important to know is that every individual is unique and so are the symbols and messages in their own dream language. For example, you may interpret what a bird, cat, or dog means in your dream from a book, but the meaning may not fit for you personally. In dreams, animals can mirror a message to you or give you a direct message if they are entering your dreams literally.

I have had animals enter my dreams on many occasions.

Yes. An animal spirit may enter your dream to give you a personal message. Or an animal companion who has crossed over may simply be visiting you within a dream.

Humans can be in other dimensions while they sleep, so they could also be meeting actual beings, correct?

Yes. In the dream state humans often travel into other dimensions or realities and do receive communications from an animal or other being. Some humans think it was just a dream, but they really were in another realm of existence.

Different cultures have different interpretations about dreams depending on their beliefs. Would you like to comment on this?

Yes. Every culture has their interpretation of what animals and other life forms mean in dreams as well as in their waking state. This depends on what they have been taught and whether or not they value that life form. For example, in China dogs may be eaten, while in America, dogs are treated like children. It is all a matter of perception and projection.

Once again, the lesson is to respect, see, feel, and know the Key Creator that lives in every being.

Yes I understand. Thank you.
You are welcome.
Council of Diverse Beings

Chapter 19

Dog: Marilyn
(A neighbor's Labrador retriever)

My spiritual body is from a different realm

Hello, Marilyn. This is a surprise. What would you like to share with me?
My person, Todd, wants me to learn how to fetch since I am a Labrador retriever. But I am not one to fetch (smile). You have always known that I am unusual. That is because I am not from this world. Todd and I have been together many times before.

Tell me more. Are you and Todd from different star systems?
No. Todd and I are from a galaxy just outside the Milky Way. Even though he is in human form and I am in dog form, we are aspects of the same soul living together to learn more about love. We can perceive the Earth plane from various perspectives by living in two separate bodies. I love Todd and he loves me. I know this could sound strange.

Our soul's intention is to enjoy Earth and to plant our vibration here as have many other souls from other star systems.

Why did you decide to come to Earth?
Earth is a diverse planet. As I mentioned we are here to enjoy ourselves, but also to spread our galaxy's vibrations and to be present in this world. Earth is going through turmoil and transition as are many galaxies in this part of the universe. Cosmic energies are shifting

so quickly that many have volunteered to be present here and to assist Earth and your solar system.

What do you know about life on Earth?

There are many beings here from various quantum planes and spaces of existence. You could compare it to the bar scene in *Star Wars*. Life on Earth did not originate on Earth. There were co-creators who had a hand in creating and deciding what was to take place on Earth. Humans are not of Earth.

All beings are created for a purpose by the Key Creator. It is relevant to know that every life form has purpose as you do. Worlds exist within worlds interdimensionlly everywhere and this includes Earth. Whether a being is the size of a pinhead or as large as a humpback whale, they are living in worlds layered within worlds not only interdimensionally, but physically, too, on land as well as within the waters and everywhere else. Every one has purpose.

Where are you from and what does your essence look like?

Todd and I (we) come from a fluid planet—not water but fluid wind-like energies. I am from beyond your universe. I am from a star system very distant from yours.

Look at me clairvoyantly. This is my original essence. It is dragonlike. I have a very long eel-like body with multiple rows of spine-like plates and fins that flow along the length of my body.

Thank you. What would you like to say to humans?

We all have access to meet and communicate with every living form. Humans have been caught in density and duality for so long that they have forgotten that communicating telepathically with all living forms is perfectly natural and the norm.

Do animals and plants on Earth remember and have access to their origins?

Yes and no. They remember their origins and have access to their home stars and planets, but some tuck that knowledge deep within their etheric bodies. A leopard on Earth is mainly focused on living his or her life as well as fulfilling his or her soul purpose. For example, a leopard can access that knowledge or let it reside in some of his or her other bodies while here on Earth or in other bodies that are living in various dimensions and planets simultaneously.

Why don't most humans recall the information that they are from other star systems?
Because of the physical structure and culture of humans, they have forgotten what they truly know. They tend to get lost by following other humans rather than listening to their spirit and heart. There are various codes in the human subconscious, DNA, and multiple chakra systems and bodies that are being activated to raise the consciousness of humankind in their spiritual evolution.

Many star beings are encoded to wake up and remember who they truly are and what they know at certain times in their lives. This is connected with the global shifts that have been and are occurring. Your own codes were opened in a major way a number of years ago. And here you are talking to me. You would have never dreamed this twenty years ago. Although you did have dreams at night which were telling you about this, correct? (smile).

Yes. That's true (laugh). Are all beings on Earth star beings, or is it a matter of perspective—depending on which aspect of self you are viewing from?
Yes. And as you have recalled, a soul can distribute portions of its energy into various forms. A soul can be living in a human, cat, plant, star, etheric bacteria, a rock, and on and on. So it does depend on from which aspect of your soul you are observing things. If you are observing life as a rock on Earth, your perspective will be different than if you are observing Earth from a star system beyond the Milky Way. Or an aspect of you, living in Saturn's rings, might view the human self on Earth as being a star being or alien (laugh). Actually, it does not matter, does it?

So, it truly is a matter of which aspect of your soul you're viewing life through (smile). What fun!
Yes, it is fun.

Can you tell me more about dogs? I guess I thought you might talk more about dogs.
Why would I mainly focus on discussing dogs? Yes, I am in a dog

body, but my origin is from a very different realm and I wanted to talk about areas I felt you would be interested in.

I chose to be in a dog body because it is a way for my two aspects, Todd and me, to be joined most of the time. What these two aspects of myself see and experience can be seen by those on my home planet. Understand that universes are connected like a vast Internet system and whatever is going on can be accessed through telepathy, and consciousness travel. You understand. Everything is energy. This is the best analogy I can give.

Just because I am in a dog body, does not make me an expert on dogs. But I like being in this dog body even though it is still challenging some days for me to be a part of it. I have only been here for one year. I am very quiet for a dog, mostly clumsy. I miss my world. And so does the Todd aspect of myself even though he is not aware of this consciously. He would call you crazy, but his/my soul understands the truth. Let us bring in the Dog Elder for you to communicate with about dogs.

Thank you, Marilyn. You are a very unusual dog. I've heard you bark only twice in a year. And you just don't act like a dog. You seem to take everything in that is going on around you in such a quiet way. You have a bright, loving essence.

Thank you. This is a key reason why I chose to be in a dog body. I enjoy radiating and expressing love on Earth.

It's a wonderful gift.

Thank you. I know you can feel the love I radiate. This was fun for us to get to know each other at the basic level (laugh).

Marilyn

Chapter 20

Dog Elder

Dogs spread joy with open hearts

(The dog elder appeared to me as a white German shepherd)
Hello. Welcome. What would you like to say about dogs?
Dogs are probably humans' closest friends worldwide. They love unconditionally. Many star beings from various galaxies are in dog form on Earth. They are here to remind humans how to love and accept themselves, others, and life.

Dogs spread joy with open hearts, which is healing, and helps humans to remember who they are at the deepest level—love. The All is love.

Dogs are wonderful companions for people. For a soul to incarnate as a dog is a high mission. In some ways, dogs are more highly evolved than humans.

I wouldn't mind being a dog, so why am I in human form?
Your soul chose to be in human form to understand what it is like to be human. It is not easy to be human. Humans must deal with the ego and tend to focus on intellect, whereas a dog or other being has it easier in this sense. Yet other beings are highly intelligent. Humans simply do not recognize other animals' intelligence because they are interpreting it from their point of view of what they think intelligence is.

Are you or have you been a dog perhaps somewhere on Earth? Have you checked into this? (smile). It is not all that unusual for one aspect of a soul to meet or be around another aspect of the same soul, as you know.

Thanks. I understand. Is there an advantage to being a dog?
Yes. The soul living in a dog's physical body is of great help on Earth. This is because they are typically more grounded. Dogs can lose some of their grounding and balance, emotionally and energetically, if their humans are ungrounded most of the time. But dogs have a basic connection to Earth.

Is there any disadvantage to being a dog?
A disadvantage can be that some dogs can help out their people too much. In living with humans, dogs can absorb their person's problems and end up acting out their person's unresolved issues or even become sick. This is because dogs cannot always put up psychic boundaries which would prevent them from taking on their person's energies and those within the home environment. But many dogs can shake off or transform their person's energies by running and playing outside in nature.

I think dogs are wonderful teachers.
Dogs are great teachers. They teach humans about unconditional love and joy. What bigger lesson could there be for any being to learn? If humans would listen to dogs, they could learn a great deal about themselves and life. Dogs can teach people how to listen to them telepathically.

A dog's heart is open. Two-way communication is easy if a human opens their heart. Telepathy is the key to understanding and connecting with dogs as well as all other living forms.

Second Visit From Dog Elder

Hello again. Can you tell me if all souls in dogs are from one place?
They are not. The souls in dog bodies are not from one planet or star system. The souls who have chosen to be in dog form are souls who have also chosen to be in companionship with humans. And the species

of dog exists on a number of stars and planets in your galaxy and several others as well.

Dogs offer great service to the All. They exist in many realms spreading love and joy. They do not exist in exactly the same kind of bodies they inhabit on Earth, but in somewhat similar bodies, depending on what realm or planet you are talking about.

Dogs live throughout other universes?
Yes. Some of the forms they exist in elsewhere would be identifiable by an Earth person, but others would not.

Thank you. Dogs play very important roles with humans, don't they?
Yes. Dogs have agreed to be major players in working with humans. The souls who live in dog bodies have agreed to be guides in many ways. Dogs love unconditionally in a way that humans are still trying to learn about and to express. Unconditional love is present in humans. It is in the divine core that all living forms carry within. One could say, God or the Key Creator loves you through your dog companions as well as many other animals who live in close quarters with the human species.

What kind of missions do dogs perform on Earth?
Dogs have purpose as humans do and many who are in dog bodies are here to share with humans. Some are teachers and healers, while others are creating order and balance. There are those who spread joy, humor, and love within the households in which they reside and radiate these wonderful gifts to their human families.

Some souls desire to experience what it is like to be a dog and to experience the emotional feelings of a dog, which is very similar to how humans experience emotions.

Dogs assist people in so many ways on Earth. It would be difficult to think of Earth without dogs and the gifts they give so freely.
You are correct. Think of how many branches of service there are that dogs are a part of in relationship to humans. Dogs give from their hearts! They do not judge and are not critical of their people. What gifts dogs offer to humans. To be loved without criticism!

Dogs are incredible therapists. Many humans who have problems with trusting other humans, such as those with emotional issues, open their hearts to dogs. Dogs help and communicate telepathically with autistic children. Also, dogs benefit the elderly who are at home as well as those in nursing homes. If a human pets a dog, it lowers the human's blood pressure and de-stresses them. Dogs protect their people and property. And for the most part dogs are trustworthy companions. Dogs, cats, and other animals offer companionship to those who are lonely or physically challenged.

A dog's love is strong and steady. Dogs have a spirit of cooperation.

What do dogs mirror to humans on the spiritual level?

Dogs mirror the Creator's love to you, which resides within you. Dogs, cats, horses, and other animals offer the message that you are always living in the love of the Creator. The love you feel from your dog companion is the Key Creator loving you through them.

Dogs teach the spiritual lesson of how to live in the moment. They are living examples of how to be spontaneous and play in life.

What do you think about the way humans tend to change dogs' basic nature?

Humans have dominated and bred dogs in ways that have significantly changed their basic makeup. Humans have bred dogs to be dependent on them for a wide variety of reasons. Some of those reasons were to create dogs who could work alongside of humans. There are dogs who herd sheep. There are hunting dogs, retrievers, watchdogs, and so on.

Humans encouraged the traits that they desired to be dominant in dogs. Long ago, dogs were much more independent and yet would still work alongside humans.

Even though this is so, souls are still agreeing to incarnate into dog bodies. Some agree to do so because they know it is a short-term agreement which they want to experience. Others want to learn more about humans. Many offer to be spiritual guides for humans.

What do you think about humans trying to make dogs into children?

Some humans want to make dogs into children. When misperceptions like this are projected onto dogs and other species, this does not honor them. We ask humans to treat dogs as dog species and not as children or "humans with fur." Dogs are not humans, no other species is human. Humans are humans, dogs are dogs, cats are cats, and so it goes (loving smile).

When a soul is living in a dog body they are agreeing to be in relationship with a human and to be guided and socialized on the personality level, but not to be controlled. Dogs can teach humans how to be in partnership with them. We ask humans to spend some time watching your dog companions and listening to what they want to communicate to you telepathically. You can learn a great deal from your dog friends about yourself and life if you let them be your teachers and guides for the sake of growth and expansion.

Why do souls reincarnate more than once as dogs?

Those who return in dog form more than once do so because they are continuing to connect with a particular soul and also to learn whatever lessons need to be learned together. Some come back to reconnect with a human simply for the sake of joy and because the souls have chosen to be together again. Many souls choose to reincarnate as a dog again because, as mentioned, it is a fairly short-term experience.

What do dogs mirror to humans on the personality level?

Dogs can absorb their person's feelings and attitudes and in that regard they become mirrors. Dogs can reflect a person's issues, feelings and attitudes back to them. A dog can mirror their person's issues by acting out their person's feelings. This draws attention to the issue so the human can work it through. And sometimes the animal might have the same issue. In this regard they mirror the issue to each other. This gives both of them the opportunity to work through and resolve the issue.

Also, dogs absorb their person's love, joy, and happiness. When this is the case, a dog will mirror their person's happiness and joy in a wonderful way. This is always delightful for both human and dog. There is usually a balance of energies that are exchanged between a dog and their human friend.

I find that many humans don't want to accept responsibility for what they create within their dog companions.

When a human brings home a very young puppy, the puppy is molded into their own image and can even become like an alter ego.

Many people create much of what they see in their dog companions. This can be true on the behavioral and physical levels. If a dog misbehaves and the person does not like it, a person can act like he/she had nothing to do with that creation. But in fact, they have had a great deal to do with whatever issues they might see going on with their dog friend. Of course genetics and breed are a factor, but the immediate environment is a much larger component.

We hope humans will come to understand, with all that dogs have to offer to them, to treat them as the equal souls that they are. But it is also true that when a soul enters a dog body, that the human must offer guidelines because the soul's energies are in a dog body.

What about when a person gets an adult dog? They have baggage, right?

Of course. If someone gets a dog that is beyond puppyhood, then the dog may have baggage from past people and circumstances. And after living with their new person awhile, the dog may eventually take on their new person's energy—both positive and negative energies.

How do dogs benefit from humans?

Humans offer dogs wonderful gifts. Many humans value dogs as family members. They give their beloved companions love from their hearts. When this is the case, dogs greatly benefit from their human friends. It is important for humans to send their dog friends positive mind images and feelings since dogs pick up on whatever someone is thinking and feeling.

Dogs benefit from taking walks and playing with their human friends. Also, dogs really enjoy telepathic conversations with their person. Most dogs love being social with their person's friends. Hugs are usually appreciated by dogs (smile).

Do souls living in dog form remember who they are?

Dogs are highly intuitive. Within their core they remember who they are. Yet, some souls living in dog bodies forget who they are because of a human's dominance and abusive energies. When you take abuse and abandonment into consideration, the personality forgets who they are and sometimes their purpose. But this is no different than what happens to many humans.

There are many souls from countless galaxies and universes who volunteer to experience being a dog and to be of service. It is a quick way to experience humans and nature's beauty as well as some other species in a short time span.

Star beings living in a dog body or even cat body are cute. And it is a way for a number of star beings to assist with raising the human species' vibrations without scaring them out of their skulls. If they were to appear in their original form, it could send humans screaming down the street (laugh).

Are dogs doing interdimensional work?
Yes. Dogs are doing interdimensional work to open the doors for higher frequencies to continue to introduce a new paradigm of Earth, which is happening as we speak and will continue to shift ongoing.

Dogs care about humans, correct?
Those who have chosen to live in dog form care about the human race. They teach humans about love, patience, joy, living in the moment, respect, and how to listen to another being. They teach humans how to be in a partnership.

We encourage humans to communicate with their dog friends in order to better understand them.

Thank you for sharing with me tonight. Great information.
You are welcome. We desire for humans to look into the core essence of dog, which is love. We desire to bring out the best in humans.
Dog Elder

Chapter 21

German shepherd/wolf: Rainbow

There really is no such thing as an "alien"

Rainbow is a German shepherd/wolf hybrid. I have had the opportunity to communicate with Rainbow on many occasions.

Hello Rainbow. Good to see you. What would you like to communicate?
 I like to fly. I chose to be in a dog/wolf body to have the best of both worlds. I am dog and I am wolf. This allows me to do my healing work with people and many other beings as well as Earth. By being in a dog/wolf body, I can live with the people I live with in a neighborhood along with my other dog/wolf mate, Thunder. We are from the same star system and made the choice to incarnate together along the same timeline so we could enjoy being together while doing our work.
 I am enjoying being in a wolf/dog body as I mentioned, because I am a domesticated dog and yet retain a degree of natural wildness, which I wanted to experience while on Earth.

Whenever I see you, I notice how people are drawn to the two of you.
 Many humans love watching my sibling and me when we are running through the park. We attract humans to us because we look like wolves and our bodies are powerful and beautiful. We teach them about wolf and dog energy. I do a great deal of healing work with my people as well as with dogs and cats in the neighborhood. Also, I do healing work with

other humans. My sibling is a healer, too. She is here to offer joy and love and to share her star energy frequency in a bigger way. We came here because we add a diverse frequency to Earth.

Where are you originally from, Rainbow?

I am from a very distant star that humans do not know about. It is a rather small star system. Our galaxy is small in comparison with this one. It is about one-third the size of the Milky Way. But it is a galaxy of very high frequency, and size does not make a difference when we are talking about frequency, or anything, really. We live very close to a black hole but the black hole in our galaxy does not eat us up. This is because of the differences with frequencies in the way space exists in our galaxy. We do not live in time as you know it, but outside of time. It is hard to find words to explain all this.

Do you have a physical form on your home star?

We can create a form or live in what you would think of as a light body. Most of the time on our star we remain in light body because of the higher frequency. To have a physical body such as the ones on Earth would be too dense for our star system.

We take on physical form when we visit or choose to have experiences in denser galaxies such as the Milky Way, and the universe you know and live in. I enjoy being in this hybrid body and so does my sibling. Although she has a difficult time because her frequency is sooo high. Yet her frequency is needed on Earth to do the work she is here to do.

Why did the two of you choose dog/wolf bodies?

We chose dog/wolf bodies because dogs live with humans. The higher council who invited us to assist with Earth and humans agreed to give us dog/wolf bodies. This is because we wanted to experience wolf and dog energy.

Also, there are many hybrid species in the cosmos. In some star systems there are assistant creators who allow species mixing of DNA. This can be for the sake of learning and experimenting. Some beings' intentions in doing this work are very positive and loving. Yet there are some whose intention is not from a clear, loving heart.

Rainbow: Photo by Jacquelin Smith

Why are you here and do you like where you live now?

We are here to show people how beautiful hybrids can be. The two of us attract many humans who then benefit from simply being around our vibrations. When humans are around the two of us together, they are the receivers of all of our frequencies, which is beneficial to them with healing and balancing their energies.

Are you in contact with your family while you are on Earth?

Yes. But our focus is being on Earth to share our gifts from our star system. Our gifts are love, joy, peace, healing, and harmonious frequencies. We telepathically communicate with our star families on a regular basis. It is easier for us to communicate with them during the full moon. The moon's energies allow us to connect more easily and enhances the connection. The moon is a wondrous being whom many humans do not bother to look at or converse with. She is a reminder of all of life's phases and the continual process of transformation. Life and death, life and death, over and over, as we all experience in this cosmos in one way or another.

Do you exist on your star while you are here?

Yes. Part of my soul's energies are living on my home star while part of my energies are here on Earth as Rainbow. My soul is also living a number of other experiences even as we talk.

How many others?

I am aware of about fifty-two, give or take an experience or two. There might be some that I am living that I am simply not aware of. I am not totally aware of all that my soul is doing, but there are many of my multidimensional selves that I am aware of in the cosmos.

Do you care about humans?

Yes. We were asked to be of assistance to humans by the higher council since humans seem to be lagging a bit in their evolutionary process. No putdown intended here. Humans seem to have a more difficult time waking up and staying awake. I would not particularly want to experience being a human, although I may end up doing so at some point.

Humans are beginning to understand their multidimensional selves that various aspects of their souls are living. Being in a human body is but one lifetime experience you are living. There really is no such thing as an "alien" because souls are having many experiences simultaneously in the cosmos. So there is nothing to be afraid of here. Those you might think of as aliens are really you in the bigger picture of the All since we are all One.

Thank you. That makes sense.

Dogs are expected to cooperate and to live in harmony with humans, which we do quite well. We are asking humans to develop these same qualities that exist within them. Humans can raise their frequency by focusing on love, joy, harmony, and cooperation.

Dogs seem to be in partnership with humans. Do you agree?

Oh yes, I agree. That is why I and my colleagues from our star system agreed to come to Earth. We were asked to be in partnership with humans. Dogs have been in partnership with humans for many centuries. Dogs have helped humans to survive. One example is that of sled dogs who work side by side with their people. Dogs are terrific companions, friends, healers and wayshowers, and certainly contribute a great deal to human culture. Dogs sniff out drugs, bombs, and cancer. Dogs have skills and talents that humans do not, which makes for a good partnership.

Dogs love unconditionally, which is a huge gift to humankind.

Yes. Dogs love unconditionally, which allows humans to open their hearts and to evolve spiritually. This is why dogs are such important partners with humans even though many humans are not aware of all that dogs and other animal friends give them. And that is fine. We are doing what we are here to do.

All breeds are important in terms of what they each express. It seems many humans do not understand how important it is to understand what breed their dog is.

Yes. It is important that a human be aware of and understand a dog's breed. It is important to understand the natural instincts that come with each breed. This way a dog can live a more fulfilling life with humans. Some humans miss this point and then end up being frustrated because the dog does not do exactly what the human desires them to do. It would benefit both human and dog, or whatever animal the person lives with, for the human to read about the different breeds so there can be a better understanding and matching of energies.

Do humans act as mirrors for dogs or other animal species?

Yes. A person can mirror an issue to a dog or another animal whose soul is wanting to work through that issue. This allows for spiritual growth to take place within the dog's soul. For example, if my soul desires to learn about giving up control, then the person I live with will have control issues which are reflected to me. And sometimes, when a dog and human have the same issue, they mirror it back and forth in an effort to learn and grow together.

We are all mirrors for one another on multiple levels. Humans tend to project their feelings and issues onto their animal friends as well as other humans. The deeper issues are what the soul is working on even when a dog or human are not aware of the soul's deeper workings in the relationship.

Humans' belief in the illusion that all beings are separate confuses things. Also, it can be easy to get lost if you do not remember the truth that we are all aspects of the Key Creator regardless of what kind of body an aspect might decide to experience.

Have you been in dog or dog/wolf form before on Earth?

No. This is my first time experiencing this form on Earth along with my sibling. We are enjoying our experiences here while doing what we were sent here to do. We enjoy the beauty of Earth. It truly is a multicultural school in many ways.

Do you feel emotions on your home star?

Yes. They are a bit different from the range of emotions on Earth. But being in a dog/wolf body helps us to be in touch with some of the basic emotions we feel on our star. This is why we chose dog/wolf body. It is closer to our natural feelings of freedom and wildness. It is hard to explain. We live in groups on my home star much the way wolves live on Earth. Wolf energy is powerful. We shapeshift. You could say we are shamans. We travel in many realms while living in our dog/wolf bodies.

We have many abilities beyond what some dogs might experience due to the wonderful wolf aspect.

Thank you. What are your families like?
We live in groups in a similar way that wolves live on Earth as I just mentioned. The groups may have twenty-five individuals. Every family group is of a particular tone and frequency that distinguishes it from the other families.

We love everyone in our family the way we love ourselves. We are raised having a confident and loving view of ourselves from the time we are conceived within the family group.

How do you reproduce?
We are born from what would look like to you large cocoons of light. There is no sexual intercourse like humans experience. An entire family can decide to give birth to a new light being by first setting their intention and then bringing this light being into light form within a matter of what to you would be about three Earth days.

The family group does not take this decision lightly. Everyone in the family must be in agreement and in harmony or else the birth cannot happen. The cocoon of light is formed by the family energy. Then every family member projects part of their frequency into the cocoon and begins to create a new being. The cocoon is watched over by family members. Love and nurturing is sent into the cocoon continuously until the new being of light emerges. Its birth is celebrated with great joy and love and is part of that family group ongoing. They can be identified by their frequency.

Sounds like a beautiful way to bring life into the cosmos.
Yes, it truly is. It takes focus and energy, but it is a creation of love.

Are there male and female genders on your star?
No. We are light beings without gender.

How many beings live on your planet?
It is difficult for me to put it in terms that you would understand but I will try. We do not use numbers, even though I have given you some numbers. I am accessing what you know in order to speak about

numbers. On our star, there are many families of light beings as well as other species. I do not know how many species are on our planet. Do you know how many are on Earth? (smile).

No (laugh).
   I will say there are millions of families.

Thank you, Rainbow.
   I am happy to have this communication with you.
   Rainbow

Chapter 22

Marine Iguana Overseer

Being coldblooded does not mean that we are heartless

Hello. Welcome. It is good to see Iguana.
Hello. We have been here in this place called Earth for millions of years in one form or another. Those of us who live on the Galapagos Islands are the only marine iguanas that exist in the world. We evolved by expanding our energetic bodies in ways that allowed our physical bodies to adapt to the ocean.

Where are you from originally?
We are from another world. A world in which there was strife. A very hot planet. And even though Galapagos is fiery, it is much cooler than where we come from.

We are a species that had to leave our world. We explored many worlds clairvoyantly and otherwise to determine what would make a good home for us.

We are no longer living on our home planet but are here. We are very interested in the future of Earth. Even though we are located in a remote area, we know what is going on all over the world. Not only through clairvoyance, but through our sensory systems which we carry within us from our home world. Our world was harsh and hot. Earth is much cooler and not as harsh as where we have come from.

Earth is older than humans have predicted. Earth has been here longer than many might think. The systems used for determining age are good but not exact. We do not really care about this, but humans seem to be curious about the age and history of many things.

Marine Iguana in Galapagos: Photo by Jacquelin Smith

Why did you choose Galapagos?
Galapagos is unique in the world. There is a key Earth vortex where the four corners of the Pacific merge, where hot and cold waters come together, allowing many varied species to exist in this realm of energy.

It is fairly remote, even though humans now tour some of the islands. This is fine, but if it were to get out of balance, there would be trouble with disease being transmitted to some species. In fact, this has happened on some of the islands.

Our bodies are efficient since we are able to be on land as well as swim in the waters to feed. Just as we have adapted, humans will adapt to environments that will evolve over time.

What does your essence look like?
We look similar to how we looked physically on our planet, but we are much smaller and more dense. Our bodies are now physical rather than the in-between of physical and etheric. We could materialize and

dematerialize whenever we desired to do so. We have been on Earth a very long time and still shapeshift. Even though we are small in physical stature, we are big energies that can expand across many miles above and into the waters.

What happened to your planet?
We still look in on what used to be our home, but it is no longer how it was. The environment has changed dramatically. It is harsher and hotter and has become etheric after shifting from being more physical/etheric to now being etheric. But it still remains a part of your solar system. It is not a planet that humans can detect unless they are looking with their intuitive eyes, or clairvoyantly.

You sound sad when you tell me about this.
Yes. It is not easy to watch your home planet go through so many changes.

So humans can't see your planet, correct?
There are many planets, stars, and solar systems undetected by humans because they do not have any way to detect them etherically. Humans are so focused on the physical dense plane that they miss many worlds that are right in front of their eyes. Researchers might be gazing at a meteor or rock on the moon or Mars and miss an entire solar system that is whirling all around. This is not to judge but to encourage humans to develop their innate intuitive abilities that have been hidden from them for thousands of years.

Thank you. Humans are getting more in touch with these abilities. Tell me more about yourselves.
We can see all around us by using our auras that reach far beyond our eyesight. Much of who we are is outside of our physical bodies as is the case with humans. We, too have energy centers and systems. Our systems are quite extensive and so who we are can be in various places and spaces simultaneously. We function outside of time and space, multidimensionally and interdimensionally speaking.

We can function as individuals or/and as a group energy when helping to balance Earth's energies as well as our own energies. We know Oneness. We synchronize our energies during particular energetic alignments to do our work here on Earth. And then we go our own ways. Our bodies carry on with our individual lives as well as our group life.

Do you communicate with one another telepathically?

Yes. We communicate telepathically with each other. We also communicate with each other through the lower spectrum vibrational emissions from within our throats, eyes, and bodies. Humans cannot hear this range of frequencies. Many species communicate through these emissions.

Do you feel love even though you are a coldblooded species?

Yes. Just because we are coldblooded does not mean we do not know, feel or understand love and what it means to have heart. Being coldblooded is simply a different body function of certain species. That is all. Being coldblooded does not mean we are heartless. When humans use the term "cold-blooded" to refer to one another, it maligns us. But then again, humans have many beliefs and references that are not true in regard to most other species. The human mind and ego can certainly be a hindrance to the human species, which then affects all others.

Yes. I understand. Is Galapagos a special place on Earth and what is your role?

Yes. As mentioned, there are a number of key vortexes here. There are no energies like it elsewhere on Earth.

We are guardians along with other species watching over these vortexes, which are more powerful than I can transmit to you.

These key vortexes are not only connected to the waters, but to Earth in relationship to the alignment with the solar system including Earth's moon, the life force, and the electromagnetic energies that run deep beneath Earth.

We are glad there are humans who recognize Galapagos as unique and protect it. This is one of the better decisions humans have made. There are many gatekeepers and higher beings who live in the oceans, in the sky dimensions, and on the islands to help maintain balance energetically with Earth's meridians. The tortoise being is one of those species, along with birds, seals, crabs, dolphins, rays, and eels, who are significant protectors and interdimensional workers as well.

Do you and other species want to be where you are?

Many beings wanted to be in the Galapagos Islands because of the higher frequencies here. The councils and guardians of many planets and stars met to decide which species from various other worlds would be graced with being placed on the islands.

Since my world was shifting form, we had no choice but to leave. Fortunately, we were invited to be a part of this seeding or implanting on Earth. We were here watching over the vortexes before the islands emerged from deep within the ocean. We knew where land would take shape and form before it manifested.

How would you know?

By detecting the frequencies beneath the waters. Humans do not understand how important the frequencies within and beneath the oceans are to the makeup of this planet. They think of Earth as their planet, but this planet belongs to all star-being species.

We are glad you appreciate our essence energy and how we look physically on Earth. You embrace the All.

Thank you. We all need to remember to embrace ourselves. Are all iguanas from your planet or are there souls who have incarnated into iguana form from other realms or universes?

Those of us in Galapagos have incarnated as a group from our planet. There are other souls who are members of other cultures who are also in iguana form, mostly land iguanas and other lizard forms.

How did you come to manifest on Earth?

We were seeded on Earth through the acts of various councils and the gathering of many higher officials from many galaxies, along with assistant creators or co-creators of the Milky Way. All of them were a part of the discussions. The co-creators helped to create the physical bodies on the Earth plane by implanting DNA and other structures that you would not understand in varied combinations of energy templates and holographic structures, which allowed the souls who had volunteered or been chosen to then fill the form with a portion of their soul's energy.

How fascinating.

All of this was done over a long period of time. It was not instant. Evolution has its place in that iguanas adapted to the ocean over a long period of time. And so we became marine iguanas. But this was also programmed into our basic innate holographic structure. But the original creation of beings comes from the assistant creators.

My species was fortunate to come to this world. This is a beautiful world. Humans do not seem to appreciate what a jewel Earth is within this particular solar system.

Is Darwin's theory of evolution correct in some ways as you just mentioned?

In some ways yes. In other ways no. Life evolving on Earth was/is a mix of intervention from star beings, assistant creators, evolution, and intelligent design of the Key Creator. And why not? (laugh). The creators of this universe had a hand in all this in terms of planting seeds of DNA and other life-creating energy structures onto and into Earth. I just described how the co-creators create life and form. This process includes creating physical, etheric, and in-between fluid and light forms.

There are some truths in Darwin's evolutionary process, but it is not the entire truth. There is a creator of this universe and co-creators who are real beings who started things rolling. Let us not forget the Key Creator who created assistant creators and the All. Spirit, assistant creators, and souls' energies create the holographic structure and frequencies which then determine what species and kind of body or bodies a soul will inhabit. A soul creates bodies to experience what it desires to experience for the sake of learning and to fulfill missions throughout the multiverses.

Thank you. Did humans evolve from apes?

No. Humans did not evolve from apes. Humans were created in and of themselves by assistant creators. Humanoids have existed on other worlds and in realms long before Earth was born. There are many star beings who inhabit human bodies on Earth. Think about this. Since you are having discussions with us and so many other animals, why would humans not be included as originating from other worlds?

Yes. Of course that makes sense.

There are a number of humans who are cutting-edge, you could say, who are star beings. They are gifting Earth with their energies and are here to inspire and encourage humans to evolve as a species. They are key in assisting with the ongoing energetic transitions happening with Earth.

Other beings, such as myself, are trying to help humans remember that they are but one species who are a part of the web of life.

Do subspecies evolve from original species of birds as Darwin has written?
Yes. And you can discuss this with the birds of Galapagos. We are happy to have been seeded here on Earth. We are happy to meet you this evening. Everyone is a part of the light network. We know your essence and you know our essence. Peace, our sister. We feel your love for us.

Thank you. Blessings to you.
You are welcome. We were happy to share this with you.
Marine Iguana Overseer

Chapter 23

Waved Albatross
(Those albatross who are gathered at the Galapagos Islands)

Galapagos is the heart of the Earth in many ways

Hello. Where is your original home?
Here we are. We showed you the Pleiades this morning. We are here on Earth along with many other souls from multiverses and have been here a very long time. We were created from Spirit and DNA seeded in Earth material. We are the albatross from the Pleiades.

Many species of albatross exist in other planetary and stars systems. We exist in physical, etheric and the in-between state of beingness on many planets and stars.

Are all beings on Earth seeded and are there beings older than you?
All beings were seeded onto Earth in one way and form or another. I really do not want to go into all the aspects of the various creation phases.

Okay.
I am speaking to you from the species that I am. I am approaching you from the framework of human perceptions and your perception of time. Everything is happening simultaneously. Yet there are many different frameworks of time and those beyond time. But for the sake of

answering your question, I will say that some souls inhabiting human bodies and other bodies are very ancient souls who existed before I existed.

Do many humans remember their origins being that of other galaxies, universes, or dimensions? Do most other animals remember their origins?

Many humans are waking up and recalling that their origin is not that of Earth. Just as many, what you call "animal" species and "plant" species, have their origins which are within other star systems, universes and dimensions. It is easier for animals, plants and other species to remain connected to their soul's mission because they do not have the ego/mind to contend with. Yet there are some who do forget or put the memories of their original home on a back burner, so to speak, in order to focus on and fulfill their missions on Earth. This way, they do not get as homesick or distracted by memories. Even when they can connect to their original homes, it is still different from being fully present at home.

Thank you. It seems humans are getting more connected with their purpose for being on Earth.

Some humans have forgotten why they are here and what their missions are, but that is changing dramatically. Many are reconnecting to their soul's energy and purpose even if it is not in a fully conscious fashion. With the raising of vibrations within and around Earth, humankind's vibration is also being raised, so humans are evolving.

Are you an albatross elder?

I am an albatross elder. A number of us from the Pleiades chose to be beings with wings. Also, we wanted to be in a place on Earth where we would not be subject to as much pollution.

The albatross is but one species of the Pleiades. Or I should say that we are beings who chose the bodies we desired to inhabit. We value being able to fly above the oceans and see the islands from a bird's-eye view. In this way, we can be a part of Earth and yet we remain as Pleiadians. There are seven stars, the seven sisters. There are more life forms from these islands of stars in the sky.

Are you an elder of all albatross?

Yes. But I have personally lived as waved albatross. I loved sailing over the oceans and fulfilling my Earth mission with the Galapagos Islands as well as with the oceans and skies. I was to contribute and integrate my frequency from the Pleiades to the Galapagos Islands and its energy vortexes, which I did with joy.

Are you living on Earth now?

No. But I ride on the wings of waved albatross who sail over the oceans not only for fun and joy but to give guidance to the albatross who are in physical form.

Why are you here on Earth and why are you interested in Earth?

You are our neighbors. You are our future. We are your future. If you think in terms of time, we have been around a lot longer and have learned many lessons that humans are struggling with today. We open our hearts to you and ask that you realize that the choices you make for yourselves affect every living form on Earth and beyond. Open your eyes and hearts. We are not better than you, but we have just had more experience and are further along in our evolutionary process.

What is your mission on Earth?

We weave love and balance through the sky. We work with the sky beings and energies as well as with the sun, the moon's energies, and the stars to balance Earth's chakra systems and aura. We are not interfering, but doing what we have been asked to do by the creator of this galaxy.

Albatross have been around much longer than the human species. Yet many star beings who inhabit human forms have been around much longer than we have. Many of them are from various universes. But the physical creation of the human body on Earth is still relatively new and being challenged in numerous ways.

Being albatross, we can better understand Earth and the evolutionary process it is moving into and through.

Do you look the same on the Pleiades?

No. Perhaps our eyes are similar to those of the albatross, which is what was decided. We are not a group consciousness, but are individuals.

But we communicate telepathically so in that sense we are connected as a group or species.

We are like globes of many-colored lights with many eyes. This is the best way for me to convey what our species looks like. We can be etheric, in-between or physical.

Is your entire species inhabiting albatross bodies?

No. But many souls from our home decided to embrace this journey together. We were invited by Earth to help create diversity on Earth. Also, we came here for an adventure and to meet other beings from other galaxies.

Thank you. Can you talk about Galapagos?

On Earth, there are beings who are created from the Spirit of Water who are water spirits. The volcano beings are alive and awake in Galapagos even if it doesn't seem like they are. There are the glorious sky beings who watch over the sky.

Every island of the Galapagos is alive and has its own spirit. There is life living within life living within life. The islands live in the water beings, the water beings live connected to the land beings. The species on each island were chosen by the island and determine what species will survive living on them. Every island of the Galapagos holds various species and helps shape how every species looks and evolves.

Galapagos is a *key* energy center in the world because of currents merging from the four corners of Earth. These vortexes run deep into Earth's center. The volcanoes are very much a part of this development. They are the islands. Each island is a distinct creation from volcanoes deep beneath the waters.

Is Darwin's theory correct in some ways?

Yes. Earth determines what species can survive in her environments. Earth is continually shifting and changing herself. Humans have interfered with this natural process by eliminating forests, clearing fields, controlling where water flows in the areas where humans live, and in other numerous ways.

Darwin came to understand evolution in some ways, but not in the same way we understand evolution. Darwin discovered very important keys as to how environment determines how a being will adapt and evolve physically in order to survive.

The waters and Earth set the stage for all species to evolve and to adapt to whatever changes the environments are moving through. This encourages spiritual evolution as well as evolution with physical changes.

Waved Albatross in Galapagos: Photo by Jacquelin Smith

How do you feel about the Galapagos Islands?
I feel blessed by these islands. One day the Galapagos Islands will be gone. These islands serve Earth in many ways and even when they are gone they will still be serving Earth energetically.

How important are the Galapagos Islands to Earth?
Galapagos is the heart of the Earth in many ways! But it is also the crown. The flow. It is through the Galapagos Islands' energies that Earth is able to connect to her higher self, soul, and Creator.

Do you know the tortoises?
Yes. The tortoises were here laying the groundwork for the oceans and with Earth long before humans were even a thought. We work

interdimensionally. Every species is doing their part on Earth for Earth. We hope that you will learn from these ancient tortoise beings who know many secrets of the multiverses. They connect important energies and anchor those energies into Earth's basic holographic grid. It is a vast web of life and we do not mean that to be trite.

Every being is connected and every life depends on another life form. Everything is interwoven. Humans are recognizing this in a very real way now. Let your spirits rise and view life from a higher plane or from a bird's-eye view (smile). This is the only way to see the larger truth, to embrace the All, and to know your place in the cosmic web. Every being has their place.

Do you feel emotions?

Yes. We feel many of the same feelings humans and other species experience. The albatross mates for life. When we are separated from our mates while flying over the oceans and reunite on the islands, we have dances that express love and affection. This may be interpreted by humans as simply a mating ritual, but it is more than ritual. If you watch our dance and listen to our sounds, you will feel the love and joy abound.

Share this conversation with others. Some will hear. Some may not. But is that not true of all that is communicated? (smile).

Yes. Thank you for sharing this wonderful information.
Albatross Elder from one of the Pleiades' seven sisters

Chapter 24

Groundhog

You were my first direct alien (human) encounter here on Earth

This message is from the soul of a young groundhog whom I spotted on a path while walking in the woods. I stopped and stood still when I saw her. Within minutes she began to cross the path but stopped directly in front of me. Then she reached out and placed a front paw on my tennis shoe. Really! I was astounded and elated. I continued standing still and communicated love and light. I silently told her how beautiful she was, and that I was honored to have her paw on my shoe. Then she returned to crossing the path, but turned and came over to me a second time. She placed the same paw on my pant leg. I sent love and light again and thanked her for trusting me.

A minute later she crossed to the other side of the path and ambled into a bush. I had remained standing still. Then the groundhog turned and looked into my aura and I into hers. Our eyes never met, but our souls had met on a lovely summer's day. This was a rare and wondrous encounter—a huge gift.

The groundhog reminded me that the veils of density and duality are thinning and that boundaries between all living forms are dissolving. She and I knew we were one in spirit. (The groundhog comes to me now as I am writing this book to speak about her star origins. As I am writing this, I feel her light and love envelop me.)

Jacquelin Smith

Hello. I am so happy you have come to speak with me again.

It is joyous to see you and to speak with you again. There are no accidents. Being in a groundhog body is fun. When I met you on the path *less traveled* (laugh), I knew we were to meet. I did not have to look into your eyes. I knew you by your aura, which was radiant and bright on that day—a human whom I knew I could trust. You could have harmed me if you wanted to, but you stood strong in love and that attracted me to you. I can feel you beaming with light this moment as we speak.

Thank you. As I listen to you I am overflowing with joy, love, and gratitude. Have we known each other before?

We know each other now. That is what is important. We are on the same journey of life and spirit. All living forms are evolving in ways their souls desire.

Were you frightened of me?

I was not frightened of you, but my groundhog body has its built-in instincts, as is true for all species. So I was a bit cautious, but I stepped beyond instinct to place my paw on your foot and leg.

You were my first direct alien (human) encounter here on Earth (smile). If you were to encounter native species on Jupiter, Saturn or Sirius, you might stop and consider if they are friendly or not. But if you felt love and light emanating from their innermost self, then you would open and explore the relationships as I did with you. Many humans might think, how could a groundhog have a soul or be from another world. Why not? Why not groundhog, why not plant, why not bluejay, dolphin, or salamander?

Humans can have a challenging time seeing beyond limiting perceptions they have about other living forms.

The human species in general has a difficult time seeing beyond limiting ideas they are taught about other living forms. Also, by categorizing other life forms, humans not only box in other living forms in terms of perception, but box themselves in as well. It is difficult for humans to see the truth that we are all One. You understand about thinking outside of the box (chuckle).

Thank you. Where are you from originally?

I am a being from another realm—one in which we are multidimensional and can materialize or dematerialize at will. We can create whatever kind of body we desire to exist in for a period of time.

What do you look like and how do you communicate?

We are etheric. Our light bodies have different shapes and colors with long flowing ribbons of light. This is our natural state of being. Our species is connected telepathically. It does not matter if we are living in other universes, dimensions, or on Earth because we can hear each other clearly. Only now and then does static occur if there are too many energetic shifts happening in the electromagnetic fields in deep space or within the dimension in which I was first born.

Is your species comprised of individuals or is it a group consciousness?

It is both. We are created as individuals initially. Then we learn from our families that we can merge and become as one when it is appropriate to do so. We communicate telepathically when we are functioning as multidimensional individuals fulfilling our missions in various multiverses. When we are one in the sense of having one etheric body, then there is no need for telepathic communication.

On what occasions do you become one?

We have celebrations which could be compared to Christmas or Thanksgiving. A time when your families come together. Our family comes together too, quite literally, as one. We can do this while our other bodies are living on Earth or in other universes. A portion of my soul exists in all my bodies, yet my key light body and soul are living at home.

Thank you. Why did you choose to be a groundhog?

Living in a groundhog body along with a number of other bodies on Earth gives me/us the opportunity to explore other species on Earth. We love to explore the multiverses. We were invited to Earth long before Earth was in physical form. We are older than you have words or numbers for. We came into being not long after multiverses were forming. Not your universe but other universes.

I chose groundhog because they live close to Earth. We are not only here to explore but to help balance and uplift Earth. And we are delighted if humans and others benefit from our vibrations. Earth sent out an SOS to deep space because she knew she could use assistance in the future, which of course is really NOW.

Also, groundhog is inconspicuous. Yes, I am in other inconspicuous forms. Nothing flashy like a hummingbird or champion horse. It makes it easier for us to do our explorations and missions without much interference by living in inconspicuous bodies. We are doing what we are here to do from behind stage curtains. We desired to be in bodies that do not get entangled with the complexities of mind/ego and its misconceptions about reality. You know if you could, you would do the same after experiencing some of the challenges of what it is like to be human (laugh). We do not mean this as a put-down in any way, but are simply stating some differences because humans are wondrous creations.

It is a joy for me/us to show you who we are. You accept the many shapes and forms of beings you are meeting very quickly. There is no time to dillydally. Energies are shifting and changing at a pace that most humans cannot comprehend.

How many bodies are you living in on Earth?
I am living in three bodies currently. There are seven others from my realm who are also living on Earth. We are in fairly constant communication.

Are you from a water world or realm?
Our original bodies appear as if we could be from waters, do they not? The way jellyfish flow through the depths of the ocean, we flow through our realm/world. You would say we are very ethereal looking.

Our world is not a world as you would understand world. You understand there are worlds within worlds within worlds which are unending. Our world is an etheric realm that is similar to the oceans on Earth in its atomic and molecular structure, but it is not physical nor contained by land the way waters are on Earth. Our realm is fluid and is part of a vast network of bands of light, sound, and color that are fluid and connected multiversally. Your mind is trying to imagine this but your mind is having a hard time. Look with your intuitive eyes. Not every world is round. A band of energy can be a world or home for many beings.

Expanding, are we? (smile). We are elated that you are overjoyed with communicating with us today. You can feel the reality of these truths in your heart and soul?

Oh, yes, yes.
Feel what this feels like because this is what it feels like to resonate with truth that is being fed to you.

Fed?
Given. Shared. Fed. We are feeding your soul to uplift you and open new codes within you.

I feel so much light from you I am overflowing with light!
See? Understand? You had no idea where this communication would go or who would show up. You trusted me—the one in groundhog garb—and look at what a wondrous swirling journey this has opened for you. We feel how this makes your heart sing.

Oh yes. It's wonderful to connect essence to essence with you.
You knew what happened between us on the path in the woods was special. Humans need to remember that every being is much more than they appear to be physically. The essence that lives within every being is divine. You never could have imagined who I am, in terms of my original star essence, nor all this wondrous fun we could have if you had not looked beyond my physical body (laugh). Even though you are an animal communicator, you see yourself that you are expanding beyond layers and layers of human cultural thought. You are seeing the multiple layers of truth that make up all beings.

Ahhh, what beauty and soul-moving stories every being has to share with you, like the butterfly, cats, and many others who desire to be in conversation with you.

Yes. Thank you. This is wonderful and fun for me.
I am happy you can hear us and that we can know one another light to light.
Groundhog

Chapter 25

Large Sea Turtle

We have been here a long, long time

For several days now while lying in bed or upon awakening, I have seen a huge, beautiful sea turtle swimming around me. She communicates telepathically to me that she's waiting to converse with me.

Hello. What would you like to say?

Large and small, we are here. The Native Americans say turtle carries the world on her back. This is true in many ways. We have been here a long, long time. We are ancient beings who help set up key balancing energies with Earth and within some quadrants of your solar system. We hear Earth sing her frequencies. We know when to adjust particular chakras and meridians within Earth and oceans when Earth's energies begin to get out of balance. We are able to see many dimensions simultaneously. You are wondering why so many sea beings are communicating with you. Well, think about this. Since the oceans make up seventy percent of Earth's surface, why would there not be many of us from the sea speaking with you?

Good point. I understand.

Humans often focus on animals on dry land, but we are here below the waves and swimming with the currents doing our missions. Just our presence helps to bring balance to the oceans as is true of many of the sea beings. We are like an orchestra creating music deep in the oceans.

Living in the oceans, we see colors, worlds, dimensions, and galaxies throughout the waters that humans do not usually bother to explore from this perspective.

There are galaxies, dimensions and many worlds in the waters, aren't there?

Yes. You already know this from talking with the dolphins. There are many galaxies within and beneath the waters. There is dimension intertwined with dimension on and on throughout the oceans. Other galaxies do not exist only in deep outer space, but in deep inner space of the oceans and seas.

For a world to be a world, it does not have to be big like Jupiter; it can be the size of your thumbnail or smaller and be equally important as Earth or the sun, Ra, that shines upon Earth. This is something humans do not stop to consider. Going into outer space to explore seems to be a major focus of humans in order to see if there are life forms on Mars or Europa or elsewhere, but the irony is that if you dive into the oceans, you will find vast universes beyond most humans' comprehension. This is outside most humans' realm of thinking. But if humans open up intuitively, they will experience what I am talking about. It is a matter of heart in diving for the truth.

Thank you. Tell me more about you and your mission on Earth.

We sea turtles are about light, love, and truth. We came upon Earth with the land tortoise. The land tortoise works with land energies as well as ocean energies. Those of us in the waters work with the deeper dimensions of the bottoms of oceans and seas, and deep within Earth. We work with Earth's grids, helping to inactivate old codes and open new codes that are necessary for Earth to continue her journey through your solar system, which is integrating with unseen solar systems that will one day be seen by those who use their inner vision, sensing, knowing, and hearing.

Yes. I understand what you are talking about. Also, I would like to experience some of the ocean's multiple dimensions.

Ride on our backs through these universes now. See the multiverses, the ocean's broadened spectrum of light, sound, dimension, and color.

Yes. I see and feel these amazing dimensions. I see other beings as well who appear to be etheric.

Yes. See the other races of civilizations who dwell here in the oceans. Etheric, yet not always etheric. And some of the shapes and images you are seeing that look similar to dwellings are dwellings. Do not expect to see houses or high-rise apartments such as you have constructed on land (laugh). These ocean dwellings are for those who understand true reality and who come here to live. Take a peek. Now look through some of these dwellings. We will guide you.

There appear to be all kinds of watery etheric shapes of dwellings where many beings are living. A variety of beings are looking at me. Some of the dwellings seem like towns. (I use this term loosely.) They are more like loose structures of color and light with various shapes. Some are tall, thin, tubelike places and others are spirals of colors.

I see gardens of colors. Some beings look like flowers, others like angels. I see crystalline structures and geometric harmonies that sing together, all knowing that they are connected, and that all are a part of creating these various dimensions.

There is a wide range of dimensions—each having its own frequency. I can hear the dimensions singing in harmony. Each dimension is constructed of its own particular geometric construct and tone, which is etheric as well as connecting with a physical component, whether it be the waters, sea turtles, or sand. Vibrations travel through water faster than the speed of light. Oh, what glorious multiverses are here.

I see stars, planets, and suns. I see other solar systems, galaxies, universes, here in the ocean realm.

All beings communicate telepathically here no differently than everywhere else in the multiverses. What an incredible ride! (laugh).

We thought you would enjoy experiencing this.

Oh yes. Can you tell me more about your work on Earth.

We are helping to create the crystalline energies and shift them into various dimensions in order to help Earth on her evolutionary journey. Other living forms are acutely aware of this. We work in teams, you could say, with dolphins, whales, coral, clams, crabs, seals, birds, and many others.

Are you from another galaxy or dimension?

Yes. We wanted to share what we are doing here first. Earth is a bountiful planet to live on. We wish humans would realize how incredible their home is and take good care of it.

Who are you and what is your world like?

I am a soul from another world. Where we live is similar to water, but not truly water as on Earth. I can show you because it is difficult to find words and there really are no words in your world to describe such other worlds.

Would you like to say more about your work on Earth?

We agreed to come here with the land tortoise. Two species agreed to take on similar form, doing similar work, but some chose to live in the waters while others chose to live on dry land. For us, this completes an important energetic connection to do our task here on Earth. We anchor energies into various Earth and multidimensional grids as well as shift circuitry in terms of electromagnetic fields, forming new crystalline patterns, and balancing all of these energies.

There are many beings working with Earth's energies. We are not doing this as a service to humans, but as a love gift to Earth as a whole. You as humans are a part of raising the frequencies on Earth, but you are not the only ones doing this work. Many humans think they are the only ones raising the frequencies on Earth.

We enjoy sharing this with you. It is time for others to understand that Earth is a WHOLE being and to understand the waters on Earth.

Thank you so much for sharing and allowing me to fly with you through the dimensions and galaxies. I'm grateful. I know there is more.

We will show you more later. There are angels in the waters. Why not? Water is simply a different frequency than Earth's air and deep space. Angels are not in "heaven" as humans refer to it. Angels are everywhere.

(Then I saw the sea turtle shapeshift into an angel of sorts with wings. No, more like fins. Light was radiating from her eyes.)

We leave you with this blessing from the sea turtles.

Blessings to Earth, all planets, stars, and worlds in the oceans and beyond that are still unseen by those living in duality. Learn how to swim, dive, or fly far beyond your body and mind.

Sea Turtle

(As we finished this communication, a group of sea turtles swam in spirals around me and then spiraled into another dimension. It was a glorious experience!)

Chapter 26

Horse: Jonah

No one has arrived

Janet called and asked me to communicate with her horse Jonah, who had recently crossed over into the light. As Jonah and I communicated, it was clear that his origins were not of Earth. I asked Janet, "Are you aware that Jonah is not from Earth?" She cried, "Yes. I felt that when I got him." Janet asked me for the name of a book about this subject. I laughed, "Well, I'm writing a book about star beings in animal form." Janet yelled, "Oh, I want to read your book." This was a gift and confirmation for me to continue writing this book.

Hello, Jonah. Good to hear from you. What would you like to share today?
I am happy to be talking with you again. You were right when you told Janet that I had trouble adjusting to living in my horse skin. But Janet and I were meant to be together again. Our souls are connected from times when we lived in other dimensions, on other planets, and in other galaxies.

Being with Janet again was great because we were connected on this physical plane. A new and strange experience for both of us.

We came here to experience the physical plane, and also to help raise Earth's frequencies. Many beings are doing that as a major focus now.

Being a horse was fun while I was here. I did tend to be clumsy, especially earlier in my life. This was my first time in a horse body. I liked being in such a big, powerful body, but I had to figure out how to balance.

What planet or realm do you come from?

I come from a planet beyond Pluto that cannot be seen by your astronomers. It is not exactly in this universe and not exactly in another universe. Maybe I could say that I live on the edge between two or more universes (smile).

Are you physical on the planet you come from?

No, I am like a globe of blue/magenta/green neon lights. This is the best way for me to describe what my original essence looks like.

Are you etheric?

I am different than etheric. I am different frequencies of light.

Thank you. Why did you choose to be a horse?

I chose to be a horse because of their grace, power, and healing abilities. Also, a great deal of learning can take place between a horse and human who are in close relationship. This benefits their souls.

What was your purpose here?

I did a great deal of healing work with Janet as well as with others. The humans and other beings I worked with were at a distance from my physical body. In reality, there is no such thing as distance anyway. They had no idea that I was assisting them with healing in many and various ways, which bled into the other realms and dimensions of their beingness.

Janet and I knew each other well and others often did not understand our profoundly deep connection, but we did. And that was all that mattered.

As I mentioned, Janet and I agreed to come together on Earth and to share our frequencies with Earth. Also, I had come to help wake Janet up so she would remember her roots in the stars. She is awake and learning more about what is real and what is illusion.

It is difficult to remember what the truth is about realities when living in the physical and living in duality. But all that is changing now. Many humans are waking up to their spiritual nature and spiritual origins.

Were you here to work mainly with humans?

I worked with many humans, but also did healing with cats, dogs, and many other living forms. Some humans have a very difficult time understanding horses. I hope I opened some of their eyes to what sensitive and intelligent beings horses truly are.

I'm sure you woke up many humans. Why did you leave the physical plane?

My oversoul decided it was time for the experience of being horse to be over. My mission was completed so my soul pulled its energy back unto itself.

Do you feel the Earth's energies are changing?

Yes. Time is shifting, dimensions are shifting, veils are lifting and more humans are understanding that everything is energy. The material world is simply the stage or dream created for souls to play out various scenarios in order to learn, grow, and evolve.

No one has arrived. Just because I am from a different planet does not make me better than anyone else. I have more learning experience, but I have not arrived. I am not what you would think of as a "god."

Thank you. Tell me more about you and your species.

My species creates new worlds and galaxies that are mainly what you would call etheric. You could call us assistant creators. Creating new worlds allows us to direct our creative abilities in positive ways, much the way Monet created paintings. His soul expressed itself by creating beauty on canvas. We express ourselves and create with our multidimensional, holographic energies through our intentions. We do not have words. I am using your mind's storage codes and memories to access these things of "words."

Even while in my horse body, I did not do well understanding words. But when Janet communicated with intentions, I was superb. I do not mean this with arrogance, but it is important to love oneself as much as the Key Creator loves us.

Thank you. What else would you like to say about horses?

Horses were on Earth long before humans were put here. There are many different souls who choose horse experience. The Native Americans knew how to be in relationship with horse. Horses are wondrous teachers, healers, and guides if humans would but take time to get quiet and listen to horse wisdom. Horses are wild, free spirits, yet many have agreed to be in partnership with humans. Horses are waking people up to what wonderful beings horses are to know.

No one has ever questioned why horses have agreed to be in partnership with humans. Native Americans understood from the first meeting with horse that this was a star connection.

The personality of each horse varies depending on the soul that enters horse. And yet their upbringing shapes their behavior in huge ways that can either support or distort the expression of their essence. This is true of all forms, but no matter what occurs on the physical level, the essence remains intact.

Horses, as well as dogs, cats, and others, are excellent communicators. They have come to know humans over time more deeply than, say, baboons or lemurs, so the telepathic communication link is easier for them.

Is there a planet where there are horses or those who look like horses?

Yes. There are a number of galaxies and realms where horse-like beings exist. Some live in physical form while others live in etheric realms. Many are shapeshifters. Oh, you might be interested, unicorns are a part of the soul connection with horses. These beings reign in other realms and kingdoms that you can visit with your consciousness.

Thank you. Is this information from you or horse elders too?

Both. You could say it is a kind of mind blending, or mind bending, depending on your point of view (smile). Since I have been horse I know some things about horses while the horse elder knows all about horses.

I see that this is a joy for you to be able to see and hear my species. Ahh! This is a new opening energetically through this communication that others will be able to access now. You are a door opener unto many dimensions, planets, stars and universes. It is a part of your purpose.

So I've been told (smile). Thank you, Jonah.

You are welcome.
Jonah

Chapter 27

Horse Elder Council

*Tap into your spiritual heart and into
the essence of your other selves*

Hello. Good to meet you.
Hello. We have decided to greet you as a council of horse elders. We speak with one voice.

Great. Why did horses come to Earth?
Horses came to Earth because we were invited to do so by the assistant creators of your universe. We come from many galaxies and realms. The physical form on Earth that you refer to as horse exists in other worlds. There are some differences depending on which galaxy or realm you visit, but the basic structure is the same or very similar.

Does everyone on the council come from a different galaxy or universe?
Yes. This is why we chose to come to you as a council. But we are of one mind, one heart, one voice. Our council, which is made up of beings from twenty-six different galaxies in various universes and realms, has been joined together for billions of years.

Sounds like horse energy has been around for a very long time?
Yes. When Earth was first formed, we were invited to be one of the species to assist with helping set up frequencies for Earth. We were

asked to drum our frequencies into Earth's heart or core. The poem below is written by our council. It is a more familiar way for us to share. We are focused on flow, sound, rhythm, and emotion. Thus we agreed to create this poem for you to share with those who read this book. It may be difficult for some to accept, but there are other forms of life who create poetry in their own ways. It is a way to express and to touch others' hearts and souls.

Oh yes. Poetry truly is the soul's language.

Descended From Stars

Horses drumming across dusty plains
drumming their beat deep into Earth
awakening her core. Earth remembers stars
and rhythms of distant galaxies.

Horses drumming songs through grassy
fields that echo through sky and sun and moon.

Horses galloping in canyons, wind blowing
through manes and spirits. Wind, their companion,
spreading seeds of creation.

Horses drumming beauty and grace and wild
deep into Earth long before humans
were dreamed into being.

Horses giving up wings
drumming their beat of love with hooves
and sweat into the heart.

Thank you. This is a very moving poem about horse.
  We thought you would value this since you love poetry.

Yes. Do horses feel emotions?
  Oh yes. This is one of the reasons we were asked to have contact with humans and to be in partnership with humans.

What many humans fail to understand or remember is that all other living forms have emotions. Humans are not exclusive in this regard. This is not a putdown but simply what we have observed in some of the human species. There are many humans who love and adore horses. Lucky for us! (neighing). Yet, as you know, many horses have been used as slaves in numerous ways. They have been beaten and broken so humans could control and use them in whatever ways they desire.

What do humans need to learn about this?

One of humankind's biggest lessons is to learn to value and be in partnership with other living forms rather than controlling them. Humans do not understand what it costs the horse and themselves spiritually speaking.

How does controlling and using or abusing horses affect humans spiritually speaking?

It is simple. What we do to another we do to ourselves. We are all One. Since beings inhabit bodies, there is the illusion that there is separation. But if you drop all bodies, every being is one divine light.

A beautiful way to state the truth. Can you say more about emotion in horses?

Horses are very sensitive beings, especially with the bodies they inhabit. Emotions actually connect all living forms. Emotions are a way for all beings to mirror themselves to one another. If a horse is having a bad day and is grumpy because another horse has bullied him, you will see it in his facial expression and body gestures, as well as hear it expressed vocally. Is this any different from what many humans experience when their boss has bullied them? It is not. And if humans take the time to notice and be tuned in they will see and feel this from their horse companion.

Yes, I understand. You are telling me you have the same range of emotions as humans do? Is there more you'd like to say?

Yes. Actually there are other emotions that most humans do not experience because they have forgotten that they can feel what their multidimensional selves feel that exist in various galaxies and universes. If a human takes time to get quiet and connect with even one of their other selves, this will expand them in ways so they can remember their other selves and feel an even more expansive range of emotions.

Emotions are important. Feelings can be terrific to experience or they can feel troubling depending on the circumstances and other beings involved. If you feel what is in your heart, there is a wide range of emotions from many experiences throughout your life. And if you tap into your spiritual heart and into the essence of your other selves, you will experience a much wider range of emotions, as I mentioned.

I like the idea of tapping into the spiritual heart. But could what you have just talked about be overwhelming for a human? How would a human tap into another self?

Here is an exercise for you to connect to other selves.

A human can sit down and become quiet. Then you can center and ground by doing relaxed breathing and feeling your feet connect to Earth. Then connect with your high self. You can imagine your high self as a globe of white light about two feet above your head. Ask your high self to show you and connect you with one of your other selves which you are ready to meet. You can ask that this connection be opened perhaps five percent. After that, you can ask for seven percent and so on so that it would not be overwhelming. It would be fun and joyful.

This sounds very positive. Are most of our other selves positive? Does the soul choose to experience all kinds of frequencies?
Not all selves are what humans refer to as being positive because the soul is balancing all of the lives it is living. So some of your selves could be a little more challenging to accept because they are living lives you might not personally resonate with. This could be referred to as darker energies or simply lower frequencies. But all is of the light and truly a part of who you are as a soul.

The soul desires to taste a wide variety of experiences. So it is not just high frequency and virtuous selves that you would encounter. The soul experiences a wide range of emotions and experiences through all of the multidimensional selves it creates in order to learn and grow. There is always a balance.

Thank you. This makes sense. Can you talk about humans riding horses? Is this a part of the partnership between humans and horses?

Yes. The souls who inhabit horses have chosen to live with humans. They have agreed to do so for some of the reasons I mentioned earlier. Horses assist humans in learning about grace, beauty, and balance. They teach humans about being centered and grounded. Horses are naturally grounded and centered, but unfortunately if horses are abused at an early age they too can lose their grounding and centeredness to an extent.

Horses agreed to allow humans to ride them as part of the partnership agreement. Horses were not created for humans, but there can be beautiful partnerships when humans and horses resonate with one another.

A very important issue when a human rides a horse is for the human to sit on the horse centered and balanced. If he or she is not centered and balanced, this throws off the horse's centeredness and balance as well. So then, both horse and human are out of balance. Horses offer humans the opportunity to learn how to not only ride from a centered and grounded place, but also how to *ride life* in a centered, balanced way.

This makes perfect sense. Do humans help horses who have been abused to regain balance and centeredness?

Yes. Fortunately, there are many wonderful humans who can help horses to regain their centeredness and balance and joy for life. And in doing this, they too regain their own centeredness and groundedness. So in this regard, it is a partnership of love, trust, and patience.

Yes. So this is also a mirroring affect?

Yes. There is mirroring between a human and a horse who are together. As one begins to heal, so does the other. So it benefits both of them.

Have you or any of the council lived in a horse body on Earth?

Yes. I have lived five lives as a horse on Earth. Every one of us on the council has been in horse form. A couple of lives I lived as horse were very difficult, but all were well worth experiencing. I loved being in a horse body because of the freedom and sense of power it gives when running through fields. I loved having a large body on Earth. Where I come from, which is a universe beyond yours, my body is quite small and bound to the planet. So, I cannot travel very far physically, but we can travel astrally and through our consciousness.

A small portion of my soul is in a horse while most of my core essence is on my home planet. I am also experiencing other lives in the cosmos. Experiencing the essence of horse adds a wonderful dimension to my lives and to my other selves.

How large are you on your home planet?
About the size of a chipmunk on Earth. On the planet from which I come there are only a few large physical forms and they are not friendly. We spend much time staying out of their way, yet we travel often beyond our bodies. This is the norm.

Thank you. Sounds kind of rough.
It can be, but for the most part life is good on my planet.

I'm glad to hear that. You have pretty much addressed this question but I'll ask anyway, are horses here to serve humans?
No. We are not here to serve humans but to be in partnership with them. This is a big lesson humans are trying to embrace and remember. This is a lesson about cooperation, harmony and partnership. When this happens, a horse and human can experience being one as they trot or gallop through a field. This is a key lesson and a wonderful lesson the horse offers humankind since horses *can* carry humans on their backs.

Yes. All this makes sense.
We hope many people will read this message. We give it to you with love and with the hope that humans will open their hearts and see what marvelous beings horses are. There are many beings throughout the cosmos who desire to experience being a horse—not only on Earth, but in other galaxies as well because of the horse essence of beauty and grace.

What about the horses who are not in contact with humans or those being abused?
They are here to experience whatever their souls have agreed to

experience and learn. Some souls choose to experience being a wild horse who has no contact with humans. Others know coming in that they will experience abuse. They still choose to be a horse for the experience. This is the case in regard to all of the selves the soul chooses to be and experience.

Thank you. This has been wonderful.
    We have enjoyed sharing with you.
    Horse Elder Council

Chapter 28

Bat Elder

Our core vibration feels like a soft gentle breeze across your cheek

Hello. What would you like to share?
Peace. We come in peace. We have known you for a very long time. We are glad you recognize our attributes and value our beingness. Our core vibration feels like a soft gentle breeze across your cheek.

I worked with fruit bats a number of years ago and fell in love with them (smile). There are many myths about bats which aren't true. What do you think about this?
Humans create some pretty strange ideas about bats. There are many myths about bats. Humans conjure up fear when creating myths about us being bloodsucking creatures who swoop down and tangle themselves in women's hair. This is utter nonsense. We are often considered vermin by humans. The vampire bats on Earth do not attack humans or drink their blood. Vampire bats are small and drink small amounts of blood of animals and poultry.

By the way, bats can see with their eyes. Some bats see better than other bats, but bats are not blind. We use our ears along with echolocation to navigate and locate insects and objects.

What would you like humans to know?

What we want humans to understand is that the misperceptions they create about bats become strengthened and become a part of the human collective subconscious when they continue to repeat negative myths about us. This just perpetuates fear and misperceptions further. We are just trying to set the record straight with telling the truth about bats.

No one has questioned other species as to what they think or feel about humans. We choose not to judge, but work energetically to uplift human consciousness so humans can see the truth about bats and to let go of the old myths. Bats are wonderful beings who offer many gifts to Earth and humans.

Yes. I understand what you are saying.

We love Earth. We may look and seem different but there are fewer differences than humans think. We think and have feelings, too.

Humans eat cows. Sometimes with blood dripping from the steak they are eating. How interesting that humans do not take their behavior into consideration before judging other species (loving smile). This is an observation, not a judgment.

We nab insects out of the night skies. And some of our kind do feed off cows. But mosquitoes take blood, too. They are considered a pest, but bats are feared in a bigger way than mosquitoes, even with the viruses and diseases mosquitoes can inflict on humans.

Can you talk about your wonderful innate skill of echolocation?

We are unique in that we use echolocation as do dolphins, whales, and some birds. Echolocation is a spin-off from our natural talents. We are from a planet called Pletharsus, which is in another galaxy that your world is not aware of.

Echolocation is detecting through sound. We emit high frequency sounds that humans cannot hear. Sound waves bounce back to us from the objects and beings around us. This is how we can detect where they are as well as their size, shape and density. This is how we locate insects at night. It is a process of high frequency sound projection and reception.

We navigate with high frequency. Echolocation is a different way of seeing and perceiving. It is a different way of feeling and knowing. Echolocation is not fully understood by Earth's scientists and probably never will be because it involves other dimensional connections and frequencies that humans do not see or hear.

What a wonderful talent to possess. Can you tell me about your home planet and what you look like?

On our home planet the period of darkness is much longer than the period of light that shines when we remain in dark dwellings. We who are bats on our home planet have six pairs of wings rather than two that we possess on Earth. Also, we have many more eyes and mouths with which to feed and view what is around us. But even with all the eyes we have, we still do not use our eyes in a primary way, but echolocation. Once, a long, long time ago on our planet, we used our eyes. This was before the darkness grew in proportion compared to the light. It had to do with the shifting of the planets, our suns, and moons. Nights grew longer, days grew shorter. There are periods when there is only darkness. This could be compared to what humans and other species experience at Earth's South Pole for months.

Thank you. Why did you decide to come to Earth?

Part of the reason we came to inhabit Earth is that our planet was losing its friendly environment. As it grew more hostile, in terms of temperature changes, it became more difficult to thrive. We felt our species would not survive. We sought out other habitats and Earth seemed a good fit for the greatest number of our needs.

There are other species on our planet as well. Some are dinosaur-like beings. You might look at them and think they were on Earth long ago. I think the creators of your solar system may have extracted DNA from these beings to use when experimenting with beings who would do well on Earth. My planet and the species on my planet were around long before Earth was born.

Again, we look similar to how we looked but not exactly. We were seeded on Earth with the help of a council of elders who oversee a number of galaxies in our particular quadrant of deep space. Our DNA was implanted on Earth so we could survive.

Earth was the place for us. Also, many other beings were being asked to come to Earth, so it has worked out for us in very positive ways. Although, it is still interesting and challenging to coexist with humans who have many misperceptions about who we are.

We do not harm humans and take only what we need in order for our species to continue to survive.

Are you from a group consciousness or do you exist as individuals?
We are individual souls in the way you think of individual souls. But we are connected through the bat collective consciousness just as humans are connected to the human collective consciousness. We are always connected to this consciousness and can tune into it whenever we desire to be linked to bat vibration.

There are also many souls living in bat costume (smile) who are from other dimensions and worlds other than my home planet. These souls have asked to experience bat energy in the physical realm on Earth.

I have experienced the wonderful gentleness of bats.
Yes, we know. You have fed fruit bats small pieces of fruit from your fingertips. You have seen how gently they took it from your hand. You have felt their silky fragile yet strong wings. You have looked into their eyes and felt the heart-to-heart connection. And you fell in love with bats even more than you already were.

Yes. How did you know about these experiences?
We are able to see the pictures stored within your mind and to know your feelings.

Great! How is your species doing on Earth now?
Our species is evolving in a different way because of being on Earth, but it is in the agreement that our souls made with the councils. All souls make agreements with one another in various ways.

What kind of work are you doing on Earth?
We are on Earth hoping to teach humans how to expand beyond false beliefs about bats and other living forms as well. A being that looks scary can be gentle, beautiful, and loving. And sometimes a being that looks familiar and beautiful on the outside can be ugly and not so loving on the inside.

We are happy on Earth even though there are some big differences between our home and Earth. We are sending all living forms on Earth love and light. Our frequency adds diversity on Earth.

We send out love vibrations when we appear to be asleep upside down in caves or other dwellings. We are building high frequency bridges that we hope humans will walk across in terms of learning that there are countless beings who live beyond Earth.

What would you like to say to humans?

If humans can see and feel the spark of the Key Creator's light in all living forms, they are seeing truth. Then humans can take the next step and accept beings on Earth and those from other universes who look perhaps a bit strange, ugly, or threatening (from a human perspective), but who only have good intentions for the All.

Humans are evolving. We are all evolving. And it can take great faith to make the leap from accepting Earth beings to accepting otherworldly beings. But let us face it (laugh), the beings on Earth *are* from other star systems and universes. Many humans simply have not thought of or accepted this possibility as being real. So, the ETs have already landed or arrived (laugh).

The human species was also seeded, but this thought can be threatening and upsetting to humankind's cultural and religious beliefs. Humans have been controlled by many of the religious organizations as well as governments who desire to keep the truth from them.

Every being of the All is of the stars, of the Key Creator and assistant creators. This is what is true and real.

Follow your hearts! Look into the Creator within you and feel the truth. The illusions of old ways of thinking and being are dropping away. Humans will be left with only the truth. Hurrah! we say from a loving place because you will be free and see the light within and all around you. You will remember who you are.

We are all joined by the Key Creator who created our souls. And our souls are wonderful, are they not? We are all One—one breath, one light, one love.

We are here to assist with opening hearts and minds. When we chose to be a part of Earth's energies, we were not aware of how we would be viewed by humans. So this is a learning process for us as well and we, too, are learning and evolving.

Jacquelin Smith

Bats are wonderful! They are very important to Earth's ecosystem. Could you say something about this?

Bats are a part of the balance of Earth's entire ecosystem. Bats disperse seeds and pollinate plants that are vital to the rain forest's survival. Also, we eat many insects, which helps maintain balance with the insect population as well as the overall balance of forests.

We come with open spirits and gifts that we offer you. We ask humans to look beyond the fear and old myths about bats. Feel our core vibration that will feel like a soft gentle breeze across your cheek.

Bats are the most endangered land mammal in North America and are disappearing worldwide. Are bats going to be remaining on Earth?

Yes. Our intention is to remain on Earth. We love Earth and are continuing to do the work we agreed to do here. But, it is becoming more difficult for our bodies to survive when Earth's entire ecosystem is changing dramatically. This is not only because of humankind's lack of caring about the bigger and long-term picture of things, but because of the interdimensional shifts occurring. These shifts involve the sun's radiation affecting the electromagnetic energies in and around Earth. And this sometimes interferes with our echolocation senses, and we depend on echolocation to navigate.

Thank you. What can bats teach humans or mirror to them?

Humans often think of us as reflecting the dark side of themselves or another, but actually we reflect light in the dark. We are not of the darkness, but we do feed in the dark.

We reflect how you can live and navigate through the darkness whether that be in literal or figurative terms. Humans tend to fear the dark, but the dark is not necessarily a negative energy. It is just a different energy from the light of day and everything in-between. It just is and will be ongoing. And how could you see the stars and planets without the night? (smile).

On Earth there is the theme of light and dark. They are of the same spectrum but just different aspects of the full spectrum of energies. On Earth, light and dark are gifts that show contrast and beauty.

Yes. Thank you for this wonderful conversation.

We thank you for sharing our messages. This has meaning.
Bat Elder

Chapter 29

Sea Horse

We are born of water

Hello. Welcome. Please tell me about you and your world.

Hello. You can call us star horses (smile). We greet you with joy this evening. The oceans of Earth are different from the oceans on our water planet. Our planet of sorts is composed of various vibrations and densities of liquids. Not truly water, but yet close to the element of water. It is difficult to find words for compositions of vibrations and liquids that simply do not exist in your world.

We were born of water. Our planet and moons were dwindling. Our species gathered together to decide where we could travel to in order to continue our species.

We are much older than Earth. We are of a galaxy of what you would call highly evolved beings. Our bodies that are living on Earth are somewhat similar to how they were originally on our planet and moons, but were much larger.

In coming to Earth, it was decided by our species and councils to be smaller and, therefore, inconspicuous. We come from a planet where we can reproduce another of our species from within one body. We accepted the proposal to be male and female on Earth with the male birthing the young. The male fertilizes the female's eggs which she places within his pouch. This shows humans that all things are possible with various living forms. This can help you expand your minds. We invite you to explore other living forms on land and in the waters. This can remind humans that every living form is unique. Also, to remind humans that the countless living forms on Earth are actually from other realms and worlds.

Thank you. Are you an elder? Are you living on Earth or have you lived on Earth?
Yes, I have lived on Earth. I left the Earth plane about five years ago in terms of Earth time. I am not an elder but the elders can speak through me to share information about our species. Yet, I am connected to the sea horses living on Earth in physical bodies.

Is your species a group consciousness or does it consist of individuals?
Our species consists of individuals. We are also connected energetically and can communicate telepathically with one another at will and with ease.

Is your liquid planet in the Milky Way galaxy?
No. Our planet does not exist any longer. But when it did exist it was in another galaxy.

How old are you?
There is not a number I can give you. We do not use or think in terms of numbers or time.

But you mentioned you are older than the Earth?
Oh yes. Much older than Earth.

Thank you. How did you come into physical being on Earth?
Our DNA was preserved by a council who implanted it into physical bodies which our souls and council (consisting of those from many galaxies) projected into being into Earth's oceans.

Our planet is no longer. We consider being on Earth an adventure as well as the survival of our species. We also exist in a few other interdimensional realms, in similar yet altered forms. We exist in etheric, pure energy, as well as fluid or water world.

What kind of work are you doing in the oceans?

Our species moves with grace as you can see. We vibrate to the higher frequencies which we multiply within Earth's waters. Even though we are physically petite, our energy fields can expand for hundreds of miles and through hundreds of multidimensional galaxies and star systems from within the waters.

We shine starlight and moonlight. We integrate the starlight and moonlight energies into Earth's bodies. This helps Earth, as well as all on planet earth, rise to a higher state of being and frequency. We are behind the scenes, angels, you could say. If you listen, you can hear our souls singing.

Beautiful!

If you look at our auras you will see how expansive we are and can be. If you look at our star essence, we radiate rainbows of unearthly colors. We are glad to be on Earth. At some point, we will be teleported to another world, but not for a long time to come in terms of Earth time.

Are you here to learn or are you here to mainly assist the Earth?

We continue to learn about Earth. We have met many beings from various galaxies, worlds and dimensions by converging together here on Earth during this developmental stage that Earth is moving through. Earth has become a hub or station of sorts for many beings to converge, to meet, and to grow as well as assist Earth in her growing process. Earth is alive as you are, even though she is a different physical form than you are.

Are your souls continuing to evolve and grow while being on Earth?

Yes. One's soul is always evolving. The Key Creator is always evolving, shifting and changing. Universes are always evolving into something new and wondrous. This means a galaxy or universe is always transforming into a new creation emerging from past or old energy. Yet it is only old energy if you place this in a time frame, which I am doing, since you live in time.

We came to Earth to survive. There are other realms we could have traveled to but coming to Earth was a choice we made. Earth asked for higher frequencies to help her rise from the denser frequencies. We and the council agreed that this would be a good plan for all concerned.

Are you here to assist humans? What would you like to say to humans?
We are here to help the "whole" of Earth, not just one or two species. The whole of Earth includes the entire Earth and all living forms. Humans tend to focus on themselves as being the most important species. Of course, this is from the humans' point of view (smile). From this way of thinking comes imbalance, greed, and hoarding of Earth's resources. We do not say this from a place of judgment, but from having observed humans for thousands of years. There was a balance when there were fewer humans. This was when humans connected to all living forms telepathically and understood they were but one of many species.

It would greatly benefit humans to open their hearts to other beings and listen to them, as they once did. More and more humans are doing this now.

"Being" is absent from most humans' lives. If you watch us, notice how we flow with the waters' currents and with all that is around us. This keeps us in balance and harmony with ourselves and the All.

Unfortunately, the flow of water energy is being disrupted by what is being dumped into the oceans. We hope humans will remember their interconnectedness with the waters, Earth, the sky, the wind, the sun and moon. And to grow beyond this and to connect with stars, quasars, other universes, and the beings who reside throughout the cosmos. We are all family in spirit.

Thank you for this very informative conversation.
We thank you, too.
Star Horse

Chapter 30

Roach

**Thoughts and emotions you send
us you send to yourselves**

Hello. I am glad to see you. What would you like to share with me?
We who come to you this evening are joyful to speak with you. We are many and we are one. We are of one consciousness that has many bodies. We were on Earth long before human beings existed in any form on Earth. We traveled here billions of years ago. We agreed to come to Earth. You will find this difficult to believe, but our DNA was hidden in what you would call junk material that crashed onto Earth. It was intentional on our part to come to Earth.

Thank you. Are you an elder?
Yes and no. We are the group speaking with one voice. We cannot be divided.

Where do you come from?
We come from a star system that humans do not know. If you look into the light of what you refer to as the past, from some of the most distant galaxies, that is where we have come from.

Do you come from a planet, star or dimension?
We come from a nebula within a star system. You could call it a

dimension. There are countless dimensions within nebulae where stars are constantly being born.

Do you have physical bodies where you come from and do you look the same as you do on Earth?

We look similar to how we look on Earth but are much smaller. We have altered some of our physical traits to adapt to Earth. But our essence is the same and intact. The divine light within us is present. We have the ability to fly as well as crawl in the denser energies. It is not a world that is like Earth. It is difficult to find words for what there is no words for.

We shapeshift. We can be physical, etheric or in-between. We understand how to access the energies of various dimensions in order to survive. We can materialize or dematerialize. We sense energies around us in the way a dog or cat senses energies. For example, dogs and cats know when an earthquake or storm is coming. We have the same innate capabilities.

How do you communicate with one another?

We emit a frequency that can be heard if you listen with your intuitive ears. It is a frequency humans cannot hear audibly because it is not within their range. Roaches speak with one another through frequency and telepathy. We are in constant contact with one another even though we are in individual bodies on Earth.

Are all cockroaches/roaches on Earth of your group consciousness?

No. Our group consciousness from afar inhabits many cockroach bodies and some other bodies as well. But we want to focus on our original roach bodies created for us by the overseer of our group soul. And within the group soul we are always linked telepathically.

Are there other souls from other star systems who inhabit roach bodies?

Yes. They must approach the council and at times the overseer and ask if they can experience becoming a physical roach on Earth or elsewhere. This can be done.

Do roaches exist in other galaxies, dimensions, and universes?

Yes. In the sense that our essence exists within many different types of bodies throughout particular quadrants of specific universes.

Thank you. Very interesting. What would you like to say to humans?

Many people abhor who we are even though they do not really know us. We know how to survive regardless of circumstances. And in this way we are teachers. We know how to adjust to environmental shifts that were happening in the beginning and will be ongoing. This is the natural order of every living form including Earth.

We are children of God. It was different on Earth before humans appeared. It certainly is challenging living with humans. We continue to adjust to humankind's energy despite the fact that most do not accept us as being the Creator's children.

Your misperceptions, disgust and fear of us is an energy that is not uplifting for the *whole*. And if it does not uplift the whole, it does not uplift humans. Remember, we are all interconnected. Thoughts and emotions you send us you send to yourselves. We ask humans to take a look at these issues and to recall how they respected us long ago for gifts that we offer Earth.

Who has seen the radiant light of spirit shine from within roaches? The Creator's spark dwells within us. We know you have seen our light, but this has come through your evolutionary growth in being an animal communicator.

Do you feel humans have invaded your places on Earth?

It could be said that humans have invaded our places, yet you think of us as invading your world (smile). Whose world is this? Good question, we think. Earth belongs to no one but herself. Most beings living on her body are aware of this and respect Earth as another being.

Since humans have taken form on Earth, many evolutionary changes have taken place within DNA that has been experimented with by more than one group of assistant creator beings.

Do you feel humans are evolving?

All beings are in the process of evolving in one way or another. It is not for us to judge, but the question or point becomes this: Have humans evolved spiritually in terms of knowing and respecting their connection to all living forms regardless of what the physical form or etheric form may look like? Humans are becoming more aware of the divine within them. This is very important for their own spiritual and consciousness evolution. And this is true not only for themselves but for all other beings as well.

Humans project fear and hate onto roaches, which must feel horrible. Are humans projecting their shadow selves onto you? What about the mirroring affect?

In many ways yes. Think of being in our shells knowing that a particular species' intention is to exterminate us. How might that feel to you to be loathed so deeply, to be feared so profoundly? Yet we understand there is a deeper truth here about all this in that humans have many misperceptions about roaches, as they do snakes and bats.

It is not always easy, as I have mentioned, to live with humans' energies. Humans fear us and think we are ugly pests. Since humans think in metaphor and image, they project their fear and hatred of their own shadow aspect onto our physical form.

If humans look into our souls, they will see the divine light flowing from roaches. We ask you to contemplate this. Look into the divine light within us.

If we chose to put ourselves into your shoes and think about what humans reflect to us—hmmm. What do you think we might say? (smile). We could focus on the shadow aspect of humans or the light. We recognize both and remember that the Creator's light lives within humans as in every being. We choose to come from a balanced viewpoint of who humans are.

What higher lesson do you mirror to humans?

We offer humans the opportunity to accept and love their own shadow aspects and to acknowledge the Creator's spirit that lives within all living forms. We offer them the opportunity to integrate all aspects of themselves.

We are hoping to help humans discover the truth beneath the illusion of physical form. All beings are the Creator's children. No exception. Let humans not judge a being by the form they inhabit—whether it be a bird, ant, or cockroach. Open your hearts and see the wonderful traits that roaches and others possess. We know how to survive. We do not harm Earth nor anyone else. Yes, we eat, but that is the natural process when in physical form. Right? (smile). Roaches are an integral part of Earth's landscape from the beginning.

It must be difficult for roaches to deal with humans. How do you do it?
We often can transcend and transmute the lower vibrations into love. Sometimes the energies can be difficult to transcend and transmute depending on how many humans are living in close proximity to us.

Thank you for sharing how you raise lower frequencies to love. Thank you for doing so. What else would you like to share with humans?
It is our physical nature to search for food and eat as it is yours in order to survive and thrive in an environment that nourishes. Roaches can show up in homes whether they are clean or not. Sometimes our communities are not created in an ideal environment because humans occupy so much land.

We live everywhere on Earth. We have watched humans exterminate us from their homes, which was perhaps once our home. On some level you reflect our worst nightmare because of your strong feelings and intentions to displace us, to wipe us from the face of Earth if it were possible. Yet, what we do as a species is profound in terms of balancing Earth's energies and ecosystems. We offer diversity and balance. Before humans existed on Earth, we did not have the extreme polarities of energies that now exist. Earth still belonged to herself and nourished and fed us. We are hoping humans will give thanks and give back to Earth in bigger ways. Humans are but one of many species created, and invited to be on Earth. This is not judgment but simply the truth. We love Earth.

How intelligent are roaches and how do you understand the evolutionary process?
We are much more intelligent than you might guess. We have the ability to relate to and be in relationship with humans on a one-to-one basis as some humans have discovered.

Just because we appear in what you consider repelling bodies does not mean we are not intelligent or more advanced than some other species. We understand the evolutionary process in a more in-depth way than humans understand their own evolutionary process at this point in time. We do not mean this with arrogance. It is just a fact. The human species on Earth is much younger than our soul group. We have been a part of councils long before humans were a thought. And long before some of the assistant creators began creating new galaxies and worlds. One might refer to us as one of the ancient races or civilizations. But humans, as you think of them, exist in other realms and galaxies, and are in various states of spiritual development.

The humans on Earth are becoming more aware of their connection to all other living forms in a conscious way, which benefits the All.

We interact and function as community. We care about our young. We care about our star system, our home, which still exists in the twenty-seventh dimension. We care about Earth. Earth is our mother in this sense because we have been here since her beginning.

You are so eloquent in your communications.
Thank you. This is our natural flow which we are sharing with you.

How were things in the beginning on Earth?
It was vastly different in the beginning. Many beings were here from various planets and star systems. The intention was to seed Earth with diverse life forms. In one way it is an experiment of sorts. It could be said that humans are catalysts in a sense, pushing other beings to continue to grow and expand. And we, too, are catalysts for humans.

What can humans learn from roaches?
Humans can learn a great deal from us about surviving, adapting, and knowing Earth in a more intimate way. Study how we live, how we commune, and tune in to how we feel. Yes, we have feelings. We are not rote beings without emotions or wisdom. We invite you to listen and learn from us. We are not above you, we have simply had more time to evolve and learn about life. You will be delighted if you communicate with us telepathically. We have much we would like to share with humans.

These are our energies and intentions which we offer to you with gratitude.

Thank you. I respect and love roaches, as you know. Roaches had visited my home and I sent them love and light. They communicated this to others in their community who then showed up in my home. Then, I communicated with the roaches telling them that I admired them, but asked if they could move to a particular place outside my home. Within two days they had fulfilled my request. I teach that if we approach roaches and other living forms with love and respect, this sets the stage for telepathic communication and cooperation between species. Do you agree?

Yes. Intention is basic to everything. If you greet us with love and positive intention we feel that vibration. Then we can be open and more willing to negotiate as long as humans have reasonable requests. But we ask that humans listen to us as well.

Yes. That makes sense. Thank you. I have enjoyed our conversation.

We have as well.

Roaches

CHAPTER 31

LLAMA: JOCELYN

Having conversations with Earth would greatly benefit humans

Jocelyn is a female wild breed of llama with whom I communicated while she was living in her physical body. She was a beautiful guanaco llama who was the color of a deer. Jocelyn was a wonderful teacher for Marion, her guardian, as well as for other humans and for the llama herd.

Hello, Jocelyn. How are you doing in spirit form?
   Greetings to you, my friend. It is good to talk with you again. I had a wonderful time being a llama on Earth, but I was certainly ready to leave my body when I did. My soul was ready to evacuate the body after living twenty-two years. I came to enjoy and love my llama body and being a part of a herd. I am glad to be spirit once again.

What did you learn being in llama form?
   I came to understand a lot about humans. Marion showed me the capacity that humans have to love. It truly was wonderful. Our souls have been connected for a very long time. Marion has experienced being a llama, so she truly understood me.

Is every llama from the same soul group or consciousness?
   No. There are souls who have chosen to experience llama energy

who are not of the group I belong to. I live beyond the stars of this galaxy. I am from another dimension of high frequency—one of love and light. There are species from other realms and universes who are visiting Earth by inhabiting llama bodies.

I am of a group consciousness, yet we are also individuals. Our consciousness can inhabit numerous bodies simultaneously. This really is not any different from your soul, in the sense that a soul is living multiple lives simultaneously. Our group consciousness simply inhabits a number of given bodies simultaneously in order to do the work we have come to do on Earth and elsewhere.

Being in llama, we are introducing our energies to Earth in a pretty big way these days to help raise Earth's frequencies. You can feel our frequency if you tune into our essence.

Thank you. How was your life as a llama?
I was the queen of the mound. Marion understood me in a way that most humans could not. This is because our souls are connected on a deep level. She knew who I was and am, and I know who she is. Marion is from within the same frequency range I have come from. She, too, is helping to integrate these energies by loving and taking care of llamas. She chose to be human to experience being human. There is great love between us.

I enjoyed looking majestic standing on the mound in spring and summer. Just look at the photo Marion sent you (smile). Marion always told me how beautiful my body was and I agreed (smile).

It is good to be free of a body for now, beyond the limitations of ears, fur and hooves, even though it was and is a wonderful experience. I can still experience this through the other llamas (of my particular species) by simply looking through their eyes and feeling their bodies. A human would put it this way: having my cake and eating it, too (laugh).

That must be fun! (laugh). By the way, I could always feel the love between you and Marion. Why did you come to Earth?
I mentioned that we came here to do our work introducing our frequency to Earth so humans and others can become accustomed to other frequencies that are different from their own. We are part of a council who is helping life forms remember the bigger picture that they have forgotten. Earth is but one small planet living amongst countless other universes. Part of our mission is to assist humans in raising their

consciousness—not only in terms of frequency but in expanding how they think about other living forms. We are "jogging" their memories on the subconscious and soul level.

Thank you. By the way, you have a wonderful sense of humor.
I love having a dry sense of humor (smile). This is who I am at my core. Many souls who live in what you refer to as animal bodies have wonderful humor. Unfortunately, many humans miss this.

Yes, you're right about that. What do you look like in the dimension you come from?
You could say we look like a wisp of a blue cloud. We are interdimensional travelers and time travelers. We do not look like llamas in our world. But we chose llama because they are not sought after as food, but more as novelty. Humans are curious about us since we are different from a horse, cow, or chicken. Not better, just different. And I liked being different (grin). My eyes as a llama were a star being's eyes and Marion could see this.

I know you visit the llama herd. Can they sense and see you?
Yes. I visit the other llamas often. I can appear and then disappear in a flash. Some of the llamas see me and then I vanish. I continue to communicate with the others telepathically who are in llama bodies. We are all able to remain in contact regardless of where a body might be that we inhabit.

While in my body, I enjoyed playing jokes on some of my fellow species in llama form. Even though the group consciousness, in our case, inhabits many llamas, we still have our individual frequencies and personalities while in physical form. And this is really fun for us! We enjoy this diversity of soul essence.

Has your group consciousness tried to inhabit one body at a time?
For a group consciousness to inhabit one body on Earth is not a wise choice. We tried this long ago, but the body could not hold the energy and we had to vacate a body by dying. We have learned that it works best if we inhabit a number of bodies simultaneously, and why not? This anchors in the frequencies we are introducing in a more direct and stronger way.

Jacquelin Smith

Jocelyn: Photo by Minnette Elder

Does your species or realm have a name?

No. We come from a higher frequency. If you listen, you can hear it. It may sound like a choir toning or singing notes but not words.

Do you communicate with Earth?

Yes. We have conversations with Earth. We connect with her essence and listen to her telepathically as a being. Having conversations with Earth would greatly benefit humans, if they would take the time to relax and listen. Humans know how to do this. It is just a matter of connecting with the innate ability that all beings have to listen to one another.

What gifts do you offer the Earth?

We bring light and love from higher dimensions. The frequencies we bring are a part of creating the new paradigm of peace and love on Earth. We, along with many other species, were asked to assist Earth in this way.

We may seem a strange lot, yet we are not (laugh). We are your brothers and sisters. There are so many realms, worlds, star systems and universes that you can come to know. Embrace the All. You are connected to everything in the cosmos.

Thank you.

Good communicating with you again.
Jocelyn, Queen of the Mound

Chapter 32

Polar Bear and Bear Species Council

Bear energy protects the Earth and gateways

Good day. I am happy to see bears. What would you like to share?
We of the bear species are joyful to be present with you today. Bear energy is around you and has been for a long time.

Yes. I often communicate with polar bears. What would you like to say about polar bears?
We polar bears are waning in numbers with the weather pattern changes. The glaciers are melting. We have been losing our habitat on Earth gradually and now it is quickening. Many are not aware of this, but in the land of ice and cold waters there are numerous dimensions which intersect at the North Pole. This is also true for the South Pole.

What is your role on Earth as bear?
We are gatekeepers, along with the grizzly bears and others, of the interdimensional doors that allow particular energies to manifest on Earth or to exit Earth. This is not only true for souls coming and going, but of frequencies from other galaxies that have been manifesting on and within the Earth plane and deep into Earth long before humans existed. There were many other species at the South and North Poles

(which is what they are called today, but long ago this was not so) before humans entered through the gateways or portals.

What is your origin and your intention on Earth?
We are from another dimension of what you could say is from deep within Earth. We agreed to become physical to monitor the beings/energies that enter Earth. We can appear and disappear at will. Humans are not around to observe this. Also, we are guiding and monitoring the energetic shifts taking place within this universe. We are intended to be gatekeepers.

As our physical bodies begin to fade and as we shift into, once again, the inner Earth dimensions or worlds, you could say there will be other gatekeepers to watch over the interdimensional gateways.

Thank you. Are you an elder on the council?
Yes. I am one of the elders and have been in existence longer than you can imagine with your mind. Before being in bear form, I had been in what you would call a dinosaur during an earlier period on Earth. I was Stegosaurus (smile). But I existed before Earth came into form.

If you existed before the Earth came into being how could you be from within the Earth?
Good question. The soul of Earth existed long before she manifested her physical body. There were councils and creators who helped with this birthing process. Not only with Earth but with your entire solar system.

That makes sense. Can you say more about the new energies affecting Earth?
The crystalline light, which is pouring onto Earth interdimensionally, is integrating into Earth's key energy centers and core. This raises the frequencies around and within Earth. You call this Earth. Long before humans were in form, we called this by a frequency or tone, rather than having a word. Ooommmaaahhh.

Thank you. Tell me more about the energies at the poles.
The energies of Earth are of purer vibration at the North and South Poles where there are fewer humans. It is pristine frequency. We live in

Star Origins and Wisdom of Animals

harmony with other species who live in these areas and in harmony with nature.

What changes do you see coming to Earth? Do you know about changes in the Milky Way galaxy?

Soon the gates that we have been overseeing will change and are changing in the sense of the tones or frequencies that are coming through now and ongoing. The sun, Uma, (this is the tone) is changing in frequency. The Milky Way is aligning with the sun and this solar system in ways that are shifting Ooommmaaahhh (Earth) dramatically as well as all the other planets in this solar system in terms of frequencies.

As the energies continue to shift, we are having great challenges with the physical changes taking place on Earth as well as within our bodies. These result from the changes within Uma as well as Earth, moon, and other heavenly bodies. Those that are seen will be shifting into other dimensions and those that are invisible to humans currently, will become visible as the new Earth continues in to be birthed.

I'm sad polar bears and other species are having such a difficult time surviving in the new environments that are developing at the poles.

We welcome your concern. Being sad will not help us, but since you are in human form we understand your feelings. We, too, feel sad at times. We miss the solid ice which energizes us and allows us to survive and travel to various areas. But this is part of the shifting energies of the new Earth rising. Bear species will return to our original home and continue to help with the development of the new Earth. Some would call us sacred. We are of a higher frequency in order to be gatekeepers.

Are other species gatekeepers? What will happen to them?

There are various species who are gatekeepers for many interdimensional gateways. Understand that many species who are leaving will simply transform into spirit form and then perhaps take on new forms of species as well as older forms of species which humans are not aware of at this point in time.

Do you enjoy the cold? And tell me more about Earth changes.

This world of ice and cold water is very comfortable for us in light of where we have come from. The ice is crystalline. The waters are crystalline. The higher frequencies now emerging integrate the crystalline energies in and around Earth. And the sun, Uma, has its part, too, with raising the frequencies. It is a harmonious dance of transformation that is happening now and will continue. The energies whirl and swirl within and around Uma, sweeping things clean so Earth can continue to expand as a being and shift into crystalline light.

Also, there is more than one Earth. We could say there are actually three Earths: dense Earth, another Earth consisting of love and light frequencies, and an in-between Earth. Every being evolves at their own pace, existing in whichever frequencies are appropriate for them. Every being will continue to evolve and move into higher and higher frequencies until they return to pure love and light.

Eventually, Earth will return to its original spiritual form, not unlike all beings who make up Creation.

This is wonderful information. Will you say more about bear energy and your mission?

Bear energy protects Earth and gateways. We help tear away Earth's old energies and welcome in the higher frequencies and beings to do their missions. Bear is strong and solid. Bear is smart and perceptive. We can see better than any biologist or researcher has ever estimated. We can sense and see all around us with our intuitive skills.

Come dance with us on the ice and feel the power that is here. It is a quiet strong power that helps to balance and maintain Earth. And as this shifts, the balances of Earth will shift.

We do not fear leaving the physical plane, though being in bear form suits our spiritual energies well, so you can feel our essence. This is why we were asked to be gatekeepers by several councils when Earth, Ooommmaaahhh, was very young.

Long ago Earth was very hot and waters boiled. We have seen Earth transform through various environmental changes and species. We love and care about Earth and the All. Our focus is to support Earth and to assist with energies that enter Earth. You could say we "filter" the energies that could potentially bombard Earth. This includes preventing certain frequencies and beings from entering Earth's energy fields.

Just because we live in the North Pole area physically does not mean we cannot affect other areas of Earth. There are many other species who are a part of this picture which I am painting for you. Remember, we are all connected. We are able to communicate with bears all over the world and other beings who inhabit animal, rock, tree, wind, water form and other forms.

Why do you care about Earth?
We come from another dimension or world from within Earth as I mentioned. She is a part of our invisible solar system you could say. We care deeply and fiercely for Earth as we do our young. Earth is not that old compared to many other planets in the scheme of evolution. Earth is very young, and she is evolving as quickly as possible.

Earth is a young soul?
Yes and no. Earth has lived other lifetimes as other forms. Not all of her other lives have been as a planet. Humans think of Earth as "big," and do not usually consider her a living being, so how could she possibly have been or be a different form? Energy of a soul creates the form in order to learn its lessons. Earth was created by assistant creators, but previously her soul could have experienced being a sea, asteroid, a star, moon, a cat or dog. We love Earth with our heart and soul.

What will the ice melting mean for Earth?
As ice transforms into waters, it changes shape and form. Nonetheless, it is the same, but Earth will do what she needs to do to reclaim balance and harmony, hoping humans will understand. Yet even then, there is and still will be a re-balancing of Earth. New species are rising from the ashes with a fuller spectrum of frequencies, which will be fitting for Earth.

We bears carry the full spectrum of frequencies. As ice melts, waters will integrate the fuller spectrum of higher frequencies more deeply for further evolutionary leaps. Remember the ancient knowledge and love as consciousness. This expands the All with spiritual integrity and will help humans recall how to connect directly which all living forms and the All. This is what you call God talking with Itself (smile).

Makes total sense. Thank you very much.
You are welcome. Love love love.
Polar and other bears

Chapter 33

Grasshopper Council

Love is the underlying code of the All

Hello. Thanks for visiting me tonight.
We are here—the grasshoppers. We bring song to Earth. Not in the way that you might think of song, but it is song all the same. Frequency is song.

Are you elders?
We are of a council of twelve elders, along with forty-seven other beings who serve on committees overseeing various aspects of our world(s).

Where do you come from?
We come from a world that is of shimmering silver. See it? It is not water and it is not like that of your land. It has a density of frequency. See how it shimmers throughout regardless from what angle you might view it.

Yes, it's beautiful. How big is your world? I seem to see it as rather small.
Smaller compared to what—your Earth or sun or the universe? (smile).

Ahhh, compared to the Earth.
You could think of our world as being small in comparison to many

others, including Earth. Yet there are worlds that are smaller than ours in terms of how you view them by size. Size means nothing to us. A world is a world. Being smaller does not diminish its place or relevance in Creation.

I agree. I wasn't trying to indicate that because your world is small that it isn't relevant.

Humans tend to compare this to that and that to this, do you not? (smile). It is not something that we of our world are familiar with. Everything simply is. We are not being critical, but asking you to expand your mind to include new ways of thinking and being. If most humans compare Earth to let us say, a world the size of a pea, most would say Earth was more valuable because it is bigger.

I understand. Thank you for reminding me of how easy it is to fall into the trap of comparing things in regard to size. It's easy for humans to attach a judgment about size and relevance without thinking about it. Where is your world?

Our world is within Earth's energies, yet it is also in a distant galaxy, where it first came into existence. For example, if you split an atom and place an aspect of it in one country and another aspect in another country or in a distant universe, all aspects of the atom respond simultaneously to a stimulus that is given to one aspect of the atom. This is true if you have four or more aspects of an atom split and placed in various localities. Our world(s) are connected energetically and respond to one another psychically in a way that is not yet understood by humankind. Our world is in more than one place and space and dimension simultaneously in various quantum fields.

How interesting! Is your world more than two energy worlds or dimensions?

Yes. Our world is established in many realities or what you would consider many realities. But then again, there is more than one Earth because Earth exists in various dimensions of frequencies, too (smile).

Why are you on Earth? And say more about your worlds.

We have come to flourish on Earth. We agreed to help Earth's ecosystem to flourish as well. Since one of our worlds is within Earth's matrix system, many of us chose to come here and live in physical form.

We are living in various realities and dimensions simultaneously. We understand how difficult it is for the human to imagine this since the mind focuses on linear time and understanding. So it can be challenging for some humans to grasp these natural basics. It is just a difference. We are not being condescending.

Thank you. Do you look the same on your mother planet?

Very similar but much, much larger. When we first inhabited Earth long ago we were much larger. We agreed to downscale our physical bodies in order to fit in with the ecosystems of that time in a balanced, harmonious way.

How do you feel about being on Earth?

We enjoy being on Earth for a multitude of reasons. It is beautiful in its energy. Earth has taken on the challenge of being host to many diversified beings.

Are you shapeshifters?

We are shapeshifters as are many beings. Humans, too, are shapeshifters but they have forgotten how to shift their consciousness. You personally know how to do this because of your in-depth experience with animal communication and shamanic work. You remembered that your consciousness can wing its way through the sky with a bird, or swim beneath the sea with a dolphin, or travel anywhere in Creation and be there instantly.

Humans are remembering the divinity within them.

Yes. Humans are awakening to their divine selves, whereas most other beings remain attuned naturally with their divine cores. The human ego and mind, along with other factors, function differently from those of many other beings..

Why have humans forgotten, or lost touch with, the divine within?

In a certain way, the human species was put to sleep by, I will say a more evolved creator, for the misuse of their power long, long ago. There is much more beyond the eighty-eight percent of the subconscious that most humans do not tap into and use. Many humans are not consciously aware of their multidimensional selves while many other beings are aware of their multiple other selves. This is not intended to judge, but only to give the facts.

I suppose you could call this the "Fall." There came a time when humans misused power and were put to sleep on many levels. The hope was/is that they can eventually learn lessons about using power based on love. Power without love disconnects a being from the Key Creator within.

Love is always the underlying code of the Key Creator. Humans are not the only species to misuse power, so do not feel guilty about this. It just is.

Thank you for this information. Tell me more about grasshoppers.

We grasshoppers weave our loving energies through grasses, gardens, fields, and everywhere else on Earth. This is communion for all living forms on Earth. Humans are being guided back into harmony and connectedness with all of Creation.

More humans are now thinking about life on other planets. This is a positive step. There will be leaps in evolution as Earth shifts and grows.

Yes, what we call leaping is fun. It is innate for us to leap because of the physical form we inhabit. It is efficient.

Imagine what it would be like to leap as we do. We are referring to a leap of fifteen of your body heights. And being able to do so in whatever direction you desire. Fun!! (smile). As we leap, we are weaving together patterns of energy, new templates and matrixes throughout many dimensions. We are galactic travelers and light workers.

Thank you. This has been enlightening and fun.

We bless you in your endeavors. We are grateful for this conversation with you. Most beings are so misunderstood in terms of who they truly are.

Council of Grasshoppers

Chapter 34

Firefly

We fireflies bring wonderment to Earth

Hello. Where do you come from?
We come from a world of fire. We have not been here as long as many other beings of light from other universes. Yet we were here before the human species, as you know it, walked the Earth. Actually, we have been in various forms throughout Earth's history.

Are you a firefly elder?
Yes. I speak for the firefly species of our home planet. I am a spokesbeing.

Tell me more about yourselves.
We are small beings physically on Earth, but much larger in reality. Our physical bodies are small on Earth in comparison to other, what you call, animals or insects. But our energy fields extend far beyond what you might think. As a group, our energy fields together flow outward for many miles. Remember that a point of light can be an entire universe.

When our light glows, it is mainly for sharing and spreading the Creator's light. This reminds all beings of beauty and love which every being is drawn to in one way or another.

The energy we radiate is amazing when considering how small our bodies are on Earth. On our home planet, our bodies are large as your big houses. Our planet feeds us light. On our planet we do not eat in the sense of eating the way humans do. It is a welcome experience for us to fulfill our mission in sharing our light and to remind the world of the beauty of the light.

Are you individuals or a group consciousness?
We are both. We can be a group consciousness or be individuals.

What is your mission on Earth?
We fireflies bring wonderment to Earth. Many smile as they observe us lighting up the night. There is great power in our energy fields. The light that glows on and off from within our bodies is part of our mating rituals, but it is part of how our bodies function. Just as a human walks or sings, we light up. Our mission is to spread light and love.

We bring light into this world. Because we come from a fire world, Earth has been an adjustment for our species. We enjoy being in Earth's environment flying among bushes and trees. We love the green. Our planet has green but not in the way Earth has green. You could call it an interdimensional green (smile).

Tell me more about your world.
Our world is one of fire. We are fire beings who enjoy flying on dark evenings during summer on Earth. This is an adventure we enjoy very much.

Our planet is much larger than Earth. In fact, you might call it a star, but we call it a planet of fire. It is not quite like your sun but is similar. There are a variety of living beings where we come from.

We have wings of fire light. It is the only way I know how to describe this. We are able to see multiple spectrums of energy, colors and dimensions, and hear their frequencies simultaneously. We are multidimensional etheric beings, so we process life in a different way than humans do.

Do you come from this universe?
No. We come from an etheric universe that is not far beyond the Milky Way galaxy—one that your astronomers cannot detect. But it can be experienced, if you let your consciousness travel to our planet.

Thanks. I can feel your planet. It is truly fire. Please tell me more about your mission on Earth.

As mentioned, we are here to bring light and love unto Earth. We found out about Earth through a few other species who communicated to us that they found it to be an interesting planet. We agree. There are many beings from diverse backgrounds and dimensions who have converged here for their own particular reasons. All this is a part of the Creator's divine plan.

Our main focus is not assisting humans, yet we interact with them. We are mainly here to interact with trees, bushes, grasses, and Earth. Our light helps to balance Earth meridians as well as her aura. Along the way, it is an adventure for us to encounter the incredible diversity that envelops planet Earth.

New patterns of interdimensional energies are and have been being created by the higher echelon of Creators. So be watching. New templates, new holographic sacred geometric paradigms are creating something new and wondrous. It is time. We play our part in this with countless other beings.

Can you communicate with those on your home planet?

Yes. We are connected to those on my home planet, but we are not in constant communication. We have certain "frequency frames," or what you might call "time frames," when we communicate with those who are overseeing our endeavors on Earth. They are also able to look through our energy bodies and view Earth.

Thank you. What would you like to share with humans?

Is it not wondrous to see our species' as lights after the sun has retreated for the night? Children and adults love us. Some children catch us with their hands and put us in jars with holes punched in the lid. Some of us die in this way, yet we are ambassadors with a mission to teach about light and love.

Some kill our kind for the light, but after we are dead, there is no living light. Humans can learn from us best by observing us rather than dissecting us.

We share our light and love freely with the All—the trees, the children, the night, the plants, and other living beings. We have only positive intentions in being on Earth. Feel our light next time you are around one of us. You can also feel our light right now if you close your eyes and connect with our light by seeing us within your mind's eye.

Think about how our small bodies can radiate so much light. Think about how much light you have within you that shines just as bright, even though it is expressed in a different way. You can see someone who is a happy glow, can you not?

Oh yes. And others are attracted to their light and love.

Yes. And this is how it is with us when we glow. Humans are drawn to us, especially children, because they are open to wonderment. Teach children how to observe us without harming us. Teach them that all living forms are better off being free. It can be fun for children to put us and other insects in jars, but teach them to respect us as beings and to release us after containing us for a very short time. A good lesson for all.

Anything else you would like to share with humans?

Humans are beginning to better understand the many realities that their own soul exists in simultaneously. It is all beyond time and space as you know it. While on Earth, we fireflies retain our abilities to be connected to our multiple selves. We see spectrums of light and hear spectrums of frequencies that humans do not hear but could hear if they listen intuitively. If humans listen from their seat of intuition, or their primal animal self, they can experience all these energies, too. It is within them, but generally humans turn an eye away from their instinctive animal self and intuitive selves. They end up living from only a small aspect of themselves rather than from who they are as a "whole" being. Some aspects of humans are asleep.

Though many other living forms may exist in a smaller physical form, they are living from their "wholeness" rather than from one or several aspects of the self. Many beings without physical brains are living from a deeper sense of wholeness. This may upset the human ego, but our intention is to share the truth with you as we understand it. Humans are moving toward embracing their wholeness. Since you are human we felt you would be interested in hearing some of our observations in regard to humans.

Are you going to continue living on Earth?

We will be here awhile longer. The global problems with pollution and energetic climate shifts are causing our numbers to dwindle. Many of my family have already returned to our home. We are beginning new phases of our work in etheric form. This way we can work interdimensionally with integrating the higher frequencies in this universe.

Thank you. This has been uplifting and lighthearted. Blessings.

Your brothers and sisters of the cosmos thank you for being receptive to what we have shared.

Firefly Elder

Chapter 35

Raccoon

Love is the greatest gift we can give to
one another regardless of species

Last week while walking through the woods, I spotted a young raccoon. I stood still and watched her look through decaying logs. She walked about fifteen feet in front of me. She glanced my way a few times as she washed her paws in the river. I was delighted to watch this raccoon living her life. I sent her love and told her how wonderful she was.

Days later I found the raccoon's body not far from her hollow. Her body was very close to where I had been standing. I felt sad and said prayers for her soul's smooth transition. I communicated to her that she was loved and admired while on this Earth. She was young and didn't have a long life, yet I knew that her soul was here as long as it had chosen to be here.

A couple of days later the raccoon showed up to communicate with me.

Hello! This is a wonderful surprise to see you.

I am happy to be here and to communicate with you. Do you really think it was coincidence that you and I observed each other on the path? (laugh).

No.

I knew you were watching me. I felt your love and knew there was nothing for me to fear. You had the opportunity to watch a raccoon "living" for a brief time. And I had the opportunity to experience love from a human for a brief time. We can learn a great deal in a matter of minutes or less if we are open.

I felt your open-heartedness and my spirit leapt with joy. You radiated joy and love in response to my presence. What an amazing lesson to learn—**love is the greatest gift we can give to one another regardless of species.** I knew you could see my light.

Yes. I agree. Thank you. Love transcends what some might refer to as species barriers. Are you from another world?

By coincidence, I happen to be from another world (laugh). You had asked Spirit to give you a sign if you should continue writing this book or not. And there I was! Coincidence? (smile).

Humans often view raccoons as nuisances, but I think raccoons are beautiful.

Raccoons are thought of in negative terms by many humans. Humans refer to us as pests who rip through garbage. You saw me in my natural state of living and loved me. No matter what costume I wear, I am born of the Key Creator.

What is your star origin—home star or planet?

My star origin is of one of the stars in Sirius—actually Sirius B. I chose to be in raccoon garb for a short time to experience how things are on Earth. I have been here before, but it has been some time. I was not here long, but enjoyed my experience on Earth.

I appeared to you as a young raccoon. The truth is that I am very old. I am older than Earth. And though my origin is from Sirius B, I existed in another universe as pure love. But we are all created from love, are we not? (smile).

Yes. What does your essence from Sirius B look like?

I am a light body. This is the best way for me to describe it in a way that you will understand. The light body that I am on Sirius is a beautiful white glow whose etheric shape is similar to that of a rose but in light body form.

Are you an individual or are you from a group consciousness?

I am from a community. My species is individuals who live in community. I do not look like a raccoon on my blue home star. We have light bodies and can materialize and dematerialize depending on what form is called for in the moment.

When my young raccoon body was alive, the others from my star could see Earth through my eyes—kind of like looking through a camera lens, but different because they can see all the dimensions holographically.

Is this what I experienced years ago when I saw a raccoon on the roof of the townhouse next door? Yet the being was way too big to truly be a raccoon. And seconds later, that raccoon or being disappeared. Immediately, I heard a raccoon scampering on my roof over my bedroom.

That experience was one of our kind manifesting on your neighbor's roof for a matter of seconds and then dematerializing and materializing on your roof. Then the being shapeshifted back to his original form of light body.

Thank you. I thought so. Do many of your species choose to live in raccoon form on Earth?

Many in our community choose to be raccoons when experiencing Earth. This is because the life span of a raccoon is not too long. And we get to experience the beauty and diversity of your world. There are many species from Sirius just as there are many species on Earth and her moon.

Are there souls from other stars, planets, or dimensions who experience being raccoons?

Yes. A number of us from Sirius B have experienced being in raccoon form, but others from our community have chosen to experience being chipmunks, squirrels, camels, zebras, and other forms. It all depends on what experience each soul wants to have and what form is best that will help us to fulfill whatever missions we have chosen to complete.

There are those from other galaxies and universes who have been and will be in raccoon form. You yourself have been in monkey, cat, etheric, and other forms.

Thank you. Each of us has a spiritual origin. It seems to me every being that exists is considered a star being or a being from another world or realm depending on one's perspective. Is this accurate?

Yes. Earth was seeded long ago with a multitude of beings from various realms, worlds, stars and dimensions throughout this universe and beyond.

Your spiritual origin is that of a star being or a being from another universe when looking through the humans' perspective about what constitutes a "star" being. This is viewing every being as separate from you. Humans consider beings who are not from Earth as "alien." The cosmic joke is that all beings on Earth originated from the Key Creator, from your universe as well as other galaxies and universes. **So there is no "them out there" and "us here." Every being is everywhere! We are all energy.**

I could refer to you as "star being" if I am perceiving you from Sirius B. But I do not view life or beings in this way. We are all part of one another. Let me use an analogy. If you live in the U.S. and have distant relatives who visit you from Italy, they may look different, speak a different language, and have different customs culturally, but they are still relatives, correct?

Yes.

I may look different than you because I am not living in a human body, but we are all relatives! Every living being possesses the divine light and energy which connects us all. We are one big cosmic family (smile).

Thanks for the analogy. I feel our exchange is one of joy and love.

The exchange you and I had and are having will not be forgotten. Our exchange was and is important to both of us. I was waiting for you. And on some level you were waiting for me. Our souls were waiting to connect.

What else would you like to say?

Love and joy are what my species is about. It is always important for humans to remember to take time to experience love, joy, and connection with all living beings. Raccoons, chipmunks, and others have so much joy and love to offer Earth. Earth feels and absorbs our love, joy, and spontaneity.

I feel like all the beings in the woods bless one another. And when dogs walk through woods they appreciate the vital, living energies.

Dogs bless the wooded areas and the wooded areas bless the dogs. The woods and other living forms are exchanging boundless love, joy, and beauty with one another. Humans can be a part of this exchange if they open and become receptive to all these gifts as they walk through the woods slowly (smile).

Yes. The exchanges are amazing, like the one you and I experienced in the woods.

Yes. Look what can happen when one is open and listening to others.

What would you like to share with humans?

All living forms offer the gift of growth to each another. Every being, every form of energy that exists is continually changing and shifting. This offers every being the opportunity to grow spiritually, regardless of what planet, star, universe, or dimension the being exists on or within.

My species is different from yours, of course. Yet no species is higher or lower than another regardless of whatever stage of evolution a species is experiencing. Each species has their own unique qualities, gifts, and talents which they offer to one another and to the All.

If humans will open their hearts they will see that all life is of equal value.

We do not have ego on my star. The ego can lead humans astray with misperceptions. Hold to the truth that we are all One, and you cannot go wrong. It really is that simple and that difficult for humans (smile).

Yes, I understand. Do you have ships or how do you travel?

We travel through intention. We can be anywhere we want instantaneously by setting our intention. We have no need for physical spacecraft as some species do. You could say we become a beam of light and appear at the desired destination.

Also, we can project an aspect of our consciousness near a physical form and can view things through that one's eyes and senses in order to look around. If we decide to live as a raccoon or other form, we project a part of our spirit into the form just as your soul does.

Thank you for this wonderful conversation and for our exchange in the woods while you were in raccoon form. I am grateful for these gifts.

So am I. You are meant to write about the underlying realities of soul essence of those inhabiting what humans call "animal" forms on Earth. The term "animal" separates humans from the rest of the world and beyond. There is no such term or category where I come from.

I understand. Thank you.

I enjoyed this communication spirit to spirit and heart to heart.

Thank you, me too.
Bye.
Raccoon

Chapter 36

Serpent Creator

Snakes bless the world by offering their gifts of healing

I have done hundreds of drawings of feathered rainbow serpents and other serpents for a number of years. The drawings simply came through me. I wasn't sure if the drawings were symbolic of kundalini energies within me and/or in the cosmos. In all my drawings there are other star systems that were intertwined with serpents or snakes. After every drawing, I feel the energy of the drawing with my hands and heart.

After the following conversation with snake creator, I knew on an innate level that my drawings of serpent were not symbolic, but were of actual being(s). Also before having this conversation with Serpent, I had drawn serpents with feathery wings. I wondered what this what about. I had not known that the Aztec name for Serpent is Quetzalcoatl, which means "sacred bird with beautiful feathers." Needless to say, I was stunned, for I had not studied or seen pictures of this before.

The following conversation validated what I had come to know and feel after years of drawings.

(Note: the words "serpent" and "snake" are used interchangeably.)

Hello. Welcome! I've been drawing you, I think, for quite awhile. This is great to meet you. Tell me about yourself.

I am the serpent creator. We have spoken or, I will say, communed many times in other dimensions—other dimensions that you are not accustomed to being aware of in a conscious way. Yes. We have been connecting through the drawings you have been doing and continue to do since they possess my energy. Drawing me is you being creative and creating, which is what the Key Creator is all about.

I am a creator. You are a creator. I am an assistant creator in the sense of learning how to create galaxies and worlds that are not only within your range of living on Earth but beyond. I am a multidimensional being existing in many dimensions and star systems.

Serpent energy is creative, wise, and powerful. The serpent energy, which many humans refer to as the kundalini energy, is coiled at the base of the root chakra. When it uncoils it snakes along the spine and activates one (chakra) energy center at a time. This allows a person or being to clear away energy blocks and to evolve spiritually. This process can take place not only in humans but in other life forms as well, whether they are in a physical body or not. Life force is my energy. I am primal and psychic energy.

Thank you. I can feel your clear energy. What is your origin?

Serpent was created by the Key Creator and lives in multiple dimensions, worlds, and universes simultaneously. You would think of me as originating in multiple dimensions. I am not from a particular planet or galaxy. My origin is that of many dimensions. I continue to evolve as all creations do.

Thank you. Are you the feathered rainbow serpent?

Yes. I can appear however I desire to appear. Many humans have seen me in visions and dreams and within other dimensions as feathered serpent or a combination of what you think of as serpent and bird.

Are the souls who inhabit snakes on Earth from the same dimensional spaces that you are from?

No. As I mentioned, there can be beings who want to have the experience of being snake in physical form. Some souls want to better understand snake energy, creator energy, healing energy which is connected to chakra systems. My energy is part of the chakra systems and more, as I have explained. There is more than one chakra system. There are many. As humans discover their interdimensional and multidimensional selves, they will discover the other chakra systems that exist in various dimensions and existences.

Are you a creator?

I am an assistant creator who was created by the Key Creator. I am not the ultimate Creator. I am but one of many assistant creators who create worlds, galaxies, universes and dimensions. Those of us who have learned to create in this way meet in higher frequency dimensions to commune and communicate about what we are creating and learning in the process.

I am not a creator who insists on ultimate power over the worlds and beings which I create. But there have been struggles between a number of creators who want to lord it over certain galaxies and even universes.

What about Earth? Did you create Earth?

I had a hand, (smile) you could say, in brainstorming with a council about what purpose Earth could serve. Earth is filled with inhabitants of various cultures from other universes.

I can expand and manifest my energy far beyond what you can imagine. My energies can bring galaxies into existence or change the flow of a universe if it is in agreement with several other creators. You could say we are co-creators. This is not to boast about my energies, but to let you know about them since you were asking. Every being is intended to be creative and to co-create with the Key Creator or the light and love and consciousness that flows through every aspect of the *whole.*

Why do you look like a serpent?

Serpent energy helped create Earth, as I have mentioned. Serpent is ancient and part of Earth's fundamental energy. If you look at snakes on Earth, they are very much in touch with Earth's innate vibrations. Snakes are fluid and flow in a natural way, which is the same way my energies flow throughout this universe. The snake body is the perfect body for living on Earth and for continuing to assist Earth, as well as watching over her.

Are you one or many beings?

I am one and yet many beings. I have many assistants who assist me in the council's creations. We are all interconnected. Just as you consist of multidimensional selves, so does serpent. This is why we are sometimes portrayed as having more than one head or viewed as having other serpent beings around us.

Did the council you are a part of help beings from other star systems and universes to have a physical body on Earth?

Yes. Our council designed physical bodies for beings from other galaxies and universes that would fit their needs for Earth. Their DNA was placed into those bodies. Also, DNA was placed on Earth for particular types of bodies to develop and grow. This offered them the opportunity to experience a physical body if they had not experienced one before or to house the essence where they came from in a way that was comfortable for them. For example, a light being from Mars might want to experience being a firefly on Earth. Or a very small being from another star system might want to experience being an elephant on Earth. A large being from Jupiter might want to experience being an ant. A being from a fire planet might desire to live with the desert, or a being from a water planet might need to live in the ocean. Or a being from a fire planet might decide to experience living as a being who swims in waters. Understand?

Yes. Thank you. Your light is so bright and beautiful, it's almost blinding! There are many cultures who honor and worship serpent, saying that serpent created life in the universe or created the universe. What would you like to say about this?

Many ancients have seen me in visions and dreams as the feathered serpent. You too have seen me in visions. The Mayan and Aztec people saw serpent with rainbow colors and feathers. I am a rainbow serpent or some might see me as serpent without rainbows or feathers. I create, I heal, I transform. See the truth of me now. The rainbows that many visionaries perceive are the spectrums of frequencies that I am, that I possess, and express. Yes. I had a hand in creating the universe in which you are currently living.

How beautiful! What about all the negative and positive myths that have been created about serpents? How would you like to respond to them?

Many myths have been created about serpents by humans. There are both negative and positive portrayals of serpent. One of the major myths created by humans in certain cultures is that serpents are evil. The Bible portrays the serpent as the one who deceived Eve, who then deceived Adam. But this is not the case. This story has led many humans astray. (By the way, the Tree of Life is one of heart, and spirit-felt love for all of the Creator's creations.) The writer was telling this story in a symbolic way. The serpent is blamed for leading Eve astray, but the truth is that when the shadow side of humans awakened, the mind and ego is what led Adam and Eve astray. The serpent was used as a metaphor for evil as well as for the ego. The writer of Genesis was projecting his own fear and ego onto serpent, which he had identified as evil in his own mind. Serpent energy has nothing to do with evil or the ego. Serpent assisted in creating your universe, Earth, and a number of beings on Earth.

Because in some cultures snakes are labeled evil, humans respond from a place of fear and kill snakes. All this happens from being taught myths which have led to misperceptions about who snakes or serpents truly are. Some humans would rather blame it all on the "serpent" rather than looking within and realizing that their species sometimes makes choices that do not serve them or others well. Serpent became a scapegoat.

Yes. This makes sense. We humans find it easy to get lost in our misperceptions and egos, don't we? (laugh).

Yes. This is why it is important to see beyond the projections and illusions that some humans create, leading themselves astray. What can seem or look like a monster or evil to humans usually is not. What can seem like a friendly, beautiful-looking human may be someone whose ego is running the show by creating misperceptions which may mislead or even harm fellow humans and other beings. This is not to judge humans but to simply point out how looks can be deceiving. The ego is the deceiver that thinks the material plane is real when it is illusion. Humans forget that they are spirits experiencing what it is like to be human and that their souls have chosen to be in human form in order to learn and grow.

How can humans move beyond their fear of snakes?

If a human will allow themselves to stop and feel the fear when they see a snake rather than screaming and running, or killing a snake, they could respond from a centered place and make a different choice. If the human feels the fear and moves beyond it, he or she can then choose to view the snake from heart energy and see the divine within the snake. In doing this, a human is truly evolving into a new being—shedding their old skin (smile). How can you then kill a snake who is not bothering you?

This is not to say that you should pick up a venomous snake without thinking because snakes respond from instinct. But if you send snakes love from a safe distance, they will feel the love and respond with love in kind. But it is important to respect the snake's boundaries as well.

Aren't more humans getting in touch with the divine within?

Yes. The good news is that many humans are allowing their minds and hearts to expand and are questioning others' opinions. More humans are reconnecting to the divinity within in a conscious way.

This is teaching humans, once again, how to trust the divine within rather than blindly following and trusting someone else's perceptions or beliefs. This is helping humans to evolve in a bigger way now. With all the new frequencies that humans are experiencing, as well as Earth, every being is being asked to remember that the divine within is who they truly are. And ultimately that we are all One. I am you and you are me. Now that might be a scary thought for a human, correct? (smile).

Yes (laugh). Does evil exist? And how can humans feel what rings true for them?

Truly, there is no evil. There are very dark energies or lower frequencies that exist in the cosmos but there is no true evil. Light and dark are just different aspects and frequencies of the energy spectrum. And when a story like the Adam and Eve story is written, humans unwittingly accept it often without questioning its origins. This story was written long ago and the misperceptions are still being perpetuated because of this being in the Bible. Yet, this is how misperceptions are created and continue in humankind's collective unconscious.

In order for people to move beyond ego and mind misperceptions, they must question the source of the stories. They must ask the divine within to show them what is true and real.

There are many cultures who hold the serpent sacred.

If you look to other cultures, the serpent is sacred and revered. Serpent is not to be feared or killed, but to be honored for the gifts it has given to this universe as well as to Earth as assistant creators. Serpent brings gifts to Mother Earth, other galaxies and universes. This is the truth about serpent.

I know you mentioned that serpent exists and is known beyond this universe?

Yes. Serpent is not only known to Earth beings, but to many others who live in existing dimensions that swaddle Earth and beyond. There are worlds within worlds, dimensions within dimensions and so on. Serpent works in many other galaxies and universes.

Many cultures worship and worshipped serpent, correct?

Many of the ancient worlds worshipped serpent. These include Africa, India, Mexico, Peru, China, Britain, Greece, Persia, Egypt, and others. So there must be a basis for this, correct? (smile). Some considered serpents gods and goddesses. We are in that we are assistant creators, but we are not the Key Creator. This was so until religious sects developed their own beliefs, which led them away from the truth. This introduced prejudices against serpent.

The snake is greatly maligned in a number of cultures. What do you think and feel about this?

Is it not ironic? (laugh). Here I am one of the creators of Earth and yet I am highly maligned by humans. Yet I am not maligned by other species. Of course, the Key Creator is the ultimate Creator of the All. Still, it is interesting how the human mind projects myths and fears onto snake and other beings, which keeps them living in constricting constructs of misperceptions. And the misinformation continues if humans do not embrace the truth. And as I mentioned, the snake is revered and worshipped in many cultures as well. It is a matter of perspective. And I want to mention that I do not have any desire to be worshipped. The idea of worship is something created within humans' minds a long time ago when humans were misled by some power-hungry assistant creators who insisted on being worshipped. Humans have forgotten that they too are wondrous co-creators.

I do not experience hurt feelings about this, if that is what you are asking. I just understand that this is where the human species is in terms of their evolutionary process. No judgments about any of this. It just is. But I do desire for humans to be who they truly are as a species and to be all that they can be. They are magnificent beings. If they only knew how magnificent!

I think many people in America and perhaps in some other countries have trouble thinking of a creator in serpent form.

It is difficult for humans to accept that a creator could look different from a human. Most imagine God to be an old wise man sitting in the sky, but this is myth, as you know. So it can be difficult for a human to understand or relate to the snake creator energy. You see me in snake form because that is the form I take on when humans see me in visions and dreams. Remember I am an energy.

What is your connection to snakes on Earth?

The snakes on Earth are ambassadors of higher frequencies. They are my children, but so are many other species. The snakes on Earth allow me to keep my pulse on what is happening globally without time being involved. There is no such time element as "an instant" because there is no time. But I know NOW what is going on globally, not only through snakes but many other beings.

Tell me about the snakes on Earth.

The snake children on Earth can have a tough life because of many humans' attitudes towards them. Yet, they know it will not be a long life, or not for most, so they agreed to incarnate physically into a snake body for adventure, or sometimes to honor me as the serpent creator. Snakes on Earth and elsewhere have my energy but so do many other beings. Serpents in one way or another exist throughout the universe and beyond, as I have mentioned.

Snakes truly "know" the Earth, don't they?

Yes. Snakes truly understand everything that is happening in and around Earth. They know when an earthquake is going to happen or when a volcano is going to erupt. Animals know this, too, but snake is close to Earth. Snake glides on Earth's skin and know her intimately. You understand this as an animal communicator and snake lover.

I have had many wonderful communications and experiences with snakes. I have always cared about snakes and often feel protective of them.

Snakes as well as other animals have their gifts and talents to share. You yourself held a friend's boa, Dash, and knew immediately that he was a healer. And the next day you felt snake energy in your aura. Dash communicated with you to let you know that he had placed snake medicine in your aura as a gift from him. And you were honored and grateful. These kinds of relationships can develop when hearts are open.

Yes. My hope is that more humans will open their hearts to snakes and see them for the beautiful beings that they are. What missions do snakes have on Earth? Are they helping humans evolve?

Snake has many missions. The snake is keeper of Earth's skin. The snake is also the gatekeeper for the inner dimensions of Earth. Snake also works interdimensionally. We have the ability to project our frequencies to Earth's core, to create and transform the sacred geometry, to shift or introduce new energies into the holographic Earths. Everything is holographic, as you know. We continue to introduce and anchor in new frequencies into Earth's core for the well-being of all life on Earth and beyond. Also, we assist Earth in being in sync with the rest of the paradigm shifts happening in your universe, as well as the new frequencies of other solar systems being integrated into what is currently existing in what you know as the Milky Way.

The snakes on Earth are healers in various ways. They help heal Earth. Snake carries the same life force frequencies that are coiled in the base of a human's spine. This is the serpent or kundalini energy. When this energy uncoils, humans experience the energies snaking through their chakra centers (energy centers) one at a time. This allows them to experience a raising in consciousness in their evolutionary process as spiritual beings. This is especially the case if they work in a conscious way with the energies and their chakra systems. Snakes on Earth, as well as my energy in various dimensions, assist humans in their evolutionary process.

Serpent energy is basic and important to Earth, isn't it?

Serpent energy is basic to Earth energy. Serpent will continue to usher in the new paradigm. Is not it ironic, as I mentioned, that sometimes what some humans think is evil, such as serpent, is truly of the Key Creator's light? The human mind can become boxed in by limiting beliefs about others and the cosmos.

Snakes live all over the globe. This was my intention as well as several other creators' intention. We can know what is going on all of the time. We do not interfere in any way, but simply enjoy observing the creation of Earth and the interactions of those living on Earth. I am saying this in a way you can understand.

What a wondrous ability for snake to be so close to Earth that snake truly *knows* Earth, understands her, and assists her in many and necessary ways.

Are there serpents who misuse their power? I've heard serpent contains light and dark as well as constructive and destructive energies.

Good question. From a human's point of view, with living in a framework of time and space, and living in physical form, you view energies as negative or positive, when in reality there is only light. There are gradations of light and frequencies. Many beings live in various frequencies and carry various frequencies. So there is the full spectrum that ranges from lower to higher frequencies. Every frequency has a purpose. What humans might view as negative simply is and has purpose, too. This is why serpent is sometimes viewed as what you would call the light and dark. Some assistant creators carry a number of frequencies while others carry fewer frequencies. Serpent carries a wide range of frequencies.

Every being has a choice in how they choose to use the frequencies that they carry. Remember that the dark and light are truly the same, but only what you would call opposite aspects within the same spectrum of frequencies.

The kundalini energy we have been communicating about can be used in a constructive way. It can be destructive if a person or being does not understand what is happening to them and does not play a part in cooperating with the energies that are snaking through their chakra systems. It truly is a dance.

Thank you. Is Earth going through a kundalini awakening?

Yes. Earth has energy centers (chakra systems) too. As the frequencies are being raised throughout your universe, so, too, are Earth's frequencies being raised. Earth is rising out of duality and shifting into higher frequency dimensions where duality and opposite poles do not exist in ways that you think about them. Earth is shedding the framework of time and actually space as you know it. Earth is shifting into the vibrations of what humans might think of as heaven, which are the higher frequencies of love, joy, and peace.

Thank you. Tell me about more about serpent and what you know about DNA.

Serpent power is far reaching. We create galaxies as well as universes and are a part of the councils that make decisions about DNA and bodies, as I have mentioned. One cannot have the physical form on Earth without DNA.

There are "banks" or what I will call templates or holographic filing cabinets filled with DNA of some of the first beings who existed from the beginning. They truly are the ancient ones.

The Key Creator has created countless assistants. We assist in creating the All. We honor, respect, and are guided by the Key Creator of the All since the very beginning.

What about the beginning of the cosmos?

The beginning is not linear as you have seen in visions. Many universes, stars, worlds, planets, galaxies, dimensions were created in the NOW–simultaneously. How is that for a mindblowing truth! (smile). Humans think and live in a linear fashion, but is not how it really is (smile). I am not making fun, but sharing the basic truth about realities which are beyond time and space as you know it.

Yes. Quantum realities, dimensions and other realities? I really don't have words for this (smile).

Yes.

Since you helped create Earth, why is there duality? Why fear and hate?

It was not this way when Earth was first created. There was another creator or actually two who interfered with the original creations of

Earth and those living on Earth from her origin. There is a much longer history to all of this. It is not appropriate to open this door.

I respect that. But if you are of higher frequency along with other creators, and all is light, then how could others interfere with this?
Because they are assistant creators who are like scientists who "play" with DNA and frequency to see what they can do because they can. As I mentioned, there is a gradation of frequencies so there is a gradation of assistant creators.

Thank you. That makes sense. Are serpents teachers and healers?
Yes. Serpents are wonderful teachers and healers. They can open your heart if you let them. They offer healing for the body along with countless other energetic healings. As we discussed, you had the experience with Dash the boa, who is a healer.

What would you like humans to know?
As I mentioned, you want to respect a snake's boundaries. It would not be wise to simply send out love and then try to pick up a snake. Of course it is not wise to pick up a rattlesnake or other venomous snake. If you center and ground and gently send love from your heart to a snake's heart, they receive this wonderful energy. And then you can gently pick up a nonvenomous snake and feel their wonderful energies that they offer.

Snakes feel smooth as clay, like Earth herself. As an assistant creator, I breathed serpent energy into Earth during creation. Serpent is a profound energy. I create from love. This may sound like an ego-based statement, but this is simply the truth about serpent energy.

See how great you feel right now. In fact, you are glowing with light. Feel it. You are trusting the light and wisdom from within yourself. This is a wonderful opening for you tonight. Now we can commune with nothing standing between us. Now we meet in communion, light to light. Feel my blessing heal you, uplift you. You know the truth of this deep in your soul.

Yes. I can feel your healing energy. Why do you use the word "commune" rather than "communication"?
Even though you sense us communicating telepathically, we are

communing. We are resonating with one another heart to heart and light to light, which is beyond telepathy. Trust your soul. Trust your inner divinity. You are meant to share these conversations with others. Those who are ready will feel the truth in their gut and heart. Some will weep.

I love you. I love Earth and every being that exists in this universe.

Do you know Q? (Q is the letter I use to represent his name.) He is a star being whom I have communicated with since 1982.

I know many star being cultures. Yes, Q knows me and I know Q since the beginning, my beloved. I am not Key Creator, as mentioned, but one of the creators who loves and creates from love.

Anything else you would you like to say to humans about what they can learn from snakes?

Snakes bless the world by offering their gifts of healing. They listen to Earth, and know how to flow. Snakes live in woods, deserts, waters, in every environment.

Serpent encourages humans to flow with their instinctive, primal selves. If humans pay attention to how snakes vibrate with Earth, they can be in tune with Earth, with themselves, and all other species.

When more humans open their hearts and see and feel the true essence, or the divine, within serpent and/or snakes on Earth, humans will experience the oneness of the All. Then humans will be better prepared to meet more beings from other galaxies and universes. Understand? And what irony (laugh) because star beings have been inhabiting Earth since the beginning. This is not intended to poke fun at your species, but it is amusing, is it not?

As I mentioned earlier, if humans will feel their fear and move beyond it, they can feel and know the divine within every snake and within themselves as well.

Oh yes. I teach workshops showing others how to look at and feel an animal's essence. This helps us humans to move beyond fears that we might have about particular species, such as snakes (smile).

Yes, exactly. Teach the children the truth about all living beings. This will help humans expand and move beyond fear and limiting beliefs about other life forms as well as themselves, their own species, and other species.

What do serpents reflect to humans?
Humans view serpents as symbols in countless ways and on countless levels. It all depends on from which perspective humans views serpents. Serpent energy can reflect to humans their ego and shadow states. We can reflect this because of the way in which many humans have been led to think about us. But serpent can mirror the ability to shed old habits, transmute toxins within the body, emotions, and behavior patterns the way a snake sheds old skin. Serpent mirrors the energy of healing and transforming into a new being and new life.

For some, serpents reflect one's fear of their primal energies. Others think of the serpent as the being who created the universe. It is all a matter of perception. I am communing with you to share who serpents truly are as spiritual beings, in hopes that humans will move beyond their old belief structures and embrace the truth.

The serpent can reflect constructive and destructive energies to humans, depending once again on perspective.

Are you referring to the kundalini energy? What would you like to say about the kundalini energies?
The kundalini energies that rise through the energy centers help humans and other beings as well to move beyond energetic blocks that have been formed through many lifetimes. The kundalini rising can help a human evolve in many ways. It can help them become aware of the powerful life force within them. But if someone does not remain aware and flow with the energies and learn to embrace and harness them to some extent, the kundalini or serpent energy can be destructive in various ways.

There is opportunity for great healing through this process with what you think of as the light and the shadow aspects of self-integrating, which results in wholeness. This gives humans the opportunity to integrate all of who they are and to fulfill their potential as spiritual beings to live as whole and powerful beings while in a body. The kundalini process is a gift.

As the frequencies continue to be raised within and around Earth, humans are experiencing this awakening, this raising in consciousness, and healing process en masse.

This makes sense. Thank you for this wonderful gift of communion on the evening of the new moon.
    You are welcome. We will commune again.
    Serpent Creator

When this experience of communion was completed with serpent, my body was so hot from the energy that I had to cool off my body. My chakras had definitely been activated.

Chapter 37

Electric Eel

We are benders of light and beings of bending light

Hello. It is a pleasure to meet you. Are you an elder or group consciousness or other?

Hello. We are one and yet we can experience being individuals. It all depends on how we set our intention. We can be anywhere in a flash. Earth has not been of much interest to us, but we were asked to take form on Earth as electric eels. We do better in the waters than on land. Water is a perfect conductor for light, for electricity. And we choose to live in a smooth, sleek physical body on Earth.

We are overseers of many universes.

Thank you. What does your star essence look like?

We are light and do not have physical bodies, yet we have light bodies. We are brilliant gold and green frequencies or beings of light who have a shape similar to what you call boomerangs (smile).

We are benders of light and beings of bending light. We are able to bend and guide light in order to do our interdimensional weavings of energy which creates and connects countless universes with what you might call etheric threads of frequency.

We are able to shapeshift universes.

Jacquelin Smith

Fascinating. Where are you from originally?

We are from Amereta, which is the eighth universe beyond your universe.

Is Amereta a star, a planet, or another dimension?

Amereta is interdimensional. It is not a planet or star. Amereta encompasses a number of star systems and universes.

Do you inhabit any other species on Earth besides the electric eel?

No.

What is your name? Do the individuals of your species have names?

We do not have names but are identified by our particular tones. We are tones. We are light. We are these descriptions from your perspective.

If you don't have names why does the eighth universe have the name "Amereta"?

We did not create this name. There are other species who created this name or, we could say, vibration, for the interdimensional area from which we come.

Thank you. Do you experience emotions?

Yes. We may seem aloof, but we are simply not emotional as are humans. We do experience emotions. You experience emotions from within your emotional and physical bodies on Earth. We feel joy and love, and radiate these essence qualities in our universe, which also radiate outward vibrationally to other universes. Remember there is no time and space. It is all about perception.

Thank you. Anything you would like to add about perception?

To you we are far away, yet in reality we are very close. Flying through a wormhole or simply shifting into our universe can be done in an instant through your consciousness. You personally have experienced these shifts into many other worlds and universes.

Yes. Why did you choose to come to Earth?

We were invited by a council of creators who basically extracted our

DNA and created electric eel bodies through a blueprint. We have been here since the beginning.

For you it would seem like a long time, but for us it is not. Not everyone from our universe is on Earth. We were asked to manifest on twelve other planets. Some are physical, some are etheric, some are like water worlds, yet not really water. They are more like a fluid with no density, or a type of density that you cannot relate to.

If you are light bodies how could the council extract DNA? Doesn't DNA only exist within physical matter?

There are different frequencies of DNA, which we could refer to as multidimensional DNA. DNA exists in many other realms and densities of bodies, including light bodies. Humans are not familiar with this but yet it exists. You know that there is a spectrum of frequencies. Expand that spectrum that humans are familiar with about one hundred times and this would include our frequency as well as that of many other beings. So DNA exists in our light bodies. This is the best way for us to put this into words or what you call a concept.

Do you look like eels in your universe?

As mentioned, the eel body reflects our energy to the best of its ability in physical form on Earth; yet our essence form is a loose form of light body we exist in. Our auras can extend for many miles beyond our bodies without any effort. This is natural for us.

What kind of work are you doing on Earth and in other universes?

We came here to introduce our frequencies to Earth. This is to let humans and others know and experience the higher frequencies that have always existed. We are tones or frequencies that weave at least twelve other universes together through strands of frequencies and/or etheric DNA. We are part of a council of overseers who assist in orchestrating order and the evolutionary process in many universes.

Wow! Sounds like you're very busy!

All of creation is woven together in frequencies and the etheric DNA of the Key Creator. DNA is a word you understand better than any other word I can think of. See, let us show you.

Oh, I am seeing patterns of two spirals. Now I see countless helixes that seem to be at the core, but at the core of what?

The core of the Key Creator.

Yes. Thank you for letting me see the DNA clairvoyantly. Tell me more about DNA in humans and on Earth.

Every being on Earth has DNA codes. Those codes are activated when particular frequencies are set into motion within Earth as well as in Earth's electromagnetic fields. There would not be an Earth or life on Earth without DNA. DNA was introduced in creating Earth, your solar system, the very stars, and the universe as you know it.

We encoded our frequencies of DNA into the being you know as Earth. Our DNA is anchored at Earth's core. The waters' ability to speedily conduct our electrical frequencies through the waters and into Earth allowed and allows for efficiency and flow in the creations of energies and matter.

We were/are part of a group of councils who layered the basic DNA grids into Earth. Earth is a living being and is encoded with many templates of frequencies and information. As Earth continued to evolve, many beings from the cosmos seeded Earth with their own frequencies of DNA with the assistance of many intergalactic councils.

What changes are going on with the Earth now?

Many of Earth's codes are being activated now and are ongoing in relationship to the higher frequencies that are penetrating Earth, her energy centers, and her aura. Earth is moving through new areas of space and receiving frequencies that she has never received before. Dramatic shifts in Earth are affecting all inhabitants of Earth in ways that will assist in their evolutionary process in a positive way. This is true not only for Earth but is happening throughout your entire solar system. These frequencies which are new for Earth are activating her specific energy centers or chakras. Big awakenings and shifts are occurring throughout your universe. This is the evolutionary process of the All. This affects other universes and within your universe as well.

Thank you. This makes sense. Are you on any planets I'm familiar with?

We are currently on Pluto—no longer called a planet by some of Earth's scientists. The label or name does not matter. We identify worlds, stars, and other beings in the multiverses by tones, frequencies and auras, and mainly by their core essence as beings. Pluto is viewed as small by your scientists, yet it is much larger than you would imagine.

Every planet and star has an essence?

Yes. Your astronomers and others do not consider the "essence" of a being or think of a planet or star or universe as a being or beings. All worlds labeled as planets and stars are living, breathing beings. Whether they are physical, etheric, or gaseous, from your viewpoint, is irrelevant to us. It is always the "core essence" of a being that matters.

Take time to look at and feel the core essences of planets, stars, and other universes using your inner vision and feeling. It is inspiring!

I will do this. Are you in contact with others of your home species?

We are all connected as I mentioned. We are one and yet can be individual if we so choose—like being electric eels. We are in contact telepathically and on the soul level, but are distanced from a portion of this while living in physical form within Earth's density. Even though water seems dense, it is not. We are able to travel through the waters by projecting our energy forms through the various dimensions and worlds that exist within waters.

Do you communicate with the others from your home?

Yes. I communicate on a regular basis with my extended family through tones and frequencies. No words. It is an instant connection with tone and frequency.

How many are in your family?

My family is one (smile). And my family is thousands. I think that would be the number in terms of Earth numbers.

Thousands?

Yes. We are one family. Yet we can also belong to smaller families or clusters. I belong to a smaller family whom I am fond of and close to. But our families are not like those on Earth. We do not have reproduction in the way you do. Our one large family can procreate. And the smaller families can procreate. We create new light beings of our species by joining together as one energetically.

How big is your universe?
The word "big" is a human perception. Big compared to...? (smile).

Big compared to our universe? Oh, this isn't an intelligent question (laugh).
I understand, but we do not compare sizes of anything in my universe. So I cannot answer this. It is like asking how big is God—understand? And everything is connected, so there is no way to truly separate one universe from another, although I did refer to the universe from which I come as being eighth from your universe. Some universes can contain the same frequencies, while others contain frequencies that are totally different. This is how I distinguish your universe from mine and many others. This is the best way for me to explain it.

Thank you. Tell me more about existing as a being of bending light.
Yes. That is our essence. I am bending light, and bend light beyond time and space. We can be anywhere we desire. When viewing things from Earth, there are many universes and very distant galaxies where light is bending, but I will make a distinction. We are bending light beings. We cannot be pinned down individually unless we manifest through forms such as electric eels. This form simply allows us to anchor in the basic DNA grids and patterns with Earth's basic design. This form allows us to continue doing interdimensional weavings. There are many species and councils who are a part of this creation process.

You were a part of creating the DNA grids of Earth's basic design? Can you say more about the council(s)?
Yes, the basic DNA creations are a part of our purpose here on Earth. Of course there are assistant creators who were a major part of this. Here is an analogy. Let us say you have a number of CEOs who gather together at a conference in order to plan and create a larger conglomerate. This larger conglomerate will involve creating a number of companies and divisions. There are those who will run some of the companies and divisions and assist the CEOs. Perhaps there will be engineers, construction teams, planners, detail people and so on to make everything happen. This is simplified but gives you a basic understanding of the organization of the divine and assistant creators. Teams and teams of beings help to make everything happen. Together, we all manifest the dream, which is the Key Creator's dream.

What do you mean by "dream"?

Every being sets their intentions and the dream manifests. It takes everyone's energies to put things into action to manifest the dream.

For example, an idea is first dreamed of and then manifested. Let us say a human dreams of weaving a blanket. Next the human buys the materials needed to create the blanket on the physical level. Just like the weaving of a blanket, so it is with the creation of countless universes. This includes living forms that are created by assistant creators and the Key Creator—all of us doing our missions in manifesting and fulfilling the dream.

Yes, I can imagine this. How beautiful! What do you think and feel about humans?

You are not my favorite species, I must admit, but I have enjoyed our communications. Those of us in eel form are not comfortable with the way humans take without giving and not giving much back to Earth.

I understand. How is Earth doing in her process?

Earth agreed to harbor many life forms from various aspects of the cosmos. She is shifting and evolving at a highly accelerated rate now.

Earth is expanding into a new being creating multiple dimensions of love, peace, and harmony. We are assisting with this process to raise Earth's inner frequencies. We are setting up new DNA grids, holographic constructs, and what you think of as sacred geometric energies. This shifts all energies at her core, which, in the end, is your core, and all beings' core. Your universe is changing shape and other universes are being integrated within your universe as the Key Creator dreams and creates a new dream.

Thank you. I have enjoyed our conversation.

You are welcome. We also enjoyed it.
Electric Eel

Chapter 38

Gorilla Elder

The spiritual awakening is not centered on humans but is Earth centered

I'll never forget crouching among seven mountain gorillas in Rwanda as they chomped on wild celery and moved through the jungle with grace. As I remained still, I observed one juvenile who sat quietly watching a caterpillar crawl along an old tree branch. I felt the gorilla troop's gentleness, love, and power in a way that touched me deeply. I will forever cherish resting in the midst of these amazing beings who have blessed not only me but Mother Earth.

Hello. Are you a gorilla elder?
Yes. You can think of me as an elder. I speak for the gorillas.

Where do you come from?
We are from another dimension which is linked with other dimensions that funnel through Earth. In one sense you can say we are from Earth, but not in any physical sense. The dimension our souls live in is very similar to Earth but not as dense.

The dimensions you come from are less dense but still have density?
Yes. You could say it is an alternative reality or parallel reality. The dimension or world which we come from has jungles, oceans, skies, and

soil. Yet, it is not quite like the environment we inhabit on Earth. We come from a higher frequency dimension where there is harmony among all living beings. There are other beings who live in this dimension who also inhabit Earth in physical form.

As we move physically in the other dimension, it is like moving through air and we can walk or fly through any objects. We are not limited or constrained by physical barriers. Let us put it this way, our reality is like a multidimensional, transparent watercolor painting. We can see through all forms, which are loosely structured, whether it be jungle, sky, soil, a bird, or water. Imagine if you could move through all objects on Earth this freely. This is how it is in the dimension in which we live.

Thank you. Are you originally from that dimension?
No, but we have existed in that dimension since Earth was formed. Before existing in Earth's inner dimension, we existed in a different galaxy in another universe.

We agreed to come to Earth because the head council told us that there was a wonderful experiment about to happen. We are a gentle species and were informed that our frequency would be but one of many diversified frequencies that would add dimension, grace and awakening to Earth and others existing on the physical plane. So we agreed to become physical on Earth to be a part of the celebration of all creation.

Is your original home physical like Earth?
No. It is very similar to the dimension we exist in, which is linked to Earth via many other dimensions. There are countless dimensions that exist in and around Earth—in fact, so many it would make your head swim. But every dimension has order.

Are you assisting with the changes Earth is experiencing?
Yes. We are upholding our agreement and continuing to implant our frequency deep into Earth to help her shift into higher dimensions. This is happening now. We live in the now, in the moment. We are. We do not think or live in a linear way as humans do.

As the energetic shifts continue globally and beyond, the higher frequencies assist every being in their own evolutionary process. So many species are moving on in order to evolve spiritually. Numerous species are preparing to leave the Earth plane. Some of those leaving are gorillas, elephants, whales, dolphins, birds, insects, plants, and countless others.

Are you a group consciousness or individuals or other?

We are both. We can be one and we can be many. It depends on which frequency we are vibrating with. I can choose what frequency to vibrate with, which will determine if I am, in that moment, of one consciousness or if I am an individual, etheric, physical, or other. There are many in-between states of being that exist.

Are some of us on the physical plane living in higher dimensions now?

Yes and no. Many who have made agreements with a wide variety of councils in various sectors are assisting in the awakening process for humans and other species on Earth. The spiritual awakening is not centered on humans but is Earth-centered. And all beings who live on Earth are shifting and evolving along with her.

Many are assisting Earth, including humans, with her transition and integration of higher frequencies as well as preparing her for the integration of another solar system and other universes into your own universes.

Thank you. I am happy that there are so many wonderful beings who are assisting Earth and those of us who live on her. What do you look like in your original form?

We are etheric, yet have a very low density, as is the dimension of which I have spoken about. We do not look like the gorilla bodies that are present on Earth. We are much larger in etheric bodies. The dimension we live in has certain frequencies as does every dimension.

How large are your etheric bodies?

Oh, one of us is about the size of a redwood tree in terms of height and aura. And our consciousness spans outward for many miles. This is an analogy so you can better understand our energy.

In our dimension or world colors are bright neon colors. We have colors that Earth does not possess. See how the colors run together as in a watercolor painting?

Yes. I can see them clairvoyantly.

There are not any definitive lines or boundaries of living beings. The jungles on Earth are very well defined. Our species knew we would do best in jungles because of the primal energies jungles possess. A jungle is a living being. We communicate with the jungle and the jungle communicates with us in a way that few understand. And since you have sat among mountain gorillas and trekked through the jungle, you now understand firsthand, correct?

Yes. When I first stepped into the jungle, I had to stop, breathe, and center because I was overwhelmed and in awe of the jungle's primal energies. I felt the jungle as a living being. I've been communicating with many other species in regard to extinction. How do gorillas feel about remaining or not remaining on Earth?

We no longer wish to exist in the circumstances that are taking place on Earth. We continue to assist with raising the vibrations with humans and Earth, but we are now in the process of completing our mission and are preparing to return to our original home beyond Earth. With the interdimensional shifts taking place, we are no longer needed on Earth as we once were. We appreciate the humans who have worked so hard to save our species, but we are looking forward to returning home. Our species can continue to assist Earth from our original home.

As the energetic shifts continue globally and beyond, the higher frequencies assist every being in their own evolutionary process. As we mentioned, many species are moving on in order to evolve spiritually.

Do gorillas desire assistance with healing and/or transcending this world?

What will assist us in the greatest way is to simply send us love and light. If you send us energy for healing, that energy can be utilized and integrated by us for our upcoming transcendence.

It is natural for gorillas and other species to leave Earth as the higher frequencies integrate with Earth, creating a new paradigm. This is part of the reason why we agreed to come to Earth in the first place. Earth is a beautiful planet. With all of the environmental and energetic shifts our mission is almost complete. We continue to help Earth integrate the Gorilla Soul frequency, which is one of teaching harmony and peace.

It sounds like the souls inhabiting gorillas are looking forward to leaving their physical bodies.

Every species offers their own specific frequency to Earth. Remember, our souls are happy to ascend, so do not focus on our physical bodies. The loss of the body can be compared to a snake shedding old skin. Yet this does not mean that you should not help other species whenever you can; if an animal needs assistance and you can help them, then do so.

Mountain Gorilla in Africa: Photo by Jacquelin Smith

Do you feel humans are out of balance with nature?

There are more humans on Earth than Earth can handle. Humans have gotten out of balance with nature in numerous ways. There are so many humans on Earth that Earth can no longer meet all their needs. And this is in part what has created many imbalances on Earth.

We hope humans will become more responsible with procreation. May humans think about the entire world when considering their own needs and desires. We ask humans to make more responsible choices. This is not intended to be a judgment. We desire for you to understand and acknowledge the truth of what we are communicating to you.

When a number of species are wiped out, the entire ecosystem eventually breaks down. This is what you have been and are witnessing on Earth. But there is purpose and lessons to be learned from everything that happens (smile).

It seems that humans are remembering that other living forms are valuable in and of themselves. But we humans still tend to think we are the most evolved species on Earth.

Yes. Many humans are remembering that other living forms on Earth are very valuable and are actually needed for balance and harmony. Humans still do not treat us as equals on Earth, yet we are equal. We ask humans to learn to see and treat other species as equals rather than looking down upon others. Humans can learn a great deal from all species if they open their hearts, listen, and learn from them.

Many gorillas in zoos have shared with me how difficult it is for them to be contained even when in a natural habitat. Is it the best choice to "save" specific species by placing them in zoos?

Every soul is strategically placed in this world depending on what frequency they are radiating for the sake of balance of Earth and within the ecosystems. Gorillas and other animals in zoos agreed to be ambassadors in order to help wake humans up to the awe-inspiring diversity of the Creator's beings who live on Earth.

What humans are trying to remember is that beings whom you refer to as "animals" are of equal value in every way, and this includes the precious soul of every being.

Because of the dramatic shifts happening energetically as well as environmentally, we do not desire to have our species in zoos any longer. At one time we agreed to do so, but there is an overall consensus for animals to withdraw from the Earth plane in the upcoming days. This is all fine.

Thank you. What would you like to say to humans about the energetic shifts that are happening?

Open your hearts and welcome in the higher frequencies that are bringing in countless interdimensional shifts. The three-dimensional world is crumbling as new paradigms are being created. Earth is moving through a rebirthing process. A new Earth without illusion. It will be a world of peace, love, and harmony. We have assisted her with this process and various species will continue to do so but, as mentioned, many species are leaving since their work is drawing to completion.

What about humans?

We send humans love and light. We assist humans with raising their vibrations just by our presence in this world. Your dog and cat friends who live with you are helping to raise your vibration whether you are aware of it or not, so thank them for their gifts. As humans integrate the higher frequencies into their energy bodies, they are evolving and remembering who they are as individuals, as a species and soul group. Those who inhabit human form are recalling why they have come to Earth. They, too, are assisting Earth in her journey into higher realms.

We thank you for your love and are grateful to those who care about us and other species. Sending us love and light will assist us in our journey home. Humans have such beautiful hearts. Let love and light radiate like the sun from your hearts.

What do gorillas mirror to humans?

Gorillas are shy, gentle vegetarians who do not harm unless our families are threatened. We offer humankind many lessons. Love, harmony and peace can exist in a wonderful and orderly way within a family. We love our families deeply. We are gentle with our young and teach them appropriate boundaries and order for the sake of the entire family. We know how to care for our young in responsible, loving ways. Humans could learn a great deal from watching how gorillas interact with each other within a family structure.

Play is an important part of our lives. Many humans have forgotten how to play with one another and in life. We try to maintain a balance within our families. The jungle gives us nourishment and we give the jungle nourishment by our presence. This is the way it is intended to be.

We mirror these lessons in hopes that humans will remember their roots in nature. And hope they will remember that balance comes from give and take— not just taking from nature. We do not take more than we need.

Thank you for this wonderful conversation.

We are happy to share this with you and other humans.
Gorilla Elder

Chapter 39

Bee

It is time for humans to return to a natural way of living

Hello. Good to see you. Where are you from originally?
We are creators from a far distance. We come from a universe that humans are not aware of, although some other species on Earth are aware of our universe. We traveled to Earth through a wormhole or portal from our universe into your universe.

Are you a group consciousness or individuals or other?
We are a group consciousness that lives in multiple bodies on Earth in bee form. Not every bee is from my universe, but a group of my species decided to incarnate as bees on Earth because it fit our energy so well.

Were you invited to Earth?
Yes. We were called upon to come to Earth. The higher council of intergalactic beings thought our species could contribute important frequencies and add richness to planet Earth. We sing a song that reaches beyond the buzz that we make in the physical bodies we have on Earth. Listen and you will hear it.

Thank you. Yes, I hear it. Are you a bee elder?
I am a representative communicating for bees.

Tell me about your universe. Do you come from a planet or star?

The planet from which we come is not like Earth. Our planet is purely geometric crystalline. There are very powerful spectrums of tones or notes which our planet sings. These are the frequencies of our planet. Your planet would not be able to tolerate such high frequencies. Also, there is a wide variety of species on our planet.

Everything, the All, is interconnected and divine. There is another galaxy not far from our planet. In the universe I come from, there is not any gravitational orbit of planets around a star. We just are. We have access to many wormholes that allow us to be in other universes and star systems instantly.

Interesting. Are you creators?

We have helped to create a galaxy that is not far from my universe. We created it for the sake of play as well as for the sake of creation and being creative. We create with intention and with frequencies.

How do you communicate with one another on your planet and in bee form on Earth?

We do not talk with one another on my planet. We do not have words. We communicate telepathically through tones and frequencies.

In bee form on Earth, we communicate on multiple levels of frequency, dance, scents, and telepathic communication. This is what a beehive does well on Earth. It is a hive's mind.

We are sharing this with humans so they can understand multiple forms of communication as well as telepathic connection. The bee bodies are in a way extraneous. If you look at the spirit of an entire hive, you will see the formation of our spirit as a collective one rather than as individuals. Since you live in a physical world, most humans see the individual bodies of bees. But if they look beyond the bodies, they will see and feel the spirit of one—of the hive.

What forms have you helped to create?

We have created some of the flower beings that exist on Earth. The planet from which we come has numerous flower and plant beings. We carried some of their DNA with us and then created the physical forms which they inhabit on Earth.

We have helped to create a few of the life forms on Earth. We work in conjunction with all species of bees. We work side by side with butterflies and also some insect beings.

What does your species look like?

On my planet, as I mentioned, we are a group species. We vibrate at a very high frequency and, therefore, have bodies of light. We are very small in comparison to the size of the bee bodies that we inhabit on Earth.

As a group consciousness, we are about as big as a human fist, if you want a comparison. Even though we can inhabit individual bodies, we are telepathically connected at all times. The size of a fist is an example of how compact our energy can be, but we can expand outward and be as large as we desire. So, there really is no set size since we are light, but I am trying to convey other ways of thinking about other realities to you.

How can your group consciousness be the size of a fist when you said you are very small in comparison to the bee bodies you inhabit?

What I mean is that the amount of light or consciousness is less within and around a single body than when we are a group not inhabiting physical bodies. I am attempting to describe with size and comparison, which is not something we do. So, I hope I have not confused you or made errors in my comparisons.

Thank you. How large is your planet?

Once again, if using a comparison, our planet is about the size of Earth's moon. Yet, our planet is crystalline, and it is not round like the moon. Our planet is geometric and holographic. There are other species on our planet, as I have mentioned. I call it a planet so that you have something to relate to; but in actuality our crystalline planet is not a planet but a frequency or energy based on the geometric crystalline light structure.

There are many places and spaces and dimensions in the cosmos that humans cannot begin to imagine, but they are real and do exist (smile).

Do you experience emotions?

Oh yes. We have emotions. We possess and feel many feelings. We feel love, joy, peace, anger, fear, anxiety, as well as grief.

Thank you. Do those of you in bee bodies live in harmony with one another and others?

Yes. There is no need for conflict or war such as humans experience. We live in divine flow, so there is harmony among us. And this harmony is not only with other bees but with flowers, plants, trees and most other species.

Bees seem dedicated to the hive and work as a community.

We are committed to our work on Earth as bees. And as a group consciousness our species does well being bees. Our consciousness is the hive's mind.

Thank you. Why do you sting when the consequences are death? Do you know you will die after you sting someone?

Once again, we are dedicated to the beehive consciousness. We are One. So, if one bee must sting in order to keep the hive safe, or sting because its life is threatened, this is all okay. We understand this and have a different perspective on "death" than do many humans. We understand that leaving the body is not the end of living. The spirit that leaves the bee body returns to the hive and is born through the Queen again, so it is not a big deal.

We humans could learn from what you have just shared with me.

When applying this to humans, they can learn that if something destroys their body, they return to the light, or what we would call the hive of souls. They return again in whatever form the soul desires. The body is just a vehicle for spirit to learn through. It is a matter of understanding the truth about soul and reality rather than being caught in the illusion that the physical plane is the only reality. The physical body is but one level of experience living in duality and and density. When humans know this, they are truly free.

Remember soul and spirit create the body. The personality living in a body can forget that it is just one aspect which belongs to a vast multidimensional soul. The soul created from the Key Creator truly is the whole of who you are. Understand?

Yes. Thank you. It can be easy to forget how vast our souls are when living in a fragile body on Earth.

Yes. Our species keeps this in the forefront of our beingness so that we do not stray from the path of light while in bee or some other form. We remember that we are creators, or truly co-creators with the Key Creator.

Can you say more about being co-creators, and what about harmony with the Key Creator?

The act of creation involves setting our intention and working in cooperation with frequencies, sounds, colors, and geometric and holographic energies. We create frequencies. When the frequencies are created, then there are beings/energies who cooperate with us. Do the Key Creator's creations cooperate with their Creator? Many do. Others who think they are separate from the Key Creator wall themselves off from the Key Creator by listening to the ego/mind. If humans and others would listen to the Key Creator/or the divine within, they would be aligned with the Key Creator and their souls. This would help them to make better choices in life's journey.

It seems easier for humans, humanoid species, and some other species who exist in the cosmos to forget who they are and that they have missions to fulfill. This is not a criticism, simply an observation.

What is your mission as bees on Earth?

We help maintain order and harmony. Bees are weavers. In weaving frequencies we create various dimensions and galaxies. We weave frequencies together, which actually assists Earth in maintaining balance, order, harmony, and beauty.

Recently bees have been dying off in large numbers. Can you address this?

We cannot stay alive in the numbers we once were, due to humankind's practices with pesticides and many other chemicals. Also, humans are asking much more of us in terms of pollinating larger fields, more crops, trees and plants. This has stretched us beyond our bodies' capabilities to do what humans ask of us. All of this is too much for our physical bodies.

There were many bees to balance and create harmony and beauty among many plants, trees, and other species on Earth. How will flowers and fruit trees and other species survive without us pollinating them? Our relationship with flowers and trees is one of harmony. Without bees, all of these beings are being adversely affected, as are many food sources which humans need to survive.

And now you are seeing the results of humans using lethal chemicals, which has lowered our immune systems. There is the problem of pesticides, but there are also other issues that have worn down our immune systems. Some of the other issues involve bacterias and viruses. There is not one simple reason as to why bees are dying, because it is a multilevel problem. Also, there is the key issue of imbalance which humans have helped to create on Earth in an attempt to meet their needs.

We have come to visit Earth as well as do our part in serving the glorious garden of Earth. At this time, a number of us are returning home, but many are staying here in spirit form. We will once again be bees in order to help maintain harmony, order, beauty, and song.

What would you like humans to understand about the effects of pollution/chemicals in regard to many other species?

Pay attention. We are barometers for what is going on generally with pollution and chemical levels in the environment. What is happening to us will eventually happen to humans and other species as well. In fact, it has been and is happening even as we communicate. What we are mirroring to humans is what pesticides are doing to all species that come into contact with these chemicals. Environmental pollution, radiation energies, and many other kinds of pollution affect everyone.

Humans have been given many warnings about what happens when various kinds of pollution take place as well as interact with one another.

How can we bring balance back to Earth? What would you like to say to humans?

It is time for humans to return to a natural way of living. Humans are seeking ways to feed large masses of their own kind, which is positive. But this needs to be done without the use of toxic chemicals and without the overuse of chemicals.

We desire for humans to focus on living together in harmony as we do in our hives. Many of us who are dying and crossing over into the light will help to raise Earth's vibrations. We hope you are listening.

All living forms are connected and interdependent. Humans have had this reflected back to their species again and again in a multitude of ways through nature for many years.

Listen to your hearts! Consider shifting your emphasis to finding natural ways to interact and cooperate with the environment. Hopefully, the way we bees live our lives will inspire humans to unite and work as one hive for the sake of Earth and all living forms.

Thank you, bees, for your heartfelt messages.

You are welcome. We have enjoyed this conversation. We hope others see us for who we truly are and what we offer to Earth as well as many other species. It is always an exchange, is it not? (smile).

Yes (smile). One last question. Is there a meditation humans can do to support the Earth and those living on Earth?

Meditation

The following meditation is one humans can do to bless Earth as well as themselves.

Sit in a garden or somewhere in nature with palms facing up and become quiet. Take a few deep breaths and let your mind and body relax. Feel and focus on feeling love, harmony, and joy. Now feel your feet connect with Earth's soil. This grounds you. (You may even want to take off shoes and socks.) Feel your connection to Earth. Imagine or feel the sun filling your heart with light, love, and peace. Then, let light, love, and peace flow from the top of your head down through your entire body flowing out the bottoms of your feet and deep into Earth. Breathe deeply.

Now feel Earth's energy flow up through your feet, legs, and spinal column, and into your heart. Take a couple of deep breaths. Now radiate love, peace, and joy in every direction, blessing the Earth, the sky and all beings on and within Earth.

Then bring your focus back to your heart. Let the sunlight fill your heart again with love, joy, peace, and harmony. Feel at one with the flowers, the trees, the ladybugs, what you call weeds, the bees, and other living beings around you. (This opens you to *experiencing the oneness of the All.*)

When you are done, take a deep breath and return to your heart. Take another breath, and feel love, peace, and joy flow through the top of your head and through your entire body, flowing out the bottoms of your feet and into Earth. This will ground you.

Now follow the same steps you have just done, except this time, do the same meditation with starlight.

The starlight offers a different frequency of love, harmony, and joy to Earth, sky and all beings. Try it. You will feel how the sunlight and starlight energies weave and complement each other. This meditation blesses Earth and also balances your energy bodies.

Thank you. This is a meaningful meditation. What a great way to send love to the Earth and all other beings. This supports us not only in experiencing oneness, but with different aspects of ourself.

Yes, this supports the All.

Thank you again. This has been wonderful.

We are happy to share. It is the reason why we are here. Thank you.
Bee

Chapter 40

Dragon Council

Humans would be surprised by all the wonderful messages other living forms would like to share with them

Hello and welcome.

We are happy to be with you today. We are a council of dragons who will be communicating with you and answering any questions that you might want to ask.

You really exist? How wonderful!

Yes, we exist.

I see three bubbles of transparent rainbow light interwoven. And next to that, I see three more bubbles of transparent rainbow light interwoven. Is this the council?

Yes. This is how we come to you. This is how you are seeing us energetically. Crystalline light and more than one spectrum of colors is our essence. Let us continue.

Thank you. Did you exist in physical form on Earth with the dinosaurs or other species?

Yes, but not in great numbers. Some might say we are an archetypal energy like an angel, yet angels truly exist and so do we. We are from a very distant galaxy. You cannot even dream of how far away it is. Another universe beyond many other universes.

We exist in multiple realities and will continue to do so. Some humans have seen us, but we chose remote places to live while living in physical form on Earth. Our species did not number as many as did species of what you know as dinosaurs.

We have been worshipped but also maligned by humankind like so many other species. This does not bother us.

Do you come from a star, planet, or dimension?

We come from an interdimensional fold that exists far away in the way that you think of distance, space, and time. Yet the reality is that we are not really far away. It is a matter of perception. We live in an interdimensional fold which is our world.

What's an interdimensional fold?

A series of sequential dimensions, with sequential frequencies that are interconnected in an unusual way that creates pockets or folds of dimensions within dimensions. That is the best way we know how to explain it.

Thank you. Are there any dragons on Earth now?

We are no longer in physical form, but still exist in the higher frequency dimensions of Earth's aura. Most will not see us. But those who have clairvoyant gifts and those who can connect with higher frequencies and dimensions will be able to see us if they ask to see us. But most do not ask.

Also, by tapping into Earth's etheric memories, you will be able to connect with dragons. We are close. If you tap into the ethers, you can watch the history of Earth like a movie, and encounter many other species who are still unknown to humankind.

Why did you come to Earth?

We came to experience Earth and the other inhabitants here long ago. Memories of us are recorded in your collective subconscious as well as in the ethers. We were asked to add our frequency to Earth. We helped set up grids and meridians energetically to set the stage for many other species to be able to live on Earth in physical form.

We have the ability to create by setting our intention. This allows us to create energies which are conducive for many other energies to be anchored with Earth. I sense you are not really understanding some of this. We are having a difficult time coming up with words for what we helped set up while on Earth. We do not speak with words. Our language is one of tone, sound, frequency, and light.

Why are many humans taught that dragons are a myth? The Chinese recorded scientific facts about dragons.

This is because we seemed like such magical creatures. If you go back in time and experience a four-legged being with wings that could fly, would not that seem magical?

Yes. What do you look like in the dimensional fold in which your species lives?

You are seeing us as you described like bubbles of faint rainbow light. We live connected in groups of three. It has always been this way. You see three bubbles—these are three beings intertwined, connected. I know this is difficult for you to grasp, but this is our essence, our spirit, which you are seeing.

Are all dragons from your dimensional fold? Can a soul from another universe experience being a dragon?

Yes, a soul can decide to experience being a dragon. Yet most of the dragons are from the distant universe I speak of, with extremely high frequencies.

Thank you. Are you physical in your dimension?

We can be physical or not. We shapeshift. What you call dragon is but one form that we experience. We are living in physical as well as nonphysical realities in many dimensions and universes.

Are you individuals or a group consciousness?

Both. We are generally a form of group consciousness. We can think as one, yet we can think and live individual lives when in physical form and also etheric form depending on what universe we are living in. We live in multiple universes. My soul is living in multiple universes this moment.

How many lives are you living right now?

Thirty-two. But I have lived many lives if you want to put this into the framework of time. But if we take this out of your perception of time I would say that I am living thousands of lives in various universes.

Are you living anywhere humans might be familiar with?

I have visited Mars. Mars is not as absent of life as humans think it is. There are important connections between Earth and Mars. Venus is considered Earth's sister planet, but you have much more in common with Mars. Humans simply have trouble seeing this since they are not looking beyond physical appearances.

How interesting. Why did you visit Mars?

I visited Mars long before I came to Earth. My species helped to also set up the stage for life on Mars. Mars was inhabited long before humans were created.

Are you living on Mars now, or did you just visit?

Remember, you are living in an arbitrary framework of time. I could say that I am still visiting and/or existing on Mars.

When you say "I," are you communicating as one voice for the entire council?

When I was on Mars, it was the council. Sometimes I may say "I" or "we." As I mentioned, we can be individual or group consciousness, but in physical form we are individuals.

What types of life forms did you encounter on Mars?

A variety of life forms existed on Mars in physical form as well as energetic frequencies. (Many life forms still exist on Mars.) There is always a spectrum of frequencies. Souls choose what frequency that they will best resonate with and then form the type of body that suits the frequency. There is a full spectrum of different kinds of bodies ranging from the density of physical form to a very high frequency of light beings who simply exist as, you could say, points of light.

You have met one species from Mars years ago. Remember?

Yes. Thank you for reminding me. It was a group consciousness that came to me to communicate a message. They looked like the sparkles on a river on a sunny day.

Yes. They are beautiful lights.

Thank you. By the way, did dragons breathe fire?

Yes. Not quite in the way that is described by humans, but we did breathe fire. It is difficult to explain. When you venture back to the period of time in which we existed, there were many species of beings which your archeologists have not even thought about. Yet, some are coming to light right now as we speak. Yesterday, you sat down in an office and on the cover of a magazine was a newly discovered dinosaur that looks like a dog with the head of a bird, beak and all. Would this have been considered before? These discoveries will help humans to continue stretching their perceptions in a way that will only help them evolve. There are many beings who naturally breathe fire throughout the cosmos.

We can breathe fire because this is what is natural for us. No different than birds singing or humans speaking words. Our DNA, our genes, are programmed for breathing fire. We will leave it at that. It makes no sense to describe the biological process as to how this is possible. Besides, the process is not anything that your researchers would understand because they do not have the basic tools to understand it. The breathing of fire not only involves DNA, but higher frequencies, and aspects of the multidimensional beings that we are. We do not intend for this to sound arrogant or condescending in any way. This simply is the reality of fire breathing.

People are always fascinated watching dragons breathe fire in films.

One of the reasons why we were invited to come to Earth was because we could help set up the ground floor so to speak, the grids on and within Earth and meridians. We created these energies from the flames of light which flowed from our mouths.

Light or fire?

Is there really a difference? We could focus on the fiery light through our intention and create various dimensions and frequencies in and around Earth. You could say we are some of the original assistant creators and midwives who helped give birth to Earth.

Fascinating. This is amazing and makes sense. Have you had much interaction with humans?

Yes, but not extensive interaction with humans. We were told that we would play a significant role in setting up Earth energies. We mostly did our work from behind the scenes. Yet the magic of the dragon form we had on Earth helped humans to expand their minds about what was possible.

So, the three-bubble light council is speaking to me with one voice?

Yes.

You truly are magical beings. Every culture has stories they tell about you. Children across the Earth are told stories about dragons. There are many stories about dragons being slain by knights.

Thank you. Humans interject their ego, and imagination into experiences or into what they have heard and create myths. Our kind was slain by those whom you might call knights, but there was no honor in the way we were destroyed. There are many other myths that still enshroud many species on Earth. Our hope is that misperceptions about many species are fading as Earth frequencies are being raised. The old beliefs are fading away as the truth is recognized.

Humans are becoming more conscious of the truth that all beings are of equal value. What would you like to say to humans?

Humans are evolving and learning how to look beyond the physical bodies of beings and into the essence of a being or beings. Of course, this is paramount if humans are to make the leap of seeing and accepting that other species' origins are not of Earth, but from many other dimensions, stars and universes.

Humans can learn a great deal by thinking and feeling from their divine hearts and by listening to what other species wish to communicate to them. Humans would be surprised by all the wonderful messages other living forms would like to share with them. Listen to what each species communicates and move beyond the mythical stories and false beliefs which only create misunderstandings, fear, and alienation.

We were/are happy to set up grids and meridians and to bring our frequency into Earth's aura. We also wanted to bring magic and to help expand not only humankind's mind but that of other species as well.

Before humans appeared, Earth was like a melting pot. For example, think of all the people who flooded into New York from various countries to have a better life or to experience a different way of life. This might be a way to think of Earth.

Why did you come to Earth?
Earth was willing, and agreed to open her shores and heart so others from all over the cosmos could come and experience physical life as well as to assist Earth with her divine process.

Do you and others continue to learn in the lives we all live?
Oh yes. Learning never ends, whether learning is conscious or subconscious. Just by being, one is always surrounded and living in energies, and learning.

There are many dimensions that humans have a hard time imagining. The truth is there are countless realities. All beings continue learning regardless of what reality and realm they live in.

Thank you for your gifts and for conversing with me.
We are elated to share this with you so that others may understand. It is always good to love regardless of what another species might think of you. Consider loving all species, all beings. The divine shines from within every being, shines in every atom.

Thank you.
You are welcome.
Dragon Council

Chapter 41

Dragonfly

We stitch together and heal any wounds within or around Earth

As I stood in the woods by a tree, five dragonflies landed on green leaves. I laughed and silently said, "Hello. Wouldn't it be wondrous to see seven of you?" Within seconds two more dragonflies appeared in the same tree. Then, I heard them singing tones with one voice.

Hello. Nice to see you. What would you like to share about yourselves?

We were here long before humans. It is through our singing that we offer Earth love, joy, balance, and beauty. We are etheric or energy beings that are one and yet many. If you look at a dragonfly's body, you can see how delicately we are sculpted. This makes it easier for us to move in and out of many dimensions. We also shapeshift easily. We are interdimensional travelers from another star system, one that is filled with love and joy. We could refer to it as an angelic realm. We are like tiny points of light. This is a description that you can understand. But if you look at our dragonfly auras, you can see that we are much larger than you might have guessed (smile).

Yes. I can see how far your auras extend. Can you expand them outward even further?

Oh yes. It is great fun for us to expand our auras. We enjoy spreading joy and love and beauty. We are messengers.

What messages would you like to share?

Our messages are of love, joy, and beauty. We are of a higher realm than are many other species. We are very common, as you know, yet we are connected to even higher beings who watch over us while on Earth.

Who are these higher beings you're connected to?

The higher beings are from and exist within the star system that is beyond the star systems that your astronomers are familiar with. We are connected in a kind of symbiotic relationship.

Can you say more about your relationship with the higher beings whom you are connected with energetically?

We are connected energetically naturally. It is a mutual and beneficial relationship of energies. While we are on Earth, the higher beings are able to view what is going on with Earth through us. Also, they are able to view all the beings from many and various dimensions and star systems in the cosmos. This viewing is positive. These higher beings care about the evolutionary process of many worlds—not just Earth. Nature is of key interest to them. You might refer to some of them as naturalists. They are interested in trees, animals, plants, the weather cycles, the solar system cycles, and so on. There are others who are interested in other beings and worlds in the cosmos. They are all part of a higher council that oversees balance and order in the cosmos.

Interesting. Are you a group consciousness?

Yes. We are a group consciousness but can inhabit individual bodies. We are always connected to one another by our species' frequency so that we can communicate whenever it is desired or needed. Our communications are not through words, but through singing.

Can you say more about your singing?

Our singing blesses Earth in a multitude of ways. Our singing helps maintain balance, peace, joy, and love. Those from the higher realms are raising our frequencies in order to raise Earth's frequencies. When humans and other beings are around us, this allows integration of higher frequencies.

Are you here to assist humans?
We are not all that focused on humans. We are focused on Earth and the whole of life on Earth. Part of the reason why there are many and various species on Earth is to create peace, love, harmony, and balance between and within all living forms.

Was this planned?
You could say this is an experiment to see how beings from countless corners of the cosmos can get along on Earth. Earth offered to host this gathering and the experiment is ongoing.

Can you say more about your mission on Earth?
Part of our mission is to uplift Earth. We help maintain order within dimensions. We stitch together and heal any wounds within or around Earth. This includes Earth's aura. You can think of Earth's aura as fabric that can become torn at times and needs to be stitched together. We are menders and healers in this regard.

Can humans hear your songs?
Yes. If humans sit and listen to our singing, they can open up and expand in wondrous ways. We help beings to open up and expand when they are around us. This is what is natural for us.

What great gifts you are giving! There are many different subspecies of dragonflies worldwide. Are you all connected and do you all work together on the mission you've just described?
We are all connected regardless of how we may look physically. All of us are focused on the mission of love, joy, beauty, balance, and peace for Earth. There are physical differences because of the slight differences in frequencies. This allows for the best body to be designed for the mission and frequency of that aspect of our group consciousness.

We are a multidimensional group consciousness that can express itself in many kinds of bodies, including light bodies, etheric bodies, physical bodies, water bodies, and others.

Water bodies?

Yes. We can create a fluid form which you would think of as water, if we need to do so.

Do you have a water body form on Earth?

I have not. But there are some who have taken on forms of beings who live in and near water.

Thank you. Are all dragonflies from one star?

We originated as a species on one star and then the higher beings seeded a number of other stars and worlds so that we would become numerous and be able to fulfill our divine purpose. Our species is scattered throughout the cosmos. But we do not look like the dragonflies on Earth in these other existences.

Can any soul choose to experience being a dragonfly?

Any soul can choose to be a dragonfly. They must go through the higher council of beings which we are connected with. They have final say as to whether they feel a soul is ready to have a dragonfly experience.

Is it difficult for you to be in physical form with having such a high frequency? Also, is it challenging to be connected to even higher frequency beings while in a body?

While we are in physical form on Earth, our frequency is living outside of the physical form in another dimension. Yet an aspect of our frequency is living in every dragonfly body. We must have the physical bodies in order to better fulfill our mission on Earth. So, no, it is not difficult to have the physical form on the Earth plane. It is enjoyable for us to interact with the many wonderful species of plants, flowers, trees, rivers, rocks, and the living air. We find it to be a pleasure and we love feeling the sun's warmth and light.

Thank you. Do you have trees, animals, or other beings on your star?

Remember, those whom you refer to as animals are beings from various aspects of the cosmos. Yes, there are other beings on our star or stars, yet they do not look like the physical forms of beings on Earth. They are very different, although we have beings who look similar to the plant and tree beings who live on Earth. The trees and plants on Earth are living beings, yet are not recognized as such by most humans.

The plant and tree beings on our star of origin are not physically stationary like those on Earth. The souls in plants and trees on Earth are not actually stationary. They are dancing and visit many other realms with their spirits. Most humans are not aware of who the tree and plant beings truly are.

Yes, I understand. I often watch tree and plant beings dance, especially at night.
The tree and plants beings' spirits often dance and travel more at night. The energies are different and quieter during the night.

Do you feel and experience emotions?
Oh yes. We feel love, joy, peace, happiness, pain, and sadness as do humans. We express these feelings in different ways than humans, but we feel emotions and express them.

Thank you. Are you an aspect of the higher beings whom you have mentioned or are you separate from them?
Well, all of us are ONE LIGHT anyway, so is it really important? (laugh).

I guess I'm curious if you're an aspect of them or if you are a separate group consciousness yet connected to them.
You could say we are an extension of one another. One aspect of life needs another aspect of life. They oversee us on our journeys throughout many galaxies and universes. Every creation is created to experience and fulfill what it is created for by the Key Creator.

Thank you for sharing your beautiful singing communications. I feel uplifted by your wonderful energy.
You are most welcome. We enjoy sharing this message for many to hear. We are messengers of love, joy, beauty, balance, and peace throughout the cosmos (big smile).
Dragonfly

After this session with the dragonflies, I felt greatly energized and as if

I was glowing. Right after this conversation, I stepped into my bedroom to grab a necklace from my dresser. I looked into the mirror and my eyes were glowing with brilliant light. My face had a whole different look. I looked about ten years younger. I realized that our conversation had helped integrate higher frequencies into my aura.

Next, the dragonfly consciousness suggested that I stand and face the sun for a few minutes, eyes closed. In doing this, I felt my vibration rise even more. Then a bright purple circle appeared in my third eye. The dragonfly communicated, "We are giving you the gift of dragonfly medicine." I was deeply honored and thanked them for this gift.

Chapter 42

Viceroy Butterfly

Every species and soul essence is wondrous and unique!

While walking through a wild prairie garden I saw a viceroy butterfly sitting on a sunflower leaf. I stood and watched him as he bathed in the afternoon light. I spontaneously reached out and put my finger under his feet. He walked onto my finger and then into the palm of my hand as if this was familiar. He explored my palm for a couple minutes. Another butterfly fluttered by and he took flight. This was a clear sign to me that this was an invitation to share in conversation at some point in time.

The next morning, hundreds of butterflies were fluttering around me etherically. They communicated with laughter, "We are waiting in the wings." What fun!

Hello. Thank you for spending a few moments in my palm. You showed how much you trusted me.

I felt the love and joy you were sending me. I knew you would not harm me. Yes, I invited you to communicate with me, which is why I chose to step onto your finger.

Who are you and what would you like to share?

My name is Clovis. I am from a very high-frequency dimension that would seem very far away to you, but if you raise your frequency it is very near.

You came to understand not long ago that a part of your soul is a butterfly, which came as a surprise to you. It is just one manifestation of your multidimensional selves that is fluttering in another dimension. Do you not think that is fun? (laugh).

Oh yes! (laugh)
Butterflies are of etheric realms, and also shapeshifters. We can shift from one dimension to another faster than you can blink your eye. We are songs. If you listen to our frequency, you will hear music. Try being in the midst of a number of butterflies. You will hear perfect harmony and what you would think of as celestial music.

I'll try it! Thank you. Are you of an angelic realm? The dragonflies shared that they were connected to what I would think of as an angelic realm.
Yes and no. Angelic in the sense of high frequency. And of course we have wings (laugh), so we fit the image that humans have of angels. We are connected to even higher frequencies who are angel-like beings. It is a kind of symbiotic relationship. This is a concept that you can understand. They have not been in physical form and remain in the higher frequencies doing work for various galaxies in terms of balancing energies and orchestrating vibrations, which is no easy task.

Are you a group consciousness or individuals?
We are both and other. We can be a group consciousness, individuals, as well as other. How to define other. Hmmm. Again, we are in a kind of symbiotic relationship with others in a higher dimension. We cannot be separated, yet we can be separate. I do not know how else to describe this since I cannot find the words.

That's okay. Thanks for trying. Does your dimension or world have a name?
It does but it is impossible to put into words because in reality it is a sound. Let me see. No, I cannot get it, at least for now.

Why do you have a name? Very few beings have given me names. Names do not really seem to be relevant.
Names are not relevant. What is relevant is the sound and vibration of every being. I have a name, yes. Some beings have names and some do not. It is just this way. No way to explain the reasoning, although those

of the higher realms are sound frequencies. I am a frequency and so are you. You have a name. And Clovis is the closest I can come to putting my name sound into a word that you will understand and feel.

Are you an elder, Clovis?

I am a representative of the butterfly realm. The higher echelon, so to speak, knew you would get a kick out of our meeting in the prairie garden and my stepping onto your finger. You knew intuitively to hold out your hand, and I knew to climb aboard. It was orchestrated by higher forces.

Wow! I'm very grateful for our physical meeting. You are very beautiful! Do you feel emotions, Clovis?

Oh yes. What is delightful about being on Earth is that we feel the sunlight, the rain, the touch of a flower's petal or milkweed. We feel joy, love, peace, beauty, sadness, and pain. Not in the exact same way humans do, but in the same basic way.

What does your true essence look like, Clovis?

I am frequency and light and sound—see?

Oh yes. Your energies expand outward really far in all directions. You possess such a huge essence for such a small body (smile). I don't mean this in a derogatory way.

My essence created this butterfly body because it is efficient for the work we are doing on Earth. It would be cumbersome to have a huge body and try to flutter at the vibratory rate that we do.

Do the higher beings whom you're connected to look through your eyes or feel through your bodies?

Yes! It is similar to when you look through binoculars or a photo lens. They are not looking through us all the time. They have their own schedule as to when they are checking out how events and energies are progressing on Earth. They are interested in how Earth is evolving, as well as the solar system you live in, as well as many others.

You mentioned that they help balance and create harmonies and celestial music, right?

Yes. In creating balance and harmony and order, the music emerges naturally.

Why are you on Earth?

Earth is beautiful, is she not? Butterflies bring beauty to this planet, do they not?

Yes.

Yet beyond the beauty we are assisting with integrating dimensions that have been kept separate, so to speak, in the past. I am putting this into words that you can relate to. We are integrating the higher frequencies in and around Earth so she can continue to evolve.

We were here long before humans arrived. We also open and close interdimensional doorways when it is appropriate. We balance the flow of energies and are often working with many dimensions simultaneously.

How is this work coming along with Earth?

Very well. We are happy to be of service and to be able to assist Earth in this way. We also work hand in hand, or wing in wing (laugh) with the bees and dragonflies, who are very much a part of this work, as well as other species. We work in harmony and create harmony and beauty in the world as well as in various aspects of the interdimensional flow and integration which I have mentioned.

Are you aware of the rest of this solar system going through big changes? The light beings I know have told me that it is.

Yes. What you know as your universe is changing dramatically. This process of Earth being raised in frequency will continue until she returns to her light form. Then other creations will manifest in various and different ways and forms from which you are accustomed.

What do you mean?

The density of Earth is being broken away from Earth like an old shell. This is also happening to all beings in physical form as well as spirit form. There are many beings who have spirit bodies. As things progress, the All will return to light or to the Key Creator. The Key

Creator will continue to create, and is always creating new creations. These are not instant shifts but a very long progression of shifts, at least from a human's point of view. From another's point of view it can appear that these shifts happen very quickly.

Sounds like we're all in for a lot of change! (smile).
Yes. But do not be concerned about all this or allow it to create fear. This is the natural process of creation. It simply is how the Key Creator and Its creations shift, evolve, transform, and continue creating.

Thank you. Do you exist on other worlds?
Yes and no. Me personally or butterflies in general?

Both.
Well, I currently exist in fifteen other dimensions and/or worlds. I am a butterfly in a few of those Self aspects, yet I am etheric without bodies in other worlds. In some places and spaces, I have bodies that you would not really understand in terms of the limiting definition of "body."

Other souls who are living butterfly existences are living multiple lives, too. And so are you.

How interesting. Do you care to elaborate about your bodies?
Well, I can have a so-called physical body that functions from a higher aspect of myself which contains a certain amount of energy; yet the higher aspect is yet another body, an etheric body, that is functioning and doing other activities that the physical body is not doing. It is more complex than this, but this is the only way I know how to explain this in a linear way.

Thank you, Clovis. This makes sense. Is this like a soul living many lives simultaneously?
Not really. Remember, what you think of as a physical body of a human has the aura and the spirit filling the body, which the soul has created. With me, there can be a "central" body that has many other bodies, which is considered one being. Maybe you could think of it like this. An octopus has eight tentacles. If you think of the head as the "central" body or Self, then the eight tentacles can all look different and

be different extensions of the Self, yet truly one body. I am explaining this from the point of view that basically all bodies are light, so do not get lost in thinking of eight separate physical bodies. It is one body. This is the best way I know how to explain this even though it is not really a clear analogy. Well, I tried (smile).

Thanks. I think I get a feel for what you are saying. Do you care about humans or are humans of any interest to you?

We think you are a colorful species, but we are not here to study the human species. There are humanoids on a number of planets in various galaxies and universes. Those on Earth are not the only ones. And all of you are connected, in terms of being humanoids, but there are some vast differences between the subspecies on Earth and those in other realms and worlds.

Are humans fairly primitive compared to those on other planets?

In some ways humans on Earth have evolved but in other ways they have not. The same is true of humanoids and other species in various aspects of the cosmos.

It is intended to be this way for the sake of learning through experience, balance, spiritual growth, and the raising of consciousness. I am sharing this with you because you asked, but we really do not have the idea of "comparing" in the realm I come from.

Every species and soul essence is wondrous and unique! And of course, you have to consider from what aspect of your many selves, multidimensionally speaking, that you are viewing this from (laugh).

Yes, (laugh). Humans love butterflies. You are all graceful and elegant.

Thank you. One of the main reasons we came to Earth was to spread beauty.

Do all butterfly species come from the same dimension you do?

No. There are various dimensions from which butterflies bloom. Not all butterflies come from one dimension or world. Many souls decide they would like to experience being a butterfly on Earth or elsewhere, just as you did. Take time to tune into your butterfly self to feel and better understand what I am communicating.

I will. What do you mean by "bloom"?

You could say we are created or born from large "energy blooms." I can only describe these blooms as looking like super-huge flowers in order for you and others to understand.

Are they flowers or something else?

They contain flower energy which has manifested on Earth but are much more than this. Butterflies need the flowers on Earth and the flowers need the butterflies and other beings. It is a symbiotic relationship based on energy/soul connections, love and creation.

Does this have any relationship to your transforming within and emerging from a chrysalis on Earth?

Yes, it does. A chrysalis is connected to plants, which connects us to the original flower/plant energy which we are connected to in other realms from which we bloom. The chrysalis is our womb.

Why go through the caterpillar stage before emerging into magnificent butterflies?

When we were invited to be a part of the Earth project, we let the council know that we needed to emerge from and be in close connection to flowers and plants. We knew this would help us adjust to Earth in a much better way and allow us to to remain connected to our original energies in other realms with the flower/plant energy blooms. Again, it is a symbiotic relationship. Yet this is true of all energies and beings, is it not? (smile).

Yes.

Being in the physical, we show humans and other species a literal transformation or metamorphosis on the physical plane. If this is possible on the physical plane, how much more potential is there in other dimensions and realms for transmutation and shapeshifting—places and spaces where you do not need wings (smile). We show you that all this is real.

It is quite a journey on Earth to begin as a caterpillar who is only able to cover a small distance physically. But after emerging from the chrysalis, wings allow us to cover vast distances globally.

Humans refer to butterflies as analogies in regard to their own transformations in life. What do you think about this?

It is an analogy that works well for humans. Many humans compare their own transformations through life and into death using butterflies as an analogy for their journey. It is the spirit's choice to experience the physical plane in being earthbound. Then as the body is left behind, you fly into higher dimensions. It is as if the spirit body has wings. And many species' spirit bodies have wings. So do many souls who inhabit human bodies.

Thank you. This makes sense. Humans are going through changes on every level, at a highly accelerated rate, it seems.

True. We did not come to Earth for the purpose of teaching humans, but we are pleased that butterflies are used as metaphors which help humans better understand their own "metamorphosis" during these great energy changes that are occurring in and around Earth. All beings on Earth are going through a raising of consciousness as well as DNA changes. Butterflies are wonderful examples of how this happens within the body, the brain, the energy centers, within the DNA itself, and within the soul.

Thank you, Clovis, for sharing from your heart. Blessings to you and all butterflies.

You are welcome. This has been fun. It is not very often that I have conversations with one of the human species. But then again, one aspect of you is, after all, a butterfly (chuckle). You have a beautiful heart. See the truth of beauty within.

Clovis

Chapter 43

Red-Tailed Hawk

Hawks spread beauty, joy, love, peace and balance

As I was walking through a prairie garden, I spotted a red-tailed hawk perched high on a tree branch about two hundred yards away. I telepathically sent the hawk love and thanked her for all the gifts that she gives to Earth. At that instant, the hawk flew toward me. She landed in the tree I was standing beneath. I looked up, she looked directly into my eyes and I heard, "Thank you for appreciating the gifts that I have to offer." With that, the hawk turned and flew across the prairie. The underside of her wings reflected the golden sun's afternoon light. As I watched her in flight, I had the privilege of seeing her bless the prairie with her wonderful life force. I saw, clairvoyantly, her energies flowing over the prairie. I stood there in awe. My heart filled with gratitude.

The following is what the hawk had to say in a conversation later on.

Hello. It's good to see you today. Thanks for the wonderful exchange of love we shared and for showing me, on the physical level, the power of love and telepathic communication.

You are welcome. It was a wonderful exchange for me as well. Many humans admire my physical body, but few actually and actively communicate with me. This was a pleasure for me.

For me as well. Why did you decide to fly over to me and look directly into my eyes?

I wanted to show you that I had heard you. I chose to acknowledge this in a physical way. This is why I flew to the tree that you were standing beneath. I wanted you and me to meet eye to eye. It is a special connection to look into each other's eyes, correct? (smile).

Oh yes. We connected spirit to spirit.

Yes. I wanted you to have this experience with a hawk. To have this kind of experience with a hawk is not like the usual experience of spirit-to-spirit connections with dogs, cats, horses, and other domesticated beings. My intention was for you to know without question that I heard you, so I responded to you.

Thank you for this gift. I saw you cover the prairie with your beautiful energies of light and love.

I knew you would be able to see my energies. I wanted you to experience this, once again, with a hawk. You are accustomed to seeing other animals, such as cats and dogs, use their energies to balance households, to heal, to spread love and joy, but experiencing this with a hawk would be a rather different experience.

Yes. Can you say more about how you use your energies and is there an interaction between you and the prairie?

Yes. This is one aspect of my mission on Earth. As I took flight over the prairie garden, I filled the entire space between my body and Earth with seeds of joy, light, and peace. I also radiated these energies in all directions. As you could see and feel, these energies filled the air as well as the prairie.

My wings are used for more than flying. There is power in my wings and power in my eyes. I project the energies of joy, light and peace from my eyes to Earth, to the trees, to the sky. And as I fly with wings spread, I can project love, joy, and peace for great distances. But I wanted you to see me specifically engaging these energies with the prairie. It is an interaction between the prairie and me—the same kind of interaction and connection you and I experienced, but I am also engaging in these kinds of interactions with plants, grasses, trees, and many other beings naturally and continuously.

This speaks to the Oneness of the All. I see beyond the physical and into the soul essence of other beings. I recognize who they are. Grass, plants, flowers, and trees have souls. They are not lesser than a human being or a dog, but equal to all beings, since all beings are of equal value. All beings are light. So one cannot categorize or linearize or create a hierarchy of beings.

Yes. I understand. It's easy for us humans to miss these intricate and important connections going on between beings whom humans don't usually bother to think about since they don't seem relevant to our lives.

Yes.

What would you like to share with humans?

In being a hawk I have a different perspective of life. I am able to view beings from the air so I gain a more inclusive view of Earth and other beings. While flying, I am able to observe the environment and the beings who live on the ground. Of course, this is important when I am searching for food.

Hawks spread beauty, joy, love, peace, and balance. We help to maintain balance energetically between Earth and heaven, you might say.

We teach humans how to look at life from a larger perspective—to view their lives from their higher self and soul so they do not get lost in whatever concern is before their eyes in any given moment. It is important to look at concerns within the framework of the "whole" of life rather than looking at this or that situation, which only fragments a being.

Hawk reminds humans to view things from a larger viewpoint, from the high self and spirit? Does this include our minds as well?

Yes. We are a reminder to you, as are other beings who fly, to look at concerns and life from a higher point of view. Remember you are souls who are experiencing what it is like to be a human. I am a soul experiencing what it is like to be a hawk.

What is it like to be a predator?

Being in a physical body we must eat in the same way humans must eat in order to survive. Humans are also a type of predator (smile). As a hawk I am an excellent hunter and kill in order to eat.

My eyes are different from human eyes. My eyes are keen and can home in on a frog, chipmunk, or rabbit while I am flying above a field or elsewhere.

I enjoy being what you call predator rather than prey. As I mentioned, because of where I come from, having wings and being a hawk is natural for me.

Thank you. By the way, what is your spiritual origin?
I come from a distant galaxy that is in what you might think of as the twelfth dimension from Earth. This is the best way for me to describe where my soul first originated, spiritually speaking. The Key Creator "inspired" me. The divine lives within all beings. The Creator is life itself.

Inspired?
Yes. The Key Creator is inspiration and any idea or intention comes from being "inspired."

Thank you. Do you come from a planet, star, or other?
My home is what you would think of as fluid and milky. Its structure is loose. There is no density such as there is on Earth. You could think of it as a world within a dimension. It is not solid, but it does have a loose form to it.

Why did your soul decide to experience being a hawk on Earth?
My essence is fluid light. I have an etheric body. I am accustomed to being able to be anywhere I want to be in an instant. I heard about Earth from a friend who had lived on Earth long ago. In fact, before humans lived on Earth. My friend said it had been an interesting experience—an adventure. I was accepted into the ranks of a few hundred souls who decided that they wanted to travel to Earth for the experience.

How do you feel about Earth?
I feel Earth is a very troubled planet. Those of us who have traveled here offer our gifts and blessings to Earth and the beings on Earth. We realize many beings came here from other galaxies and universes. Earth

can be a playground in some ways, but there is a great deal of learning for all who inhabit this planet. And Earth is evolving in ways that most humans have trouble grasping, since many have trouble thinking of Earth as a living being.

Why did you choose to be a hawk?
I was attracted to inhabiting a hawk body because hawks can fly. I would not cope well with being on Earth if I had to live on the ground. It would be very difficult energetically speaking. Hawks have wonderful lives. Also, I knew that I could have purpose in spreading love, light, peace, and joy between heaven and Earth. I use the word "heaven" because it is a word that humans can relate to. But I am speaking about multiple dimensions that exist within the spaces between Earth and moving through infinity. The hawk body suits the needs of my soul.

Thank you. Are you speaking to me as a representative or hawk elder?
I am one of many elders who are communicating to you what humans need to be remembering.

Are you referring to what you said earlier, that humans are souls experiencing being humans and that we need to remember we are soul first and foremost?
Yes. But also, we hope that you remember the love, peace, joy, and divinity that lives within you. Just as I spread my energies over Earth, so, too, can humans.

I understand. Do you have families where you come from?
Yes. Our families are different from yours. My family is a group consciousness and we have etheric bodies. We are always linked energetically.

How many members are there in your family?
I am thinking two thousand. We do not deal with numbers as humans do, but I think this is near the correct number.

Your family connections are energetic rather than like blood relatives on Earth, correct?
Yes.

Jacquelin Smith

How great to have such a large family (laugh).
　Oh it is! (laugh).

Are you connected to them while you're living on Earth?
　Yes and no. We communicate energetically or what you might think of as telepathically. We do not communicate through words, but through different tones and frequencies.

Interesting. Is this your first life on Earth?
　Yes. I am enjoying the adventure here on Earth. I will be here a couple more years and then return home.

Do you think you'll return to Earth?
　Perhaps. But I have not really decided that yet. The energies are sometimes difficult to deal with because of all the frequency changes that are taking place. I will offer my gifts and blessings to Earth, which I am happy to do. Then I will listen to find out what my soul has in store for me.

Are you communicating from your soul?
　Yes. And you are also communicating with the soul aspect of me that is in a hawk body. But until I am out of this hawk body, I am not fully experiencing the core of my soul.

Thank you. I've really enjoyed our conversation and connection.
　So have I. Remember, you too can fly.
　Red-tailed Hawk

Chapter 44

Squirrel

Open your hearts and see us for who we truly are

I glanced out of my bedroom window this morning. There were two squirrels playing by a tree. One of the squirrels chased the other squirrel across the yard and toward my chain-link fence. The squirrel being chased scampered through the fence and into my neighbor's yard. Yes, through the fence. I rubbed my eyes, thinking, "No way." Even though I have witnessed animals dematerialize and materialize, I figured I wasn't fully awake yet. Maybe the squirrel had crawled under an area where the fence wasn't secured into the ground. I checked and the fence was properly secured deep into the ground. So, I let it go. Still not quite sure if what I saw was real.

Four days later I looked out my patio door and a squirrel was walking close by the fence. As I stood watching, the squirrel jumped through the fence as if the fence wasn't there. Now I knew I really had seen what I thought I had seen days earlier! I trusted what I had just seen, but I decided to once again check for holes or open areas along the entire fence line. The fence was still secured deep into the ground.

The squirrels were showing me the truth about the interdimensional shifts. They showed me how the old frequencies and old boundaries are dissolving literally. The squirrels gave me the gift of witnessing these physical manifestations of interdimensional shifts.

Animals are showing us what we, too, can do if we raise our frequencies and believe all things are possible.

Seeing the squirrels walk through the fence as I was completing this book was a gift. In many ways, they have validated what many of the other animal souls have talked about throughout this book.

Hello. I am glad you showed up.

Hello (laugh). We showed you once and chose to show you twice what changes are happening at a rapid rate in what you think of as reality. The physical plane is illusion. When you understand the physical plane is illusion and exists mainly within your mind, then you will be able to experience other realities and dimensions beyond limiting thoughts you have about what is real and what is not.

We enjoyed showing you this twice, since you doubted what you saw with the first squirrel. It is not magic. This is about raising your frequency so that you, too, can "walk" through fences (smile). It really is fun.

Thank you for showing me the reality of walking through the fence two times. I needed to see it twice for it to sink in at a deeper level.

The interdimensional energies are shifting at an accelerated rate. Some days the frequencies are quite high and other days they are lower. This is the way Earth can maintain balance as she shifts into higher dimensions.

You are aware of all the energetic shifts going on?

How could we not be? (smile). We are very much attuned with Earth. We spend a great deal of time playing on her soil. We are close to Earth and are aligned with her energies. We are connected to Earth even while nesting in trees since trees are directly rooted into Earth. Earth's vibrations rise up through the roots and through the entire tree. We feel these vibrations as well as feeling the tree's vibrations.

What kind of relationship do you have with trees?

We love trees and trees love us. Squirrels and trees communicate telepathically with each other. The trees are living beings as we are. We live in harmony and balance with the trees and they with us. And just as all squirrels are connected to each other, so are all trees.

We are both very connected to Earth as I just explained. Sometimes when trees take on too many lower frequencies, we help clear and rebalance their energies, bringing their energies back into harmony.

All this makes perfect sense. People often think of squirrels as mundane pests. Why have you chosen to live in such close proximity to humans?

It is a choice we have made to live close by humans to remind them that they are not the only beings living in a neighborhood. This is true whether the neighborhood is urban, suburban, or rural. There are many squirrels living in neighborhoods such as yours. We are here to remind humans to connect with other beings and to connect with nature. Sometimes humans forget to connect with nature and other living beings even when they live in the midst of trees, squirrels, birds, and other beings. It would help humans to take time to create balance in their lives.

Squirrels give and help maintain balance and harmony in neighborhoods energetically. Think of all the houses, cars, and fences in a neighborhood. Without squirrels and without trees, a neighborhood would indeed be a more barren place to live. There would be a lack of balance and "living" nature and animal energy.

Yes, this makes sense. Is it difficult for you to find places to build your nests in neighborhoods?

It certainly can be a challenge. This depends on the trees in a neighborhood. Squirrels have to find ways to survive in neighborhoods and of course wherever we might live. But neighborhoods can be some of the most difficult areas for squirrels to find great locations and trees to live in.

Squirrels seem to thrive in neighborhoods. So why is it a challenge?

Well, for one thing, the streets are a challenge for us to deal with. Squirrels have to learn when to cross a street or not cross a street. We have to deal with cars and trucks that can be unpredictable. There is also the pollution from chimneys and cars. There is noise. There are humans. Understand?

Yes. I understand why this is challenging. It's challenging for me to live in a neighborhood some days (smile).

Yes, we know (laugh). Those of us living in your trees are aware of your frequency. We know that you do not think of these trees as "your" trees but the Creator's trees. This is why we decided to show you how quickly energies are shifting by walking through the fence. Fun, is it not?

Yes. Thank you for reminding me what is real. Are you here to help humans stay in touch with other beings and nature? Are you here to help them evolve? Is this part of your mission on Earth?

Our species made a choice to be in relationship with humans, although there are many squirrels who do not live in close proximity to humans. We are not here specifically for humans, but it is part of our mission to help raise their consciousness. As I mentioned, we are also here to help create balance and harmony within neighborhoods, within the world.

Squirrels live in many places on Earth. There must be many squirrels in order to assist Earth with balance and harmony, and in a way, to counter or rebalance some of the lower energies that humans create on Earth.

You must be very busy (smile).

Yes, we are busy (laugh). You would not know that from watching us. When you watch us play in the trees and in your yard, we are raising the vibrations. Humans would do better to play more.

I agree. Do you live in the moment?

Yes. But we do plan ahead with burying nuts so that we have food during the winter. We understand how to survive.

Are you one of the squirrels living in my yard?

Yes. I am speaking for the family of squirrels who live in the trees in your yard as well as for squirrels. I am a representative.

Thank you. What is your star origin?

We came here from a planet that is beyond your galaxy. The planet I come from exists within a dimension that is of high frequency with a bit of density. What I mean is that our planet's consistency has some density yet is not physical in the way what you know is physical. Its energy is of an in-between state.

Is your home planet within this universe?
No. It is within another universe that is of higher frequencies. It is in the same space as what you think of as your universe, but actually is not within your universe. Hard to put into words. We do not have words on our planet.

Are all squirrels from your planet?
The first spiritual essence of squirrel was not only on my planet but on several others as well. This is what the Creator decided.

Any soul can choose to experience living as a squirrel on Earth, or elsewhere if that is what it desires to do. And if this is in agreement with the higher councils who counsel souls as to what kinds of experiences will allow them to grow and serve the All.

There are councils who help souls decide the kinds of experiences that will help them grow and serve the All?
Yes. These councils consist of beings from various dimensions, planets, stars, and beyond. It is their role to act as what you would consider guidance counselors. There are countless councils throughout the cosmos who assist souls in reviewing what they have learned and experienced, and how they have contributed to the All. They ask the soul questions such as: what else would you like to experience and learn, and how would you like to serve the All?

I thought souls lived many lives simultaneously?
They do. A soul is living many lives at once. When the soul withdraws its energy from let us say three lives, it will think about and decide how it wants to invest that energy into other experiences and ways to serve the All. A soul may decide to experience what you would think of as a high frequency life—a life filled with love, joy, and service or deciding to live what you might think of as a lower frequency life to learn about the shadow aspects of the self or the universe. There is always the full spectrum of frequencies. And in experiencing the full spectrum of frequencies, this leads to integration and wholeness with a soul.

Thank you for explaining this. It makes sense. What would you like to say to humans?

Go outdoors. Take a walk in the woods. Touch trees. Touch green leaves. Nature and animals can only help humans get back into balance and harmony within themselves as well as with one another and Earth. When humans are out of touch with nature they are also out of touch with themselves and Spirit. Spirit lives within every plant, flower, tree, and squirrel (smile). And, of course, every living form.

What do squirrels mirror to humans?

Squirrels mirror to you the aspects of yourself that work to survive. What I mean is the part of you that stores food and plans for the future. Also, we mirror the aspect of you that needs to remember to play. In other words, inner harmony and balance. We reflect how you can live in balance and harmony within your environment. Also, we mirror how you as humans can live amongst yourselves with balance, harmony, and peace.

Look to our communities as examples of how humans can live together in a better way. Do you see squirrels killing one another?

No.

We have our squabbles, but look at how the squirrel communities live in peace on Earth. Squirrels set healthy boundaries with one another from a place of love, mutual respect, and understanding. Quite amazing when you think about it, is it not? I am not boasting for squirrels, but simply pointing out facts.

Yes. I can see how the basics of squirrel communities are a great model for humans to emulate in many ways. It would benefit humans to listen to the squirrels.

Yes. We have been communicating with humans for a very long time. We came to Earth after humans arrived. We come to humans in your dreams to help awaken you into higher consciousness. We are creating balance and harmony within neighborhoods as well as within your private living space which includes your yard.

Open your hearts and see us for who we truly are. We are ambassadors from a distant planet here on Earth to create harmony and balance. We create balance and harmony in various places and within dimensions within and around Earth. Our basic nature is to be of service. We are here to teach with love while growing from our experiences on Earth and elsewhere.

Thank you for this wonderful conversation.
　You are welcome. It is long overdue (smile).

Yes, it is (laugh).
　We will talk with you later.
　Squirrel

Chapter 45

What Is Your Animal Companion's Star Origin?

Your dog, cat, or guinea pig might be from another world. How can you know or find out? If you are ready to hear and accept what they have to communicate, just ask. It's that simple. You can communicate with any animal soul: cat, dog, guinea pig, dolphin, snake, hedgehog, gorilla, bird, or any other being.

I have taught classes and workshops on telepathic communication with animals, finding out your animal friend's star origins, as well as many other classes for more than twenty-five years. Also, I teach courses on telepathic communication with interdimensional beings and extraterrestrials because there are so many people who are wanting to communicate with our brothers and sisters throughout the cosmos.

Are you ready to delve into the deeper truth about who your cuddly dog, sweet kitty, or gorgeous horse really is in the bigger scheme of things? If you are, follow the easy guidelines I present in this chapter for you to know your animal friend at the soul level.

When I communicate with an animal, I listen to what they share. I am also able to see their star being essence and soul. You can too. The core of every being is of the Key Creator or what some call Divine.

Star Being Traits

The following are some basic physical and personality traits, and attributes that many star beings possess.

* Striking eyes. You can recognize them as being from another world. Star beings often have very large and/or unusual-looking eyes.
* Difficulty spatially with judging distances.
* A challenging time learning to fit in as a cat or dog or whatever animal form they might have chosen to live in. This can include having a difficult time socializing with other animals of their own species.
* Frequencies that just feel different. Their auras often stand out from others. For example, you may see swirling rainbows around star beings, or rainbows that shoot outward from the aura. You may see unearthly colors.
* A nature that can be friendly and affectionate, but can also seem cool and distant at times.
* Eccentric, weird, or awkward behaviors. They're expressing their unique star-being traits.
* Extreme sensitivity to the people and circumstances around them. They're psychic.
* Inability to tolerate conflict between humans.
* A tendency to stare off into space when they're actually communicating with other star beings from their home planet or doing the work they're here to do.

Difficulties Star Beings Can Encounter As Animals

Try traveling to a foreign country where you don't know the language or culture—a place where you don't know the rules. You may be labeled as quirky, dumb, or weird because you're unfamiliar with the foreign terrain. This can be the same with a star being in animal form who's adjusting to an unfamiliar body. Sometimes star beings in cat or dog bodies suddenly bark or meow—surprised at hearing this strange voice coming out of their mouths. This applies to other animals as well. We could say that they experience a dual consciousness.

The basic traits of a cat, for example, can be at the forefront, but the star self is there to one degree or another. For some, the star self is very prominent. For others, it might be less prominent, but the star self is present as a soul fulfills its purpose. Sometimes it can take a while for the star being to adjust to not only an animal body but to Earth.

Those whom we humans refer to as animals love unconditionally. Many star beings from other dimensions and worlds love unconditionally. We could refer to what we call star beings as interdimensional beings as well. The label isn't really important. One horse's soul had this to say: "It's natural for us to be drawn to be a dog, horse, bird, or other forms because of the higher vibrations they express."

Gizmo - A Star Being Who Had Trouble Adjusting to his Cat Body

Beth called me because her cat, Gizmo, had been killed by a car. She said Gizmo had acted strange and quirky during his short lifetime. Beth said he never knew he was a cat. Gizmo was clumsy and had no street smarts.

He communicated to me from his spirit that he simply didn't know what to do with his cat body. Beth tried to keep him in the house, but said it was impossible to do so.

Gizmo communicated the following to me. "I wasn't paying attention when I got hit by a car. I was looking across the street at another cat. I'm still trying to figure out this Earth stuff. I love seeing all the new sights that don't exist on the etheric planet I come from."

"I had trouble adjusting to a cat body." This is no different from the star being in the movie, *Starman*, who took on the form of a woman's husband who had died and learned clumsily how to act human. For example, Gizmo kept forgetting that he had a tail. He has a very high vibration and I could see that his origin was not Earth. He communicated, "This was only my second lifetime on Earth. I got killed one other time by a car. I have to learn to watch where I'm going. I've gotten bounced out from my body twice now.

"Part of the reason I came to this planet was to be with Beth again. I came to wake her up and help her remember where she comes from and who she really is. She is not from Earth."

Gizmo had come through a portal from a distant star in deep space to enter the body of a kitten, whom Beth picked up and carried home one summer day. Gizmo went on to show me he was from another star system. His essence was vibrant and bouncing here, there, and everywhere. These are the only words I know to describe him. Gizmo's essence is very bright light with many whirling rainbows and splashes of silver crystalline.

After sharing Gizmo's messages with Beth, she laughed and said, "I've always known I wasn't from this place."

Gizmo also communicated, "I'm everywhere at once," which expresses the wisdom and energy shared from his soul.

Max

At a conference where I gave consults, I talked with a delightful couple about their white boxer, Max, who had recently crossed over into the light.

I described his make-up, saying that he was a wonderful and open-hearted dog but had a great deal of trouble figuring out how to work his dog body. I shared that an aspect of his soul had decided to incarnate into a dog on Earth.

Jerry and Marlene laughed, "Yes, he had a very hard time. He used to stumble and was rather clumsy. And Max had blue eyes that were very unusual. At times he didn't act like a dog. We weren't sure what kind of animal Max thought he was. We weren't sure if he thought he was a human or what. Sometimes he slinked like a cat. Very weird, but we loved him so much."

Max communicated to me that he was a star being who had come from a distant galaxy and who had been on Earth four times, once as a cat. I shared this with Jerry and Marlene. They resonated with what Max had shared.

Telepathic Communication is Natural

Communication with animals is a natural way of being. This way can seem unnatural because of false notions we've been taught and have accepted about our own capabilities and those of animals.

Limiting views can block or hinder intimate communication with animals. People get bogged down in what they were taught a cat, dog, or any other animal should be. We can expand and look beyond the physical body in order to communicate with an animal's soul. For example, if we look into and connect with the essence of a being we are scared of, such as a spider, we grow and expand to embrace beings who may look very different from humans. It took me a few years to not react to some of the beings who communicated with me from other dimensions and worlds. They have taught me that there's nothing to be afraid of except my own misperceptions about them. Also, I always ask for only the highest vibration of beings to show up and it would be best for you to ask for this as well. Set your intention to attract only those beings who are of love and light and joy

When I was first learning to communicate with animals, I asked for advice from someone who knew all about it.

A wise gorilla spoke to me, "See beyond my gorilla layers to communicate with who I truly am." This enabled me to connect with his essence rather than getting lost in layers of how I expected a gorilla to be and act. I experienced his essence, feelings, and thoughts about his life and world.

The animals know who they are because they retain a clear connection to the universal intelligence and to their soul.

Reawaken

Telepathic communication is a natural way of communicating. We just need to reawaken our innate inner senses. Other animals telepathically communicate easily with one another. We must remember that we too are animals.

People often sense another's thoughts and feelings; they're just not aware of sending or receiving them. By consciously using these intuitive abilities, we can easily converse with animals. Telepathic communication with animals is a language of the heart to be experienced.

This communication is like a telephone conversation between two people. The telephone wires are the available lines of consciousness open between us that make the call possible. The electrical current, or the energy that the two beings send toward each other, flows through the telephone wires and enables the beings to connect and have a conversation.

Being human, we receive images, words, thoughts, and feelings. Animals can perceive whatever feelings and images we send, since these are the primary perceptions between us. The vibration, the intention behind the word, is translated in ways that both the animal and we can comprehend.

Telepathic Communication

Telepathy is a universal language. Telepathic communication bridges many gaps, crossing species, culture, language, and physical barriers. This natural communion enables us to understand more fully what an animal thinks and feels about a person or situation. This connection allows us to communicate with their souls in direct ways.

Nonverbal communication adds a dimension to relationships that creates a fuller and deeper connection. Heart to heart and soul to soul, we all can experience interspecies connections not only with our animal companions but with beings throughout the cosmos.

Guidelines for Communication

The guidelines for communicating with the souls of those who reside in animal bodies are very similar to those for communicating with the personality aspect of animals. The soul and personality are really one, but are different aspects of a soul's expression. If you want to learn how to communicate with animals, in general, read my book, *Animal Communication—Our Sacred Connection*.

1. Sit in a comfortable, quiet place, with or without an animal friend.
2. Center and breathe, being present in the moment with mind and body.
3. Create a heart-to-heart connection.
4. Formulate a question.
5. Send the question.

6. Be open, experience what you receive.
7. Thank your animal companion.
8. Release each other with love.

Step 1. Sit in a quiet, peaceful place where there are no distractions for you and your animal friend. If they are not with you, place a photo of them on your lap or beside you. A photo gives you the image of the animal being. Communicating through a photo with an animal is easy and natural since time and space do not actually exist. An aspect of their energy is in the photograph. Relax and get comfortable.

Now set aside any limiting beliefs you hold about yourself or beings in animal form. You might imagine putting those beliefs temporarily into an empty box on a shelf outside of the room. This enables intuition and feelings to flow more freely. Trust yourself. Believe and expect that you will have a conversation with your animal companion.

Make sure, intuitively, that you have the animal's attention, and that this is a good time for them. The calmer you are, the calmer your animal friend will be.

Before communicating, you can make eye contact for a few moments with your animal companion or touch them. Most animals directly sense your desire for communication and are cooperative. The animal may look around the room while communication is going on, but they're usually participating in the conversation. They may gaze into your eyes or sit beside you while you communicate.

Step 2. Place crystals, flowers, stones, or any sacred objects around you. This will raise your vibration. You can listen to uplifting music or sit in silence.

Now take a deep breath and center, which is to relax and be at peace. Focus on your breathing. This will shift your attention away from busy thoughts and move it towards relaxation of mind and body. This creates open and clear channels for communication to take place. Be open and spontaneous. Be the playful child. Let this be fun!

Be present, in the moment, in body and mind. You always want to be relaxed, centered, and feeling upbeat whenever you initiate a communication. Place yourself in a bubble of golden light. By doing this you raise your vibration. This makes it easier for an animal's soul to communicate with you.

When people are first learning telepathic communication in my workshops, I ask them to close their eyes. This helps them concentrate and eliminates outer distractions. In the beginning, an animal's presence can itself be a distraction. But with practice, people easily communicate with their eyes open or closed.

Step 3. Create a heart-to-heart connection. Look beyond the physical form and connect with the animal's essence. Send love from your heart to the animal's heart. A loving bond is a living current that allows thoughts and feelings to flow like water.

While sharing in this connection, remain centered. This enables you to remain clear while you send and receive messages.

Step 4. Formulate a single thought or question in your mind before you communicate telepathically. The image, thought, and feeling you're going to send needs to be clear. Here are some questions you might want to ask your animal friend: What is your star origin? What would you like to share with me about where you come from? Have we known each other before? Do you have a name? How old are you? Do you have a family where you come from? Why are you on Earth? What would you like to share with me in general? Have our souls been together in other dimensions, realms, or galaxies in the past or now?

Step 5. Send the thought, image, and feeling simultaneously to the animal. Visualize your message or question traveling along the heart-to-heart connection as if it's traveling through a telephone wire or on a ray of light from your heart to the animal's heart. Then release what you have sent. This keeps the communications clear.

You've just sent your first message, and I bet you're wondering if your animal got it. Since animals are so attuned and receptive to us, they receive our message. Trust that the animal has received the thoughts and images. Have fun and let it flow.

Step 6. To receive a response, remain quiet in mind and body. Be open and receptive. Imagine yourself as empty, waiting to receive. Listen with your heart and trust what you receive. Expect to receive from your animal friend. If you don't expect to receive anything, you probably won't. If you are thinking while trying to receive, you won't be able to hear or see what the animal's soul communicates. Relax.

Listen to what the soul describes or shows you about where they are from. If you ask for a name, your animal friend may or may not give you a name. They may share a sound or vibration with you that is their frequency rather than being a name. The same can be true if you ask them for the name of the planet, star, or dimension they are from originally. They may give you the name of a planet or star or they might share its sound or vibration with you. If you listen with your inner ears and heart, you'll be able to hear the frequency or sound they are sharing with you.

If your animal friend's spiritual origins are those of an individual, you will likely hear or perceive them as communicating with one voice. Most beings who are of a group consciousness will usually speak with one voice as well, so this is not a problem in communicating with them.

You will hear some beings talk, while other beings will sing telepathically. Go with what comes. It's all great fun.

Step 7. Thank the animal's soul for communicating with you. This lets them know that you appreciate their communications. You can imagine the telephone wire of energy dissolving between the two of you, or imagine the animal and you hanging up the phone.

Step 8. After the communication say silently, "Let us release each other with love." This automatically allows you to move back into your own energy field or personal boundaries, yet remain connected in love.

Practice And Have Fun

There is no right or wrong way to communicate. With practice, you'll find your own way of communicating with the beings who inhabit animal bodies as well as other beings who live throughout the cosmos.

Inner trust and clarity comes with time and practice. Everyone has the ability to communicate telepathically with beings who live in animal bodies as well as others who exist in dimensions and worlds beyond this universe. Communicate with love and with a joyful heart. This will attract loving beings. Your animal companions' souls are more awesome than you can imagine!

If you decide to communicate with star beings other than your animal companions, set your intention to communicate with beings who are of love and light. You'll be able to feel or sense this about them. If you don't intuitively feel love from a being, ask that being to leave. Just as there is a wide spectrum of vibrations which humans express, the same is true for other beings as well. When you radiate love and light, you will attract loving, joyful communications.

Remembering Who You Are

In communicating telepathically with the soul of your animal companion, there is a good chance that you will begin to recall memories of your own star origin. It is also possible that you will recall memories of past lives you've lived in other dimensions or star systems. You may also get in touch with lives that are simultaneous lives which you are living now in other dimensions or universes.

This is an awakening which many people are experiencing today. Let the memories come and trust what you receive. This is the next step in your evolutionary process.

These memories will remind you that you not only belong to the Earth family, but to a greater cosmic family. All beings are a part of the cosmic family. It doesn't matter what costumes souls decide to dress up in. Cats, dogs, horses, humans, praying mantises, birds, worms, and all others are of the cosmic family.

Communicating with the soul essences will fill you with love and joy. Let us remember that it is a privilege and honor to be a part of our cosmic family.

Epilogue

This very moment, as I complete this book, the full moon is shining upon me through my window.

This book is a dream come true because now others can read and revel in what these amazing beings have shared from their hearts and souls. I am honored and grateful to have been part of these incredible exchanges.

Glossary

Aura: a life field surrounding a person or object that functions as a blueprint; an invisible, electromagnetic field that surrounds a person or nonphysical being that supports and sustains their physical and nonphysical structure.

Chakra: an energy center; a whirling vortex or wheel of etheric energy, perceived by some as a lotus flower. A vortex draws in universal energy to vitalize the physical and spiritual bodies. The chakras bring about the development of our spiritual awareness. Humans possess seven major chakra centers.

Crystalline: consisting or made of crystal(s) or like crystal, clear and transparent.

Dimension: plane or realm of manifestation that exists energetically; a range of frequency vibration.

Electromagnetic field: the field created by a circuit of electrically charged particles at the atomic and subatomic levels as they flow through the human body, all things, and the planets themselves, connecting all of creation.

Etheric body: the first of a series of energetic bodies that surrounds each living thing in layers, which constitute part of its aura. When a being is nonphysical, we may refer to them as being "etheric."

Frequency: the vibration range of energy expressing itself, whether it be in physical form or nonphysical form.

Grid: a network of evenly spaced horizontal and vertical lines of energy, which include energy meridians, that lies beneath and supports all areas of Earth, whether land or water.

Hologram: a part of an entity that holds characteristics of the entire entity and therefore contains it. For example, a leaf contains the energy of the whole tree, the brain contains the energy of the whole universe (and so on).

Interdimensional: involving two or more dimensions or planes.

Multidimensional: involving multiple dimensions or planes.

Multiverse: the entirety of all that exists, comprising multiple universes of a wide range of types and multiple dimensions beyond the familiar framework of space-time.

Shapeshifting: a temporary shift in either the physical form or energetic form. A person or animal can shapeshift while still in the body by the shifting of consciousness to alter either their energetic body or their physical body to another form, such as the form of another animal or being.

Telepathy: the ability of one person to communicate with another without using sound or language; perception by one person of what another person or living form is thinking and feeling; the sending of a thought so that another person or living form receives it.

Wormhole: as conceptualized in contemporary astrophysics, a specific distortion in space-time that links one location or time with another, through an energetic path that is shorter in distance and takes less time than would be expected by measuring physical distance alone.

About The Author

Jacquelin Smith is an internationally known animal communicator and psychic who lives in Columbus, Ohio. She is a pioneer in the field of telepathic communication with animals and is one of the original animal communicators in the United States. She has been communicating with animals and has worked as a psychic with people professionally for more than thirty years.

Jacquelin has been communicating with animals, star beings, and interdimensional beings since early childhood. She has taught workshops on animal communication in various cities throughout the United States. Also, Jacquelin has taught workshops on communicating with star beings.

She offers apprenticeship programs to people who want to learn how to communicate with animals and with star beings. Her book, *Animal Communication—Our Sacred Connection*, is one of the most comprehensive books on animal communication and animals.

Jacquelin's work continues to receive media coverage through radio interviews and television talk shows.

For information about private consultations, workshops, apprenticeship programs, DVDs, books, and more visit Jacquelin's website www.jacquelinsmith.com. You can email her at jacquelinsmith@jacquelinsmith.com.